PORTRAIT OF
THE CHILTERNS

Portrait of
The CHILTERNS

by

Elizabeth Cull

Photographs by the author

For Bob & Janet
with best wishes
Elizabeth Cull

14:2:1983

ROBERT HALE · LONDON

ISBN 0 7091 9738 1

Robert Hale Limited
Clerkenwell House
Clerkenwell Green
London EC1R 0HT

Photoset in Great Britain by
Rowland Phototypesetting Ltd, Bury St Edmunds, Suffolk
and printed by St Edmundsbury Press, Bury St Edmunds, Suffolk
Bound by Woolnough Bookbinding Ltd, Northants

Contents

Illustrations

Acknowledgements

I take this opportunity of thanking all who have helped me while this book has been in preparation, have talked to me, lent me books and pamphlets, suggested lines of research and prevented me from making obvious mistakes. One in particular has read every word of the text, made many helpful suggestions, and continually encouraged me. To name any when so many have helped would be unkind, but each has my gratitude. Some, indeed, will never be known to me by name: writers of church guides, parish histories, town information booklets, and all the hundred and one leaflets and guides that pass through a writer's hands without ever finding a way into the bibliography.

There will be readers of this book who know a great deal about the Chilterns already, who have read J. H. B. Peel, H. J. Massingham, Annan Dickson, Kevin Fitzgerald, John Camp, Vera Burden, Brian Bailey, *et al.* I hope even they will find something new here, and will think kindly of me if they also find much of what they have read before; for some readers this will be their first book on the Chilterns, and they are entitled to the whole story.

All information is correct, as far as I could ascertain, at the time of going to press, but if there are errors I hope they are minor and such as will not give offence. Again, it is not possible to include every fact, anecdote, legend, church, nor even every village in a book of this length, so I have written about the things that interest me, and tried to describe the district as I see it.

There is a list of sources at the back of the book. Of the two unattributed quotations in Chapter XXII, the first is from "The Deserted Village" by Oliver Goldsmith, the second from *Songs of Travel* by R. L. Stevenson. Finally, I have to thank J. H. B. Peel for permission to quote his account of the Death of Hampden; Ian Rodger for permission to quote from his broadcast talk on Megalithic Mathematics; Macmillan & Co. for permission to quote from A. G. Macdonnell's *England Their England*, and Hodder & Stoughton for permission to quote from Arthur Mee's *Buckinghamshire*.

Elizabeth Cull

Chorleywood, 1982

Is it so small a thing
To have enjoy'd the sun,
To have lived light in the spring,
To have loved, to have thought, to have done;
To have advanced true friends, and beat down baffling foes?
Matthew Arnold
"Empedocles on Etna"

1

The Chiltern Hills

I am assured by a friend who once lived on Islay and moved down the country by degrees to settle within hailing distance of the Isle of Wight, that the further south one travels, the easier and softer life becomes. Be that as it may, there can be few people in Britain today who find life easier or pleasanter than those who live in that broad belt north of London where commuter-land shades into farming country that we call the Chilterns. No map puts a boundary to the district; centred on the Chiltern Hills, it crosses the three counties of Hertfordshire, Buckinghamshire and Oxfordshire without taking in the whole of any of them. All over Britain there are areas such as this, with neither fixed geographical outline nor official identity, yet known by name to every dweller in the land. The Cotswolds, the Mendips, the Lake District, the Border Country, Snowdonia; all bring their own image, a different and personal image for each of us.

Taken individually, none of these areas occupies much space on a map of the British Isles. And so it is with the Chilterns. Lying between London and Oxford, so close to the capital that its southern fringes are almost entangled in the suburbs, cut through by the A1, M1, M4 and M40, the accessible Chilterns are yet blessed with beauty and quietness. Undulating and green, dotted with coppices and commons, laced about by footpaths, leavened with prosperous meadow-land and arable, and sanctified by glorious beechwoods that rise to the sky, it is a gracious place in which to live and a pleasant place to visit. Little villages hide in the valleys with winding ways that lead to nowhere more important than an inn and a few cottages at the lane's end, while the hills that stride in an almost unbroken line from Dunstable Downs to the Thames unify the district and give it a name.

But there is more to the Chilterns than the Chiltern Hills. Where the Metropolitan Railway line comes in from London to Rickmansworth, Chorleywood, Amersham and Chesham it almost merits the label 'suburban'; the towns of Aylesbury and High Wycombe have their industrial estates, modern shopping precincts and multi-storey car parks; Tring and Thame, Wendover and Watlington, Great Missenden and Princes Risborough are little country towns still, bustling or peaceful according to the day, and all between are scattered the villages and farmsteads that give life and purpose to the whole. When the Chiltern countryside wakes in spring the beechwood paths are edged with massed clumps of violets and primroses, and as the trees shake out their first fresh leaves they top the slender trunks with a green haze of unimaginable delicacy. Celandines nestle under the burgeoning hedges, and on the hills yellow Brimstone butterflies dance above wild orchids hiding shyly in the grass. Summer brings a brighter charm; the hills grow yellow with cowslips, skylarks sing their hearts out above the corn, and pale, powdery Chalkhill Blue butterflies delight the eye. But the greatest glory comes as the year is dying, when leaves crisp with rime are crunched underfoot and the sky sends back the earth's soft browns and russets in a great golden glow. No surprise, then, that at weekends railway stations from Rickmansworth to Aylesbury and Tring to the Thames are busy with walkers *en route* for the Chiltern Hills and some of the best walking country this side of the Yorkshire Dales.

The district forms a triangle set slightly askew in the middle of England, on the line between the bulge of the Wash and the cut of the Bristol Channel. Aylesbury stands at the apex; Thame brings the line down in the west, Tring and Berkhamsted in the east, with Princess Risborough squarely between. Watlington, High Wycombe and Rickmansworth make a rough line across the centre, with Chinnor in the west above, Beaconsfield in the east below, and Great Missenden, Chesham and Amersham in a bunch to the right of centre. The wavy base line to the triangle is formed by the towns along the Thames, Goring, Henley, Marlow, Maidenhead and Slough; though the last two are not generally thought of as Chiltern towns.

Blue lines show where water flows: Thistle Brook starts above Aylesbury and gathers with others of its kind to make the River Thame, which flows off the map in the west beyond the town that bears its name, to join the great Thames at Dorchester. The Bulbourne flows around the reservoirs at Tring; the River Wye rises at West Wycombe and flows to the Thames at Bourne End, with water mills all along its route; the River Chess rises by Chesham and trickles through Latimer and Chorleywood to fade away in water meadows at Rickmansworth; while the tiny River Misbourne runs its entire course between Great Missenden and Chalfont St Peter. There are reservoirs above

Tring and flooded gravel pits between Denham and Rickmansworth, but the only other noticeable stretch of water is the narrow trunk of the Grand Union Canal slashing north from Rickmansworth, with arms off to Aylesbury and Wendover.

Patches of green show the beechwoods, mostly following the line of the Chiltern Hills that march across the district from north-east to south-west: Ivinghoe Beacon, Pitstone Hill, Steps Hill, Clipper Down, and after the gap at Tring, Bacombe Hill, Coombe Hill, Lodge Hill, Beacon Hill, Pulpit Hill, Longdown Hill, Whiteleaf. Another gap at Whiteleaf where Princes Risborough lies in the valley, then into Oxfordshire for Wainhill, Chinnor Hill, Crowell Hill, another Beacon Hill, Shirburn Hill, Watlington Hill, Britwell Hill, and so down to the Thames.

In truth, the name Chiltern may well have belonged to the district before it was given to the hills, for the three Chiltern Hundreds of Desborough, Burnham and Stoke were listed in Domesday, and have been grouped together since the eleventh century. Desborough Hundred rises in a line from Medmenham on the Thames to High Wycombe, then sweeps across into Oxfordshire to take in the parishes of Stokenchurch, Saunderton, Turville and Fawley, among others, and all the territory bounded roughly by the B481 and the A423. Stoke Hundred borders the Thames and includes such places as Wraysbury, Eton and Datchet, Iver, Langley, Denham and Slough, few of which would be thought of as Chiltern towns, while Burnham Hundred encompasses the area from Slough to Amersham, including all of Burnham Beeches and the ancient parishes of Chalfont St Giles, Chalfont St Peter, Beaconsfield, Chenies and Penn, among others. Most of the Hundreds that once marked out the administrative districts of the British Isles are merely historical curiosities today, and so would the Chiltern Hundreds be had they not been artificially retained as an office under the Crown. Members of Parliament may not resign, but neither may they hold a civil office of profit. So to be appointed to the Stewardship of the Chiltern Hundreds is a convenient escape route for any M.P. who wishes to disembarrass himself of his seat. The office was not always such a sinecure. In the Middle Ages these hills were the haunt of highwaymen and thieves, threatening travellers on the important through route to Oxford and the North. 'Beat a bush and start a thief' was said of the Chilterns then, and the first Steward of the Chiltern Hundreds was appointed to remedy this sad state of affairs.

The chronicler John Leland, writing of the Chilterns in 1538, said: 'All this way goeth the Chiltern Hills, al the soil being a chalke clay', and it is still this chalk which sets the character of the Chilterns. Four hundred thousand years ago, at the end of the Ice Age, the glaciers halted here, having crushed and ground before them a limestone escarpment stretching across southern England from Lyme Regis to the Wash. Our Chiltern Hills are part of this escarpment. The dip slope, untouched by the ice, fades gently down towards London and the Essex plain, but to the north the scarp falls steeply away, giving long vistas over the Vale of Aylesbury and the Oxfordshire Downs. As the ice receded the weight of its melt-waters bored and slashed at the soft chalk, striking south to the Thames and north-east to sweep from the Wash and scour out the English Channel, cutting us off from Europe. Lesser gaps were left in the chalk; one now lets the M1 through between Luton and Dunstable and another takes the Grand Union Canal at Tring, though where the M40 crosses above Stokenchurch on its way to Oxford an artificial cleft was cut in the scarp leaving startling chalk sides that seemed to rise for ever. For the first year or so after the road was built these steep chalk cliffs were smothered in summer with vivid scarlet field poppies, a wonderful sight. The poppies bloomed for only a few years, and were succeeded by a low, creeping moss working along the ledges, and now that the road has been five or six years in use a hanging, green, whin-like vegetation droops untidily down the face, almost hiding the white chalk from sight.

The Chilterns are not quite 'al chalke', in places other rocks intrude; west of High Wycombe and in Hughenden Valley there are beds of sand and loam and irregular beds of gravel, 'Reading Beds' the geologists call them. These Reading Beds are the source of Greywethers, or sarsen stones, formed by the action of water percolating through sand. Bradenham was an ancient centre for sarsen cutting, and it is thought that the big stones may have been transported from thence along the Ridgeway to Avebury in Wiltshire, to make the prehistoric stone circle there. At the eastern end of the Chilterns are found masses of Hertfordshire pudding-stone, a flint and pebble conglomerate compacted together by the great weight of ice that once lay above them. St Mary's Church, Chesham, rests on a foundation of Hertfordshire pudding-stone, and one slab of the substance unearthed at Boxmoor, near Hemel Hempstead, was twenty feet long by forty feet wide and proved indestructible. Cottagers used to keep lumps of the stuff outside their doors to ward off the evil eye. Then there are crag deposits at Berkhamsted, extensively worked gravel beds on high ground in South Hertfordshire, and pebbly clay with sand topping some of the hills in Buckinghamshire. But chalk is the heart of all, filtering out for us the purest drinking water in all England, and gardeners throughout the Chilterns tend their chalk-loving clematis and philadelphus as happy consolation for the prize rhododendrons that can never be theirs.

Nor has history passed the Chilterns by. It was at Berkhamsted in 1066 that the Saxon nobles met William the Conqueror to acknowledge his victory at Hastings, a thousand years after Cunobelinus, King of the Britons, fought the Roman legions on the hills above Wendover. There are remains of Iron Age forts and barrows all along the lie of the hills, and the whole area shows evidence of occupation since the beginning of recorded time. All Saints' Church at Wing has a rare Saxon apse, one of only four such known in Britain, and archaeological excavations have dated the crypt at the seventh century. More than one Chiltern church shows signs of Saxon workmanship; many have Norman remains, and few are less than medieval. Many have examples of wall-painting; St Nicholas's Church at Little Kimble is probably the best known, but Little Hampden's tiny church has a painting of the Weighing of Souls, and the parish church at Chalfont St Giles has fourteenth-century paintings on its whitewashed walls.

Situated so conveniently between London and Oxford, the district has been favoured by both Church and State. The Cistercians held lands in Oxfordshire and Buckinghamshire; there were abbeys in most of the larger towns at the time of the Dissolution, and a nunnery at Goring. The Black Prince held the manor of Princes Risborough and was much seen at Berkhamsted. Henry VIII kept unofficial court at Moor Park whilst in pursuit of one of his queens, and King Charles is said to have set up Nell Gwynn at Tring Park. Stately homes and great estates there are too: Cliveden, Mapledurham House, West Wycombe Park, Hughenden Manor, Mentmore, Waddesdon, Stonor Park and Rotherfield Greys; and villages such as Aldbury, Chenies, Little Hampden, Ewelme, Hambleden, Hawridge and Cholesbury, Fingest, and Little Missenden are all gems in perfect settings.

This situation of the Chilterns between London and Oxford has been a mixed blessing during the twentieth century. The growth of suburban commuter services from Euston, Marylebone and Baker Street, the building of the M1 and the M4, and the extension of the Western Avenue into the M40 means that virtually no part of the Chilterns is beyond daily reach of London, and in consequence the character of the district has altered greatly. On the surface, it has changed from a number of small towns supporting their own industries and servicing the agricultural communities round about, to a vast dormitory for city workers. In fact, the picture is not quite so gloomy as this. Though much bigger now, the towns still house workers of their own local industries, industries which have themselves grown rapidly since the war. They still provide shopping and recreational facilities for those who work the surrounding land, and the commuters who stream back from London each evening are sometimes more cherishing of their lovely environment than those who were born there and take it all for granted. It is often commuter-cash and commuter-interest that fuels the preservation and amenity societies, city-bred sharpness that detects abuse of the beloved countryside and knows how to take steps to defend it.

One other road must be mentioned: one that travels through the Chilterns not northwards from London as the railways and all the other main roads to but across the district from east to west, along the ridges of the hills from Ivinghoe to Goring. It is the Chiltern Ridgeway, part of a prehistoric route that once ran from Castle Rising in Norfolk to the mouth of the Axe at Seaton Bay. One of the old green roads of Britain, those ancient trackways and drive roads which have been travelled by man and beast since the dawn of history. Almost the whole length of this one has survived, and apart from a gap between Tring and Wendover and a short break around Nuffield in Oxfordshire, it unites the Chilterns today as it has since the Stone Age. In 1973 the Countryside Commission, in pursuit of its brief to make the countryside more easy of access, waymarked and signposted this old route, designating it as the Ridgeway Long Distance Footpath at a little official opening ceremony held on the windy summit of Ivinghoe Beacon.

The Long Distance Footpath follows the old green road for eighty miles, from Ivinghoe Beacon to Overton Hill, in Wiltshire, crossing the Thames between Goring and Streatley.

While the Wiltshire section runs long and straight across the high downs, true to the route of the old green road and touching such prehistoric remains as the Stone Circle at Avebury, Waylands Smithy, and the White Horse of White Horse Down on its way, in the more heavily developed Chilterns the new footpath has had to be patched in piecemeal where the old way has been lost. But the effort was successful; today the Ridgeway is the most popular of Britain's long distance footpaths, rivalling even the Pennine Way, and thousands of walkers travel it each year.

This, then, is the Chilterns. Something old, something new. Old towns and villages, new shops and factories, long hill walks and green byways, railways and waterways and modern fast roads. Much to discover, yet no one part of it so far from another that it cannot be reached in an hour by road or on a long day's march. A neat, compact sort of a place; well populated, yet still with remote fastnesses like Bix Bottom, Little Hampden, or Dunsmore village, that the lucky traveller comes upon only by chance. And the Chiltern people, native or incomer; recusants at one end of the Chilterns, dissenters at the other, and in between all the thousands of ordinary men and women whose lives have no record, but without whom there would be no history, and no book.

2

A Ride on the Railway

In every estate agents' office throughout the prosperous Chilterns there should be a plaque to Sir Edward Watkin, one-time Chairman of the Metropolitan Railway Company, and next to it a picture of Lord Aberconway. For it was under the chairmanship of these two men that the railway expanded into the Chilterns, making way for the extensive patchwork of commuter estates that followed along its lines.

Sir Edward was a typical Victorian self-made man. Starting as a clerk in a railway office, he worked himself up by diligence and personality into a management position, and when he took over the chairmanship of the Metropolitan Line in 1872 he probably knew more than any other man about the railway system in Britain. At that time the Met was a little City line running between Paddington and Farringdon Street; Sir Edward pooh-poohed the Board's modest ambitions for extensions from Baker Street to St John's Wood; he had his own ideas for a trans-continental network connecting Manchester with London, Dover and Paris. His ambition was never realized, but he drove the line out to the edge of the Chilterns, to Rickmansworth, Chesham and Chalfont, and when in 1891 the line bought in the Aylesbury and Buckingham Railway it was at least possible for passengers to buy a through ticket from Marylebone to Manchester, changing beyond Aylesbury at Verney Junction.

The journey through the Chilterns in those days was a delight, aptly described as

> running through lovely, magical rural England ... to wayside halts where the only passengers are milk-churns ... lonely platforms where the only tickets are bought by geese and ducks. It stops in the middle of buttercup meadows to pick up eggs and flowers. It glides past the great pile of willow branches that are maturing to make England's cricket bats. It is a dreamer among railways, a poet, kindly and absurd and lovely.*

All this on a journey that ended at Aylesbury. One could paint a very different picture today. Unfortunately ducks and geese and

---

* *England Their England*, A. G. Macdonnell, Macmillan, 1957.

milk-churns, necessary though they may be to the life of the countryside, do not generate enough traffic to run a railway. A line needs paying passengers and freight. Finding themselves short on both, the Board of the Metropolitan sought to increase passenger traffic by luring London businessmen out to live in the fresh air of the Chiltern countryside. Already new housing estates at Wembley, Ruislip and Harrow were proving good business for the Met, and under Sir Edward's chairmanship the Metropolitan Surplus Lands Committee set out to acquire suitable building land further along the line in Hertfordshire and Buckinghamshire. This led in 1919, long after Sir Edward's death, to the formation of the Metropolitan Railway Estates Company. The new company bought land for development at Northwood, Rickmansworth and Amersham, and the Chiltern commuter was born.

The term 'Metroland' was coined by an anonymous advertising man, and the slogan 'Come and live in Metroland' enticed the traveller from hoardings all along the line from Baker Street. At first plots of land were offered for buyers to build individually, but by the beginning of the 1930s the Metropolitan Railway Estates Co. was putting up its own estates of ready-built homes in the Chilterns, and it continued to build at Rickmansworth, Chorleywood and Amersham long after the Met Line itself was swallowed up by the London Passenger Transport Board in 1933. Indeed, houses were still being built on 'Railway' land after the Second World War. In 1921 the Cedars Estate at Rickmansworth was started with 'detached residences of the country-house type' selling from £975; not so expensive as the Cassiobury Estate at Watford, on the branch line, where houses started at £1,100. At that time a season ticket to Baker Street cost 21s.3d. a week, no small item in the budget, but then these houses were not built for poor men.

Gradually the estates crept out along the line: to Moor Park, to Chorleywood's Chenies Estate, and to Amersham-on-the-Hill. In the main they were built to a pattern: rows of neat, uniform residences and identical semis, though in some places more ambitious estates of detached villas were ventured. They must have looked very raw and intrusive to those already living in the little country places that were their setting, but they have weathered well and lost the 'estate' look that once they had.

There was already some commuter traffic on the Met Line, though, before the new estates were developed. People made their way from great distances to take the daily train to London, like the intrepid lady 'typewriter' who in 1923 used to alight at Chorleywood on dark winter evenings and walk home four miles through the woods that then stretched unbroken to Chalfont St Giles, lighting her way with a lanthorn. The face of the district has changed beyond recognition since those days, with new roads, motorways, and vast estates of new houses quite unconnected with Metropolitan Railway Estates, but it is still possible to walk through the woods from Chorleywood to Chalfont St Giles by bridle-ways and footpaths where violets bloom among the celandines in spring, and in late summer the hedges are a fragrant mass of honeysuckle and wild rose. A man would shed the cares of day who walked at evening between those hedges; over the stile and through the woods by Newland Park and Ashwells Farm and across green fields to the narrow way that leads beside houses with names like Tree Tops, Oak Trees and Berryn Arbour, to the Pheasant crossroads at Chalfont St Giles, where he can see off his very creditable thirst at the bottom of a pint pot.

To the traveller Chiltern-bound from London, Moor Park with its little copse beside the track its tree-lined streets and its row of discreet, countrified shops just glimpsed from the station, must seem like the beginning of the Chilterns. But Moor Park is not 'the beginning of' anything. Moor Park just *is*. Elegant, secluded and virtuous, it sweeps up its skirts like an Edwardian lady and bars itself from the world with gated roadways and a uniformed attendant, to guard its private roads from those who don't belong. Home of the famous Moor Park and Sandy Lodge golf courses and of Merchant Taylors Boys' School, it manages by constant vigilance to keep up its standards in a slip-shod world. Someone has to, after all.

The estate at Moor Park was laid out and developed in the 1930s on land bought by the Moor Park Estate Co. at the time when the mansion of Moor Park, the park and the golf courses were bought by Hertfordshire County Council. Broad avenues of individual detached houses run into Northwood and the out-lying suburbs of West London in the south, but are separated from Rickmansworth in the north by the golf course, the Batchworth meadows and the Grand Union Canal.

The mansion at Moor Park is interesting: that which stands on the site today, used by Moor Park Golf Club as a superior nineteenth hole, was built in the eighteenth century for Mr

Benjamin Styles, one of the few men to make money from the South Sea Bubble. Originally there were dainty, curved colonnades to either side of the house, terminating in little side wings with cupolas to match the Corinthian columns of the portico, but a subsequent owner with no eye for elegance or symmetry demolished them in favour of an orangery. Lord Robert Grosvenor, the first Baron Ebury, inherited the estate in the year before the Corn Laws were repealed, and built the first small golf course in the park, but the present courses were laid out in the 1920s to the order of Viscount Leverhulme, who ran the place as a country club.

The history of 'the Manor of the Moor' goes right back to King Offa. He had a timber hunting lodge on the site.

Not until the tidy bunkers and smooth green fairways have been left behind and the railway has crossed the canal and rumbled across the water meadows into sleepy old Rickmansworth, does it enter the Chilterns proper. Rickmansworth (whisper it quietly) is the station London Transport forgot. Chorleywood was another such, until an accident burned the roof off half of it in March 1980. Fluted iron pillars, canopied wooden roofs, echoing boards in the vestibule, hissing gas-fires in the waiting-rooms and layer upon layer of crusted cream paint on the walls; only the curling posters advertising the films and exhibitions of the 1980s and the parked cars that stand where once sheep and cattle pens were, tell us that we have left behind the Twenties and Thirties and that the Second World War is not still in the future.

Until 1961 Rickmansworth was the locomotive exchange point. Trains coming from London were silent, clean, character-less, electric; they made their way on into the Chilterns as huffing, puffing, fire-and-smoke serpents to delight children of all ages along the rest of the line to Aylesbury, for already steam trains were becoming a rarity. With the disappearance of the steam locos the rot really set in for Rickmansworth. Despite public outcry, the Swan Inn and the lovely old shops in the High Street, including Swannell & Sly's building (early seventeenth-century wattle and daub plastered all over with notices of auctions and farm sales), were torn down in aid of a feature-less town development programme. The old cinema has gone; Salter's Brewery and the Moussec Wine factory have gone, the big, old houses in Station Road that one saw from the train have gone, to make way for a modern shopping precinct, a new Public

Library, and Watersmeet Theatre and Civic Hall. A short stretch of Church Street still survives to show how it all was, and there is a pretty little row of cottages by the side of St Mary's churchyard, as well as an enclave of Victorian terraced houses in a little backwater between the church and The Bury, much in demand among housebuyers and showing a bright and cherished face to the world.

The Bury itself, tucked away behind tne church, was built during the time of Sir Gilbert Wakering, who in 1637 was granted a lease of the manor from the Crown. Although the house is now used as a Hertfordshire County Council Health Centre, much of its fine Jacobean panelling remains. The church of St Mary the Virgin, with its wonderful acoustics, has had a chequered career. It was set on fire by outraged parishioners whilst Cardinal Wolsey was resident at Moor Park, and further damaged by the Puritans in 1640. The present flint and stone building was put up in 1890 using the side walls and tower of the old church. Sir Arthur Blomfield designed the nave and chancel, and the fine East window commemorates the first Lord Ebury. St Mary's vicarage, set behind a high wall at the back of the High Street, is medieval, and the oldest vicarage in the county, though it is now used for offices, a new vicarage having been built in 1975.

3

Chorleywood and the Chess Valley

Chorleywood is the next stop along the line, a station where the banks on the up-line are covered in stonecrop and backed with buddleia bushes, so that London-bound passengers on summer afternoons wait amid the flutter of butterflies and the heavy drone of bumble-bees among the blossoms, 'all the live murmurs of a summer day'. The down platform is, if anything, more spectacular; separating the passengers from what used to be the sidings and is now the car park, is a hedge of broom fully eight feet tall whose pale, fragrant, almost luminous blossoms wait at evening the summer through to welcome the commuter home. No surprise that Mrs Peters, who cares for these gardens, wins awards year after year in the Station Gardens Competition, her framed commendations hanging in a row on the waiting-room walls. The station is in what used to be called Chorleywood West, though the 'West' has been dropped locally. The original village of Chorleywood lies on the A404, on the other side of Chorleywood Common.

For a place that hit the headlines a few years back as having more cars per head of the population than anywhere else in England, the present Chorleywood village is surprisingly hard to find by road. Signposted on the A404 at both Rickmansworth and Amersham, you could drive all day between the two and see no more than the church on the common and Pullen's Stores, and when at last you spotted the one sign pointing east to 'Chorleywood Station', you could still drive round to the station and away without detecting the shopping centre and thriving community that lies to the back of it. One visitor, an addict of J. R. R. Tolkien, who had quested up and down the A404 for half a morning and found the shopping centre only at his last, desperate throw, described Chorleywood as: 'Like Middle Earth; it takes you a week to find it, and when you get there it's like nowhere you've ever been before.'

Much of this side of the village was developed in late Victorian and Edwardian times, and the solid, period houses, mostly with five or six bedrooms, plenty of living space, attics and basements, are much the same today. In the Swillett, at the top of Shire Lane, are rows of Victorian terraces, while on the other side of the county boundary, which splits Chorleywood in two, is the Chenies Estate. This is a mostly post-war development where the roads are broad, gracious and tree-lined, with flowering cherries and japonicas set in grass verges. Until a few years ago an old roadman used to scythe these verges once or twice a year, carrying his scythe and a toolbag with his sharpening stone and a bite of lunch, his old dog trotting at his heels. A chatty man, he'd be ready to gossip or pass the time of day with anyone who came by, sharpening his scythe the while in a vaguely alarming manner. He'd be two or three days cleaning the verges, leaving the cut grass in sweet-smelling windrows to be gathered up by any rabbit-fancier under the age of ten. When autumn came he swopped his scythe for a bill-hook to trim the hedges and banks along the lanes towards Chalfont St Giles, and could be seen on drizzly days eating his lunch under the hedge, with a sack around his shoulders and the old dog curled up by his side, a little, lively man with rosy cheeks and bright, smiling eyes. But he retired the winter his dog died, and now the hedgerows are trimmed by a man on a tractor with a mechanical cutter which leaves the branch ends naked and raw and the lanes strewn with twigs and sharp bits of hawthorn. The verges fare no better. They are in the care of the Buckinghamshire Highways Department and are descended upon by four men in a Council lorry with brooms, shovels and a motor mower. They churn away with the mower all morning and by lunchtime they are ankle deep in a bruised and stinking mass that no rabbit would look twice at. It is supposed to be more efficient, but one can't help thinking of the old man and rueing the days that are gone.

On a little rise to the north-east of the village is the modern church of St Andrew, built in 1963, distinguished as being the last new church in a new parish to be built in England. The trend now is to amalgamate parishes and close churches rather than to expand and build new. The people of the parish had been collecting sporadically to build a new church in place of the temporary hall used as a daughter church of Chorleywood Christchurch, since a plot of land was donated for the purpose in 1912. They were told that they must find the whole cost of the church themselves, and that they must first build a new vicarage. Under the leadership of John Perry, a young vicar in his first parish, they set to work in earnest in the early 1960s, and by faith the new church was built and consecrated in May

1966. Set in green lawns, it is a modest building of brick and concrete, not so obstinately modern as to be unsympathetic to its surroundings, but still very much of its age. The plain wooden altar cross, altar rails and communion table were made by parishioners, as were the pottery communion vessels; the lectern Bible was given by the children of the Church School, and the kneelers, as always, stitched by the ladies of the parish. Bare though it is, this church is much loved by the community it serves and not unusually filled to overflowing. Never more so, of course, than at Christmastide, when the Midnight Mass sees it bright with hundreds of candles set on every ledge and shelf, so that it seems to dance in twinkling light on its little hilltop.

But all is not twentieth century: William Penn married his first wife, Gulielma Springett, at King John's Farm, a handsome, timbered house in Shepherds Lane, very well preserved and still in use as a private residence. And Bullsland Farm in the Swillett, once a separate village but now adjoining Chorleywood to the south-west, is probably sixteenth century. Set among cherry orchards, its Tudor brickwork and overhanging eaves tuck it down so neatly into the landscape as to make you feel that if you watered it, it would grow, yet through its lands runs a footpath where the signpost reads 'Chorleywood Station ¾', and from whence it is little more than half an hour by train to Baker Street or Marylebone.

The A404, across the Common from Chorleywood Station, was once part of the Marquis of Salisbury's 'Gout Road', built in the nineteenth century to connect up Hatfield to the Bath road and transport the Marquis and his aches and pains in some degree of comfort to the Spa. Chorleywood Christchurch lies on the A404, nineteenth-century flint with stone facings and a broach spire. When the spire had to be re-shingled in 1968 all the top-form children at the Church School signed their names on one of the shingles, in the presence of an old lady from the almshouses who had been a pupil at the Church School when the spire had last been shingled. Among the memorials in the churchyard is an angel with a butterfly carved at its foot, recalling that as the coffin was being lowered a butterfly settled on one of the wreaths and went down with it into the grave. Most likely a Brimstone, since it was February. The memorial commemorates Mr John Saunders Gilliat, Lord of the Manor, Member of Parliament from 1886 to 1892, Governor of the Bank of England, and a great benefactor in the parish. Another member of the Gilliat family, the Reverend J. H. G. Gilliat, was later to be vicar of Christchurch for twenty-two years.

There is a handsome memorial tablet in the church to Sir George Alexander, the actor-manager who produced all Oscar Wilde's plays. He lived at nearby Tollgate Cottage until he built Chorleywood Court, a few yards further along towards Rickmansworth, a building that doesn't show to advantage from the road. Sir Henry Wood came later to live at Appletree Cottage in Dog Kennel Lane. He was President of the Chorleywood Music Society, and sometime Guest Conductor at their concerts held between the Wars in the War Memorial Hall at Chorleywood West, when evening dress was *de rigueur* for performers and audience alike. Also in Dog Kennel Lane, next to the almshouses, is the entrance to the Chorleywood College for Girls with Little or No Sight, administered by the R.N.I.B., the only Grammar School for blind girls in England. The Manor House, opposite the church on the other side of the A404, was used as a Quaker Meeting House in William Penn's time, and part of the garden was used for a burial ground. Quaker records for 1678 state: 'Those who did not accompany Penn to America worshipped at Wilson's house in Chorleywood.'

On the other side of the A404 the Chorleywood House Estate runs down to the banks of the River Chess, a pretty little chalk stream famous for trout. The Chess gathers around Chesham, to splash and gurgle over its shallow bed alongside the B485 through Latimer, Chenies and Sarratt to Rickmansworth, where the map shows it vanishing in the Batchworth weirs. There is a lovely Chess Valley walk signposted from Chorleywood House through Beechengrove Woods and Sarratt Bottom to Chenies Mill, but unfortunately it bypasses all the villages, and all are worth seeing. There are the remains of wall-paintings in Sarratt's saddleback church, which is isolated in Sarratt Bottom with the Manor House, the Cock, and a pretty little row of almshouses, the best part of a mile from the village proper. This straggles prettily beside a generous village green on a by-road looping from Watford to Hemel Hempstead. The sleepy character of Sarratt changes dramatically every year in May, when people gather from miles around to enjoy the roundabouts and bumper-cars of the fair on the Green. There is a mini-influx of similar nature on bright Sunday mornings in spring and summer when The Boot and The Cricketers are surrounded by Landrovers, Jags and Volvos whose owners are inside having the ritual pre-lunch drink. Sarratt is a popular village, and its pleasant houses, both modest and grand, are much sought after. Stewart Granger and James Mason both lived at Sarratt (and Dirk Bogarde at Amersham) in the days when British films were still being made at Elstree Studios, and more than one present-day Sarratt resident might prove to be a household name, but they wouldn't thank me for listing them here.

A little further along the road towards Hemel Hempstead is the village of Chipperfield, scattered about a crossroads, where cricket is played on the green on summer weekends opposite the Two Brewers Inn.

A short diversion from the river walk is Latimer, one of the prettiest villages in South Buckinghamshire. Latimer vies with Chenies for the title 'Best Kept Village' and at one time one or other of them seemed always to be the holder. A handful of cottages around a triangular green, some timbered, some brick and tile, all sitting in flowers, spruced up and smartened by white picket fences, bowered in trees, Latimer oozes care and contentment. An idyllic place to live if you drive a car but, like many such villages, the back of beyond if you don't. George Gilbert Scott, the Victorian architect and church-restorer whose works can be seen throughout the Chilterns, spent much time at Latimer in his youth; is it coincidental that a large part of the village was rebuilt during the reign of the Old Queen? Still in the parish but well away from the village is the National Defence College at Latimer House, one-time residence of Lord Chesham, a Boer War veteran whose statue occupies a place of honour in the square at Aylesbury. Personnel from all the NATO countries come to this old soldier's house today to learn the business of keeping the peace, and there may be something fitting in that.

Coming back towards Chenies, Latimer Park Farm became famous earlier this century as the site of a large Roman villa. There were both Roman and Belgic sites all over Buckinghamshire and south-west Hertfordshire; St Albans (of course), Chorleywood, Sarratt, Amersham, Chesham, Great Missenden, are just a few. One old lady with a small-holding on the outskirts of Chalfont St Giles was so adept at finding bits of tile and so forth on her land as to convince herself that she lived on the site of a Roman villa; had she been removed a few miles to the north-west it might indeed have been so, for at Latimer Park Farm in 1864 excavations revealed six entire rooms, two corridors and part of the bathroom of such a villa. In 1910 two agents of Lord Chesham, to whom the farm then belonged, re-opened the site and more work was done, but not until 1963 when the new owner, Mr P.F. Cansdale, approached the Chess Valley Archaeological and Historical Society and asked them to undertake the work, was the site really investigated thoroughly and the remains of a Belgic timber villa found beneath the Roman one, showing that the Chess Valley had been settled for over two thousand years.

Latimer Park Farm, or Dell Farm as it was then known, was part of the manor of Chenies until the fourteenth century, when Sir John Cheyne held the manor then known as Isenhamsted Cheyne. But in 1376 a grant of the land was made to Adam Fraunce and his wife with the proviso that they should build there within three years, and the land passed into Latimer. In 1526 Lady Anne Sapcote, a lady who had been twice widowed and who had the manor from her mother, born a Cheyne, married Sir John Russell. He was to become first Earl of Bedford and founder of that family's fortunes. Sir John rebuilt most of the Manor House at Chenies, so Leland tells us, 'A great deal of the house is newly set-up, made of bricke and timber; and fair logginges be new erected in the garden.' These 'new logginges' were built to the west of the orangery, to serve as a nursery, and a prudent former owner constructed a tunnel leading from the main house, to use as an escape hatch in times of trouble.

Chenies remained the home of the Earls of Bedford until the middle of the seventeenth century, when they removed to Woburn. In those early years the villagers became used to the retinues of Royalty; Henry VIII was twice at the Manor House, once with Queen Anne Boleyn and once with Queen Katharine Howard. On this second occasion, when he was an old man, lame with vicious ulcer of the leg, a special bed-chamber was furnished for the King on the ground floor, while his Queen was accommodated elsewhere. But Thomas Culpeper was a member of the retinue, and driven by the itch of suspicion the ageing King left his bed to wander the house in search of his wife. Even now, it is said, in the dark hours of night, the halting footsteps of a lame man are heard stumbling along the corridors and dragging painfully upon the stair . . . All these old houses have their ghosts, and who can wonder, knowing their history?

The King held no grudge against his host for his wife's infidelity; he appointed Sir John Russell one of the sixteen

Counsellors to his infant son, and at the coronation of King Edward VI John Russell was made Great Steward of England, with an earldom. The second Earl was godfather to Sir Francis Drake, and died so deep in debt that all the contents of the manor had to be sold off to pay for his funeral. The third Earl put in hand the draining of the Cambridgeshire Fens (known to this day as the Bedford Levels); the fourth Earl removed the family to Woburn, and Chenies knew them no more until they died, and returned to lie at last in the Bedford family chapel which Sir John Russell's wife built on to St Michael's Church, Chenies, after his death in 1556. St Michael's stands so close beside the Manor House that it must surely have been built by the Isenhamsted Cheynes as an adjunct to the original manor. The lovely old Perpendicular church with its Norman font and hammer-beam roof has an austere beauty that makes the perfect foil to the richness of the Bedford Memorials, cut off in their side chapel by a glass screen from the body of the church. And the houses of Chenies village wash around the feet of the church and manor, making a perfect grouping.

The whole of the Bedford lands at Chenies were finally sold off after the sudden death of the twelfth Duke in 1953. The Manor House was bought by Alistair and Elizabeth McLeod Matthews, thereby passing back into the hands of the Cheyne family, with whom Mrs McLeod Matthews is distantly connected. Freeholds of the cottages in the village, some of them built in the middle of the nineteenth century to house the estate workers, were sold at the same time. Chenies is a model village; low, sturdy, white- or cream-washed cottages preserving a uniform neatness to two sides of the triangular green, with the church, the single-storey Church School and schoolmaster's house making up the remainder, and the unusual stepped gable of the Manor House just visible in the background. One Russell, however, returned to the district alive: Lady Ela Russell had a house built in 1895 on Bedford lands at Chorleywood. Chorleywood House stands today much as it was built for Lady Ela, a handsome brick building with stone mullions and the Bedford crest and motto, 'Che Sera Sera', high on the east wall. Lady Ela was a maiden lady of fixed ideas; she had the house built to her own design, and it wasn't until it was nearly completed that it was found that, like Noddy, she had forgotten to put in the staircase, and half the house had to be taken down again to get it in. The Chorleywood House Estate is now owned by the Council, and the lovely grounds are open for public use. The house itself is split up into Council offices on the ground floor and private flats, on long leases, on the upper floors.

4

Amersham, Chesham and Great Missenden

From Chorleywood and Chenies the railway line climbs steadily through woods and across rolling farmlands that call to mind Tennyson's lines in *The Lady of Shalott*:

> On either side the river lie
> Long fields of barley, and of rye,
> That clothe the wold and meet the sky . . .

Save that one comes, not to Tower'd Camelot but, more mundanely, to Chalfont and Latimer Station, where a branch line goes off to Chesham, five miles north-west as the crow flies. All this area, from Rickmansworth to Amersham, along the branch line to Chesham, and south of Little Chalfont to Chalfont St Giles, Chalfont St Peter and Gerrards Cross, has been built over since the First War, and more extensively since the Second. It is by far the most heavily developed part of the Chilterns, though nowhere is it 'development' as any city dweller would recognize it. Farms and woods and commons show plenty of green patches on the map, but compared with the empty acres of the Oxfordshire Chilterns this part is almost suburban.

Little Chalfont is very much post-1914; a mixed community of Council houses, private estates of bungalows, semis and modern town-houses in neat rows and closes, and smaller private estates towards Chalfont St Giles. It was known during the brief period of steam power for the traction engines and steam-ploughs of the local timber yards owned by F. Honour & Son in Lodge Lane and T. T. Boughton & Sons at Amersham Common. Steam engines in the livery of both these yards can still be seen at Chiltern fairs and rallies, and more than one garden in the district boasts a private monster, all gleaming brass and shiny black and gold paint, hidden under vast tarpaulins against the day when it sallies forth at a valiant eight miles an hour to get its picture taken by the *Bucks Examiner*.

That same newspaper was responsible in the 1960s for a letter to the editor worthy of a place in any anthology. The boys of Dr Challoner's Grammar School at Amersham had produced Brecht's *The Caucasian Chalk Circle* for their annual school play, stirring up a controversy among the parents it is difficult to comprehend in the so much more permissive climate of the Eighties. The correspondence columns of local papers fairly rang with comments, mostly against, until the whole matter was brought to a halt by a letter so apposite that, fifteen years later, I can quote it almost verbatim. It read:

> My two sons have but lately come to study at the school of Dr Challoner in Amersham, where, I am shocked to find, instead of reading the Works of the Masters they are studying the plays of one Will Shakspear, a lowly fellow, known to frequent Taverns and consort with Actors and the Like. Is this why we send our sons . . . ?

Here memory fails me, but I do recall it was 'given under my hand this day at ye sign of ye Low Chatterings, Chalfont St Giles'. I apologize to the clever lady who wrote this letter, and trust she will forgive me for not seeking her out and asking permission to reproduce it here. Not surprisingly, the editor had added at the bottom: 'This correspondence will now cease'.

Dr Challoner's Grammar School was a charity foundation of 1624, originally sited in the High Street at Old Amersham. 'Forever a free School for the Education, Institution and Instruction of Children and Youths within the age of 18 years, as well poor as rich, inhabiting within the said Parish of Amersham or in any other place, to be called the School of Dr Robert Challoner.' In 1832 there were but six boys on the roll, though there had been twenty a year or two earlier. Today there are 980 boys in the new buildings at Amersham-on-the-Hill, and over 1,000 girls at the new building, Dr Challoner's High School, at Little Chalfont. Both, at the time of writing, are competitive entry grammar schools under the care of Buckinghamshire County Council, one of the few authorities to resist the government order that all state secondary education should take place in comprehensive schools. Competition for entry to these two schools is so great that at one time it was necessary for a child to obtain upwards of 90 per cent in the eleven-plus exam to be offered a place, though of course these things change all the time.

Amersham Station, next along the line from Little Chalfont, is in the newer part of Amersham, known as Amersham-on-the-Hill. 'Old' Amersham, as it is called locally, lies at the far end of Station Road on the former London to Aylesbury coach road, now the A413. The town is first heard of in the year 1200 with the grant of a Friday Market to the Earl of Essex, then holder of the manor. Later the Friday was changed to Tuesday, but the usage died away during the nineteenth century and the only remnant is the famous Amersham Mop held every September. For many years tradition decreed that the whole High Street be closed for the Fair on the day of Amersham Mop, but nowadays the volume of traffic on the A413 is too great to permit it. The High Street is broad and well favoured, as its former name of Broadway suggests, and lined with dainty Tudor and Georgian shops, houses and cottages. The Griffin, the Crown, the Swan and the Elephant are all old hostelries, and the width of the High Street can be judged from the fact that the old Town Hall, built in 1682 to the order of Sir William Drake of Shardeloes, takes up but half the carriageway, leaving as much again for traffic to pass along the busy A413. Had the High Street been narrower, either the Town Hall would have had to be demolished, as Rickmansworth's was, or Amersham would long ago have had the bypass it sorely needs.

The Drakes of Shardeloes have long connections with Amersham; generations of the family lie in the Drake Chapel in St Mary's Church, their monuments spanning two hundred years from 1654 to 1854. The present house at Shardeloes, completed by Robert Adam in 1766 in the Palladian style, stands on a rise well back from the A413, about a mile north of the town along the road to Great Missenden. Its beautiful park was laid out by Humphry Repton, and to his order the River Misbourne, which flows through the grounds on its way to trickle along at the back of Amersham High Street, was widened into a lake. The Misbourne dried up during the long, hot, dry summer of 1977, and this lake, so long a part of the landscape, temporarily vanished. Under Shardeloes' roof today is not the one big house which needed a retinue of servants to keep it in order, but a number of highly desirable apartments leased to a few lucky owners who have full private use of the surrounding park.

But the Drakes are comparative Johnny-come-latelies to the town; preceding them by two hundred years were the first Amersham Martyrs, Lollards, followers of Wyclif, burned for their beliefs on Bury Field in 1414. Richard Turner, Walter Young and John Horwood are mentioned in the Victoria County History, while another of their number, Thomas Chase, perished at Bedford in the Bishop of Woburn's Little Ease, and in 1506 William Tilsworth's daughter was made to put the light to his funeral pyre while her husband carried wood for it. The last of the Amersham Martyrs perished in 1522, but their beliefs did not die; rather were they nurtured in secret before being revived by the seventeenth-century Dissenters, for the whole Chiltern area has a history of religious and political nonconformity, and it is no accident that this district saw the first shots of the Civil War.

On a rise between Old Amersham and Amersham-on-the-Hill, just off Station Road, is a house that caused quite a stir when it was built in 1929. The work of A.D. Connell, a follower of Le Corbusier, it consists of a number of concrete oblongs of different heights set on end against the hillside and looking out over Old Amersham. The spectacular staircase window on the tallest oblong takes up almost the whole of one wall from roof to ground, lighting the three-storey staircase from top to bottom. This building would be remarkable if built today; in 1929 it was like a slap in the face. Called 'High and Over', it is still there, together with four smaller houses of similar design built by Mr Connell's partner, Basil Ward, in 1934. Students of architectural curiosities would find it worth more than a glance, though the 1960s town houses of Highover Park that now surround it lend to High and Over a sad, quite unjustified air of *déjà vu*. With well-heeled, discerning clients to cater for, architects have built much that is good in this part of the Chilterns during the twentieth century, such as the Voysey houses at Chorleywood and Beaconsfield, Shrubs Wood at Chalfont St Giles, and the Lutyens house at Pollards Wood, Little Chalfont.

The roads going east from the old town, Gore Hill and Whielden Street, seem mere ribbons of concrete at first sight, but they lead to some of the prettiest countryside in all Buckinghamshire. Jeremiah Wharton, serving in the Parliamentary Army in the Civil War, described it as 'The sweetest country that ever I saw, and as is the country, so are the people.' A criss-cross of narrow lanes connects up the villages of Coleshill, Winchmore Hill, Penn and Tylers Green that serve the rich, rolling arable land all about them. Though you could take the bus from Amersham Station or travel these lanes by car, two wheels are the best means of locomotion here. Shut up in a car you would miss the scent of the blossoms and the air like wine, and although there is a network of footpaths, on foot you couldn't move fast enough to see it all. But drifting along on a bicycle you can inspect the lovely old red-brick farmhouses, loiter along the village greens counting the ducks on the ponds, and sample the hospitality of such inns as the Squirrel at Penn Street or the Hit and Miss at Tylers Green.

You slip back a century as you pedal along the single-track lane that winds through the woods from Winchmore Hill to Coleshill; it cuts through a beechwood where no ditch or bank separates the narrow roadway from the crumbly brown leaf-mould of the wood stretching away on either side, a leaf-mould which is covered in spring by an incomparable carpet of daffodils. The slender, unbranched trunks of the beeches rise up an infinite way above you, making a new sky of leaves instead of clouds and filtering down a new, green sunlight. On windless days the silence is almost eerie, and when rain falls it collects among the leaves in huge drops that fall with great splats into the leaf-mould.

Journeying round these villages in early summer you find verges and hedgebanks a smother of celandine and stitchwort, with delicate fronds of cow-parsley waving above and pretty little Orange-tip butterflies dancing among the blossoms. The air will be heady with the scent of summer blossom, and the horse-chestnuts, in full, glorious leaf, will be lighting up their white and deep-pink candles especially for your benefit. There are still a few black-and-white thatched cottages to be seen and plenty of Buckinghamshire brick and flint in the villages, but in the main the architecture is unremarkable, just the infinitely varied dolly-mixture of styles that go to make up an English village. Pink-washed, cream-washed, red-brick and stone, overhung by trees and decked with flowers, the houses and cottages line the lanes and cluster around the generous village greens, rubbing shoulders and nodding heads to each other in the friendliest, homeliest way. And all these villages have their history; at Stock Place, Coleshill, the poet Edmund Waller was born in March of 1606. Here, under Waller's Oak, he is presumed to have sat writing 'Go, Lovely Rose' and his other poems. Waller was a political animal, a prudent man who, though a Royalist much at home in the Court of Charles I, kept his peace with the Parliamentarians while they were in power. He loved his cousin, Lady Dorothy Sidney, and much of his poetry was written for her. But the lady would have none of him, so he bought Hall Barn, Beaconsfield, with his widowed mother and lived there until he died, and was buried there in the churchyard.

Thomas Ellwood, the Quaker, had a house near Coleshill, which in his time was a detached part of Hertfordshire. His home was used as a Quaker Meeting House at a time when such Meetings were unlawful and Quakers were being imprisoned and persecuted for their beliefs. It was then one of the few places where Friends could meet in comparative safety, for the Hertfordshire magistrates rarely stirred themselves to exercise authority there, having enough trouble under their noses at home, while the Buckinghamshire warrant was not valid in this off-shoot of Hertfordshire. One wonders if Thomas Ellwood chose his house with this in mind.

At Tylers Green the statesman Edmund Burke, also buried in the church at Beaconsfield, founded a school in 1796 for the children of French Royalists who were executed during the Revolution; it was in existence for only twenty-four years, but is still remembered in the name 'French School Meadow'. Penn, which runs into Tylers Green along the B474, is famous as the birthplace of Jack Shrimpton the highwayman, who ruled the Oxford Road so that 'scarce a coach or horseman could pass without being robbed'. There is a memorial to him, not in the church at Beaconsfield this time but in the bar of the Bull Hotel on the Oxford Road at Gerrards Cross, a hostelry which knew him well in his heyday.

On the far side of the A404 Holmer Green, once another village such as those we have been visiting, is now almost overcome by the spread of modern development. Almost, but not quite; there are still cottages along the village green, still cricket to be watched there in summer or football in winter, and still the bar of the Bat and Ball with ready welcome. But nothing to commemorate Christina Rossetti as the Pink and Lily at Speen commemorates Rupert Brooke, though she lived in the village for many years and he was but passing through. Perhaps the village took her own words too literally:

> When I am dead, my dearest,
>   Sing no sad songs for me;
> Plant thou no roses at my head
>   Nor shady cypress tree:
> Be the green grass above me
>   With showers and dew-drops wet,
> And if thou wilt, remember,
>   And, if thou wilt, forget.

From Chalfont and Latimer a branch line skirts Amersham-on-the-Hill and the superior residences of Chesham Bois to wind northwards through deep cuttings to Chesham. London Transport claims that this line is uneconomic and keeps threatening to axe it, but each time an active and vocal Users' Committee puts up a sufficiently convincing case for its retention. Certainly the loss of the line would make a big difference to Chesham residents who, given a lucky change at Chalfont and Latimer, can be in London within the hour.

The River Chess bubbles up in the old part of town at The Bury, and though residents call the town Chez'am rather than the more obvious Chesh-am, the river, in fact, takes its name from the town. It is a clear trout stream, running with a mass of white and yellow water crowfoot in a little cutting through the old town, to trickle prettily along beside the aptly named Waterside and the back road to Chenies and Latimer. There is a mill house beautifully preserved and added to beside the little weir at Chenies, before the river runs through water meadows on its way to its end at Rickmansworth. A short but truly lovely eight miles, most of which is fully accessible – though not necessarily to fishermen.

Much larger than Amersham or Rickmansworth, Chesham is really three towns in one. The oldest part, where the River Chess rises by Church Street, dates back to the fourteenth century, and is as different from the Victorian and Edwardian terraces of the town centre as it is from the high-density flats and town-houses that were built along Waterside during the 1970s, and the smart, modern estates off Chartridge Lane and White Hill. The periods are very mixed; of Church Street, for example, Pevsner says that Nos 54 and 56 are fourteenth century, No. 58 mid-Georgian, and The Bury, built for William Lowndes, one-time Secretary to the Treasury, has the date 1712 on the rain-water heads. A row of Georgian cottages leads to Wey Lane and Fullers Hill, where Germains still has one timber-framed wing dating back before the Reformation. In the High Street the Post Office, within a stone's throw of Waitrose and Sainsbury's vast modern supermarkets, dates from 1625, and on the road towards Latimer, Blackwell Hall Farm preserves its sixteenth-century leaded and mullioned windows.

'Boots, Brushes, Beer and Baptists' was the going description of the town when the Met Line joined it to Aylesbury, Amersham and Rickmansworth in 1889, but the families of boot and brushmakers that made such a success in Chesham during the nineteenth century were followed by any number of others bringing new trades to the small workshops around Townsend Road and along Waterside, and the old country town put on a brisk new workaday face. Today Chesham is third in the Chilterns' league of industrial towns, smaller only than Aylesbury and High Wycombe, and former family concerns like Webb, Jarratt the brushmakers now market their products internationally. One concern founded in Chesham around the turn of the century moved on to greater things elsewhere; the draper's shop opened in the High Street by Mr Arthur Liberty to sell, among other things, goods from his sisters' nearby silk workshops, grew into one of London's leading stores, Liberty's of Regent Street, and Mr Arthur prospered to become Sir Arthur Lasenby Liberty, Lord of the Manor at The Lee.

The Lee is one of the tiny villages set in the lattice of lanes in the Chesham, Wendover, Great Missenden triangle; here an ancient ditch and earthworks enclose a part-timbered farmhouse and an old church, a Grade 1 listed building with rare wall-paintings, a twelfth-century font and a fraction of thirteenth-century glass. Sir Arthur took the village in hand, re-routed the roads to provide a village green, rebuilt the Cock and Rabbit on a more imposing site beside the 'new' church built in the 1860s, and decorated the new green with chunks of Hertfordshire pudding-stone dug out at Lee Gate. His descendants, the Stewart-Libertys, have built houses for their estate workers of a more than usually high standard to complement the seventeenth- and eighteenth-century cottages that lie on the north side of the green, and their preservation of this picturesque village was recognized in 1980 when it was declared a Conservation Area, 'of special architectural or historical interest, the character of which it is desirable to preserve'.

Nor was 'Baptists' a frivolous description; an obstinate refusal by the men of Chesham to worship in any way but their own has led to a history of nonconformity in the town. Early in the sixteenth century Thomas Harding was put to death 'in the Dell going to Botley', which has been established as the bottom of White Hill, after being stood in the corner like a dunce and publicly preached against by Richard Woodcoke, 'Hammer of the Heretics', in St Mary's Church. As early as 1506 Thomas Harding was in trouble with the Church 'for speaking against Idolatry and Superstition'; he was tried again with his wife,

Alice, in 1515, and yet again in 1522. In 1532 he was again brought to task for praying alone instead of going to church as all good men should, discovered to be in possession of a copy of Wyclif's English Bible, and condemned to his martyrdom.

Thomas Harding was only the forerunner of many Chesham dissenters, in witness of which meeting-places and citadels of Baptists, Calvinists, Congregationalists, Quakers, Salvationists, Wesleyans, Zionists and United Free rub their plain, undecorated shoulders in the middle of the town and spread towards the outskirts, while right in the centre the lovely Perpendicular church of St Mary tries to put the record straight with a cross in the churchyard bearing the inscription: 'To the Glory of God and to the Memory of Thomas Harding, Martyr, of Dunsgrove, Chesham, who in fiery trial at the stake laid down his life for the Word of God and for the testimony of Jesus Christ in this Parish on May 30th, 1532. The Noble Army of Martyrs praise Thee.'

Any number of lovely country lanes lead away from Chesham in a panoramic semicircle east, north and west to the pretty villages of the surrounding countryside. From Botley and Ley Hill in the east they work round to Whelpley Hill and Ashley Green on the road to Berkhamsted, to the villages of Hawridge, Cholesbury, Buckland Common and St Leonards set on their high heath before Tring, and through the lovely lacing of up-and-down single-track lanes by Pednor and Chartridge and Hyde Heath back towards Amersham and Great Missenden. William Cobbett described this countryside around Chesham whilst on the first of his *Rural Rides* in 1821: 'This is most beautiful! The hedges are now full of the shepherd's-rose, honeysuckles, and all sorts of wild-flowers; so that you are upon a grass walk, with this most beautiful of all flower-gardens and shrubberies on your one hand, and with the corn on the other.' So it is in the lanes around Chesham today. There are a few houses, some old, some new, but thanks to the Green Belt the countryside is largely the unspoiled home of wild creatures and the beasts of the field, as it was in Cobbett's day.

Although Amersham is the terminus for London Transport's electric trains, British Rail's diesels from Marylebone which run over the same tracks carry on for three stations more: Great Missenden, Wendover and Aylesbury. When peace was declared in 1945 Great Missenden was a sleepy little place with one main street, three or four inns, a few surrounding cottages and a railway station on the Met Line. It was the country destination of London cycling clubs and the haunt of the Sunday hiker, and the surrounding villages of Prestwood, the Kingshills, Little Missenden, Hyde Heath, Ballinger and The Lee were planets to its tiny sun.

Today some of those who first saw this peaceful village on their weekend visits to the country are among the thousands who have come to live in the new houses and estates that have sprung up within reach of Missenden Station during the last three decades. Great Missenden itself, limited in one direction by the A413 and in the other by the railway line, has not been too greatly affected, but just along the road Prestwood has taken on quite a different aspect and become almost urban, with row upon row of new town-houses and semis. Great and Little Kingshill have been more kindly dealt with; although both villages have been added to their rural air remains. But on the far side of the A414 where Frith Hill goes due east to Chesham, the villages of Hyde Heath, South Heath and Ballinger have put on body and spread along the lanes in all directions, modest houses and bungalows rubbing shoulders with large private residences secluded behind the walls and hedges of their own acres.

These are the lanes where, every year in May, Dede Monzani ushers the two hundred or so young people who turn out annually for her twenty-mile Sponsored Walk for Spastics. Starting from Dr Challoner's Boys School at Amersham, they go along Copperkins Lane to Hyde Heath, down Frith Hill to Great Missenden, through the town to the Nags Head for a quick bite of lunch, then on through the Kingshills, Spurlands End and Holmer Green to a two-mile finishing tramp along the verges of the A404 that would kill them off like flies had not the crafty marshals at the last halt on the green at Penn Street told them that the finishing point at Old Amersham was 'just along the road'!

Always in the forefront of the walk and among the first to finish every year is Mrs Monzani's daughter Paula, herself a spastic, in her wheelchair. Mrs Monzani gathers up her walkers and marshals from the discos and dancing classes she runs on winter evenings and in school holidays in and around Amersham. Her bubbling personality and loving understanding of young people make these dances very popular, and not only do her customers have the fun of learning to dance, they also learn to give pleasure to others at her Wheelchair Evenings, where they waltz and jive their disabled partners through the bumps and thrills of a rollicking three hours of wheelchair dances. Mrs Monzani's Walks raise thousands of pounds annually, and her activities help to teach the rest of us that the disabled are just ordinary people, and not a race apart.

North of Ballinger Bottom towards The Lee, the lanes narrow down to single track and high hedges obscure the view. The way becomes more secretive and remote; the rows of smart new houses have been left behind, and only an occasional farm or cottage breaks up the countryside. Places with names like 'Cherry Tree' or 'Chiltern Haven' stand isolated in their rural fastness, though they can be no more than three miles from Missenden, Chesham or Wendover. Blooms of musky elderflower hang like old lace above the roses and honeysuckle of the June hedgerows, and between the hedges glimpses can be seen of rolling cornfields splashed blood-red with poppies, while overhead gliders from the airfield at Booker, near High Wycombe, soar like silent ghosts.

Like the lanes beyond Amersham around Winchmore Hill and Penn, this is good cycling country, seen at its best from a perch above two wheels. Somewhere as you labour up the hills and whizz down you will be startled to find yourself within the confines of Pednor Manor, where the lane cuts through. It is an odd experience to be at one moment on a country lane without a building in sight and the next in a courtyard where old red-brick houses converted from farm buildings of the sixteenth-century manor form three sides of a square on one hand, and the garages form the fourth side on the other, all enclosed between tall pillars like twisted Tudor chimney-pots, where the lane cuts through. A case for saying 'What was that?' and going back for another look.

Great Missenden is the starting place for another clear chalk stream, the River Misbourne. It is said to rise in Mobwell Meadow, opposite the Black Horse, from where it flows through the grounds of Missenden Abbey, through the village of Little Missenden and on to Amersham. It can be seen for most of the way beside the A413, until it widens into Shardeloes Lake.

The years which have so changed Great Missenden and the surrounding villages have left Little Missenden undisturbed, and it survives as a charming example of the true English village; church, manor house, farms and cottages, the river running by and over all a rural peace, total and undisturbed. What more could one ask? The manor house is Jacobean, but the church of St John the Baptist around which the village houses cluster as chicks around a hen, is truly old. The most recent part, the porch, was added in 1450, the oldest of the bells is fourteenth century, the beautiful wall-paintings uncovered in 1931 are part twelfth century, and there are Roman bricks in the chancel arch, which was built by Anglo-Saxons. Yet at the annual Missenden Festival of Music and the Arts this old church is the focal point for displaying the work of some of our most modern artists and writers, a fitting tribute to one who said: 'Behold, I make all things new'.

5

The Chalfonts, Gerrards Cross and Beaconsfield

To the south of Amersham lie Chalfont St Giles, Chalfont St Peter and Gerrards Cross, all good examples of suburban development. Chalfont St Giles is a historic village, principally noted for having sheltered the poet John Milton and his family from the Plague in 1665. With London so unsavoury, Milton wrote to his friend Thomas Ellwood, the Quaker, asking him to find a modest house for himself and his family until the Plague was over. Only two houses remain in the village from that time, Stonewells Farm on the corner of Bowstridge Lane, and the 'pretty box' Thomas Ellwood found for his friend, now preserved as 'Milton's Cottage', a museum to the poet's memory. In the event, Milton lived there only until the Great Fire had swept the capital clean before returning to his beloved London, to die there in 1674 and be buried in St Giles Church, Cripplegate.

Although his time there was so short, Milton's Cottage is the only house still in existence where the poet is known to have lived, and in 1887 the cottage was bought by public subscription as a Milton Museum to commemorate Queen Victoria's Jubilee, the Queen herself heading the list with a donation of £20. It was refurbished in 1977 as part of the Jubilee celebrations for our present Queen, and is on view to the public, together with a roomful of Milton memorabilia. It is said that the poet finished *Paradise Lost* here, and started on *Paradise Regained*. At one time, according to the curator, there was a first edition of *Paradise Lost* on view in the museum, but it was stolen in 1977 before the present burglar alarm system was installed. There is an appeal on hand to buy another.

The tower of St Giles Church can be seen rising above the village shops just off the green. It is reached through an arched entrance between the shops, and thence by an intriguing rotating lych-gate. Parts of the church are thirteenth century, and there are extensive and well-preserved fourteenth-century wall-paintings, but the church was restored by the Victorians and the attractive glass is all nineteenth century.

Well built up to both sides of the High Street and along the

connecting roads to Little Chalfont in one direction and
Beaconsfield in the other, Chalfont St Giles is almost too big
now to be called a village, but it has escaped the fate of Chalfont
St Peter which has been virtually cut in half by the A413, and
where the entry to the village has been re-developed into a
modern shopping precinct. The bypass runs where horse-drawn
traffic of yesteryear once forded the Misbourne, and the river is
buried in a culvert, making only a brief appearance between the
car park and the Greyhound Inn where its neat banks are
brightened from April to June with patches of white ramsons.
Judge Jeffreys, who lived at Bulstrode Park in the days when it
was still within the bounds of St Peter parish, held court at the
Greyhound during the 1680s. In those days the Greyhound was
a coaching inn on the London to Aylesbury road, and a smart
black and yellow coach stood in the yard to remind passers-by of
its former glories until the yard was built over in the 1970s to
make a dining-room. The arch through which the weary,
lathered horses pulled their load after the long haul from
London has been bricked up, and the garden where, much later,
afternoon teas were served to weekend hikers, has been paved
over.

Bulstrode Park is now part of Gerrards Cross, separated from
Chalfont St Peter by a fine stretch of part-wooded common. This
is a pleasant, superior suburb bisected by the A40, a place of
broad, leafy avenues and quiet private roads, bordered on all
sides by parks and commons and with the added attraction of a
reed-edged pond at Latchmoor. Part of it dates from the 1920s
and '30s, but much of the development is post-war, particularly
at Bulstrode where individually designed houses stand in large
plots along the private roads. The name 'Bulstrode' was coined
in honour of a family named Shobbington, who held the manor
at the time of the Norman invasion. They rode out on bulls to
oppose the Conqueror, who was so impressed with their
audacity that he left them in possession of their lands, whereupon they changed their name to Bulstrode and added a bull's
head to their crest.

Bulstrode Park has had a chequered career since the
infamous judge lived there. His lands and property were
sequestered when he was taken to the Tower, and the manor
was later granted to the Earl of Portland by William of Orange.
After many alterations, some by James Wyatt who was responsible for Ashridge, the house was demolished in 1860 and the

present mansion built for the Duke of Somerset. The Park changed hands many times until in the 1950s, reduced to the mansion and seventy-five acres of woodland, it was bought as a commune by the Society of Brothers, a German group formerly known as the Bruderhof. The commune lasted ten years, fighting a losing battle with rot and decay in the mansion, which had been left too long empty and open to the weather, and with encroaching woodland in the park. They eked out a frugal living by farming what land they could clear and by selling beautifully made wooden toys and garden furniture to their visitors, who came by the coachload.

Family communes were more of a rarity in the 1950s and 1960s, and in any case this one would have been something of an anomaly in well-heeled Gerrards Cross. Though the members desperately supplemented their income by selling off to collectors such bits of the mansion as could be taken away, like the garden statues and the great chandelier over the main staircase, in 1966 they admitted defeat and moved on, leaving the mansion empty once more.

It was bought by the present occupiers, the Worldwide Evangelical Crusade, who had lost their more modest headquarters in Upper Norwood as the result of a compulsory purchase order. They have cleared the land and tilled it, and with some professional help but largely by voluntary labour, have put the mansion into good order and restored much of its former beauty. The lovely, light entrance hall with its delicate plaster mouldings and wide sweep of staircase greets the visitor with that fresh, clean smell of beeswax and furniture polish that one hardly ever encounters in these days of instant shine. The daily complement at Bulstrode today is about a hundred people, including children, but the number increases by half as much again at weekends. Among other things, the buildings are used as an Evangelical Conference Centre, for youth work, and as a family home for overseas workers and missionaries who have no other base in England. They must find Bulstrode's green, rolling acres very pleasant after the arid plains of Africa or the steaming South American jungle, and the affluent shopping centre of Gerrards Cross very different from the primitive villages and settlements they are used to.

Like its next-door neighbour Gerrards Cross, the pretty little town of Beaconsfield is much favoured as a home base by well-travelled businessmen for its nearness to London Airport, only a comfortable, chauffeur-driven twenty minutes away. Beacons-field acknowledges its dual character by labelling half of itself 'Beaconsfield New Town'; here are just such tree-lined streets of solid, detached middle-class houses as are seen all over this part of the Chilterns, interspersed with little private schools preparing their pupils for greater things elsewhere, and shops along the post-war parades that grow fat on commuter incomes.

The older part of the town is different again. This is the town that Burke and Waller knew, and to which Chesterton came in the 1920s to sit in the bar at the White Hart quaffing his ale and endlessly talking. A town of seventeenth-century houses set far back along broad and noble thoroughfares, many of them now converted to offices for solicitors and surveyors or to shops for the sale of antiques. Some of the old houses along the main street have been most cleverly re-fronted, their modern leaded panes and concrete facings managing to look not at all out of place.

Right in the centre of Beaconsfield the ways cross from London to High Wycombe and from Windsor to Aylesbury, the four roads being known as Windsor End, London End, Wycombe End and Aylesbury End. St Mary's Church, where Waller and Burke lie buried, the former under a monolith in the churchyard and the latter commemorated by a modest plaque on the floor of the church (fourth pew from front, right-hand side), stands in the south-west corner of this crossing, at Windsor End. Alongside, forming three sides to a courtyard, is its former Rectory, a fine old timbered building dating from the early 1500s. The Church School, recently made redundant, has been converted to a workshop and studio by Patrick Reyntiens, the world-famous stained-glass artist who was responsible for producing John Piper's magnificent window for Coventry Cathedral. Besides creating such wonderful works of art, the studio also offers post-graduate courses in stained-glass work for professionals and a few courses for beginners in the art, reminiscent of Eric Gill's establishment at Piggotts in the 1940s.

Beaconsfield's most famous son is probably the Whig politician Edmund Burke, though he was an Irishman, born and educated in Dublin. He bought the estate of Gregories at Beaconsfield in 1768 and lived there until his death in 1797. Outspoken, rash and always broke, Burke was something of a trial to his friends and a gift to his political enemies. He was cast in that mould of men that these hills have ever sheltered, free-thinkers, intellectuals, political activists. Burke's humane attitude to the colonies, as witnessed in his speech on American Taxation in 1774, was far in advance of his time, and had his liberal advice been heeded much bad feeling between the English-speaking nations might have been avoided, and much bloodshed. The speech he made later, to open the impeachment of Warren Hastings, had the same impact on his generation as Churchill's war speeches had upon ours. He was offered a peerage as the Earl of Beaconsfield, but he turned it down. Disraeli is said to have so admired Burke that when his turn came he chose his title, Lord Beaconsfield, in Burke's honour.

Burke was a great entertainer and a man with hundreds of friends. Sheridan and Garrick were among those who stayed regularly at Gregories, and Dr Johnson came in the company of Mrs Thrale. The estate Burke bought with money borrowed from friends and maintained so perilously against bailiffs and warrants and orders for debt for nearly thirty years, and where he carried out his experiments in agriculture, often leading the horses or guiding the plough himself, now lies beneath the houses of the New Town, though the seventeenth-century Burke House still stands in the High Street. Hall Barn, in Windsor End, the house that Waller built, has been more kindly dealt with; it belongs today to Lord Burnham, who has preserved and enhanced the house in its country setting. In 1809 William Hickey took 'a pretty cottage called Little Hall Barn' near Waller's house, and settled down to write the *Memoirs* that were edited in the 1960s by Peter Quennell at Berkhamsted.

This lovely old town is the last outpost of old Buckinghamshire. Only the gnarled, ruined trunks of Burnham Beeches separate it from the modern wastes of Slough in the south, and in the west the ways cross the M4 to make for the riverside towns of Cookham and Maidenhead. Mercifully, the A40 and M40 both pass Beaconsfield by, leaving it to its peaceful devices, and though there is much development in the New Town around the railway, the old, broad High Street is beautifully preserved.

In the New Town is a feature that has put Beaconsfield on the international map: Bekonscot Model Village. Started as a hobby in 1929 by Mr Roland Callingham, its seventy-five buildings averaging two foot in height with their 1,200 tiny residents hand-carved from wood, now cover an acre of ground. The village has churches, castles, Tudor-style houses, a zoo, railway line, airport, pier and lighthouse, docks and refinery, all set among miniature trees and growing plants that leave not a square inch of bare earth in the whole complex. It is significant that the descriptive booklet is printed in three languages, for over six million visitors from all over the world have admired this society in miniature during its fifty years' existence, and in that time over £300,000 has been collected for charity. Queen Mary was a frequent visitor, and the *Bekonscot Advertiser*, printed to celebrate the village's golden jubilee in 1979, has a charming picture of her there with our own Queen, then aged eight.

The model village is now run by a committee of three people nominated by the founder's widow and three nominated by the Church Army, one of Bekonscot's charities. A staff of gardeners, modellers and administrators now keep the wheels turning at Bekonscot, and all profits realized after the running expenses have been met go to charity, an average of £20,000 every year.

Chorleywood Station

Metroland in springtime when these trees are a mass of pink or white blossom

Chenies Manor, still a family home

The River Chess at Sarratt Bottom

Old Amersham

Chesham High Street

Chalfont St Peter from Gold Hill Common

Beaconsfield

Great Missenden

Leafy Buckinghamshire—a view near Great Missenden

Tring. The Market Square and the neo-Tudor Rose and Crown

The mansion at Ashridge. The spire is a fibreglass replacement

Dean Incent's House, Berkhamsted

School House, Berkhamsted

The village pond at Aldbury

Wendover High Street

6

A Little Bit of Hertfordshire

The early 1950s were the palmy days of radio, when advertising was infra-dig and hardly anyone had telly. In those days the soft Hertfordshire burr of Sir Bernard Miles was to be heard on the air putting 'a edge' on his sickle on the 'finest bit o' shaarpenin' stone in 'Aarfordshere'. Billed as the Uncrowned King of the Chiltern Hills, he would chortle his wily way around the countryside, his accent keeping us all spellbound. If Sir Bernard was indeed a Hertfordshire man native to the Chiltern Hills, he would have been born in that narrow salient where the A41 carries a strip of Hertfordshire deep into Buckinghamshire, almost as far as the county town of Aylesbury. Here are the towns of Berkhamsted and Tring, the villages of Marsworth, Aldbury, Wigginton and Little Gaddesden, and the glories of Ashridge. There are few places where the Chiltern beechwoods can be seen to better advantage than at Frithsden ('Freesden') on the Ashridge estate, and not only are there beechwoods, but open glades and heaths and misty views of not-too-distant hills, and if you are lucky you may see a deer.

This district is part of the old hundred of Tring, ruled from Hemel Hempstead by the Dacorum District Council, though with sub-offices at both Berkhamsted and Tring reminiscent of the days when they were autonomous as 'Tring and Tring Rural' and 'Berkhamsted and Berkhamsted Rural'. There is a definite feeling of Hertfordshire in this scoop out of Buckinghamshire; busy though they are, Berkhamsted and Tring lack the air of immediacy that is about in the Buckinghamshire towns of Aylesbury and High Wycombe, without seeming either so rural as Wendover nor so long-set as Thame or Princes Risborough, and the villages seem neater, flatter and less isolated than those of leafy Buckinghamshire.

Berkhamsted and Tring bestride the A41, which forms the High Street in both towns. This was formerly the old coaching road from London to Birmingham, and before that it was part of the road the Romans built from St Albans to Cirencester and Bath, called Akeman Street. Berkhamsted is the larger town of the two, its population in 1980 being nearly 16,000.

As you drive downhill into Berkhamsted through the lanes on

the Ashridge side, there are glimpses through the trees to where the town snuggles in the cleft of the Bulbourne Valley, the older parts settled along the valley bottom and the newer estates of council houses and solid middle-class residences climbing the hills on either side. All the necessities of life can be supplied by the High Street shops, from boots to books, food to furniture. There are several large car-parks, the usual supermarkets, and some old-established department stores, though the town is not large enough to support the more famous multiples. The High Street is broad and airy with wide pavements, but it straggles untidily for the better part of two miles along the A41 with no noticeable centre since its sixteenth-century market hall burned down in 1854.

The railway line that runs parallel with the High Street is the main route from London to Carlisle, carrying some of British Rail's most modern rolling stock and whisking Berkhamsted's commuters to London in well under the hour. An imposing railway station, built when the line was opened in the year Queen Victoria came to the throne, stands in Castle Street, close to where the Grand Union Canal flows beneath the castle walls; the trees around the site and the green space beyond the canal bank lend an open and countrified aspect which is not belied, for Berkhamsted is a true country town and for all its present nondescript appearance it has a long history.

On a cold November day in 1066 all that remained of King Harold's nobles, 'Bishop Ealdred, Prince Edgar, Earl Morcar, Earl Edwin, and all the best men from London', as the Anglo-Saxon Chronicle says, waited at Berkhamsted for William the Conqueror. He had won his battle at Hastings and killed everyone in sight of any importance, and was harrying up the country looking for someone of sufficient importance to crown him King. He found him at Berkhamsted with the others, and at Westminster on Christmas Day Bishop Ealdred finally placed the crown of England upon the Conqueror's head, he first having sworn on oath 'that he would govern this nation according to the best practice of his predecessors if they [the Saxon nobles] would be loyal to him'. The Chronicle continues: 'Nevertheless, he imposed a very heavy tax on the country, and went oversea to Normandy in the spring'.* A typical absentee landlord. But the

* The Anglo-Saxon Chronicle, translated by G. N. Garmonsway, Everyman edition, 1953.

first step towards his crowning was at Berkhamsted, when the Saxon nobles bowed the knee and conceded William's victory, while he promised to be a 'Kind Lord' to them. His first act of kindness was to share out the Saxon lands between his own countrymen. His half-brother, Robert of Mortain, was granted Berkhamsted for his trouble, and Robert used the men of the town to build him a fortified castle on high land to the east.

Count Mortain's castle was protected by wooden palisades hewn from the surrounding beechwoods, but in the next century, when Thomas à Becket held the manor under Henry II, it was rebuilt with a stone keep and curtain walls. These walls seem to have suffered from thirteenth-century jerry-building, for they were breached a few years after Thomas's death by the barons in their war against King John, and had to be rebuilt once more. From then on the castle was in continuous use as a royal residence until nearly 1500, when Henry VIII moved the Court to Ashridge. One of its owners, Richard, Earl of Cornwall, was elected King of the Holy Roman Empire, the only Englishman to be so distinguished. The castle walls were breached once more by the guns of Cromwell's men in the Civil War, before being left at last to the soft, disintegrating touch of the summer suns and winter rains, and the encroaching grass and weeds.

Over the years Berkhamsted's residents found the castle a marvellous quarry for ready-cut stone, and many a local house has bits of castle wall under the foundations. The main barbican and gateway were sliced off when the railway station was built, and more ground was lost to the roads that encircle the site. Since the castle was put into the care of the Ministry of Works in 1930 the remains have been kept tidy and well cared for, though today the curtain walls serve only to retain the smooth, raised lawns that cover what is left of the ruins.

The castle has probably put Berkhamsted to a deal of trouble over the years, but there is no doubt the town owes it much. The close connection with Royalty brought trade, prosperity and privilege; the town's first Royal Charter was granted by Henry II in 1156, and more than one castle resident has been a benefactor in the town. Dr John Incent, one-time Dean of St Paul's, knew Berkhamsted as a boy when his father held office at the castle, and when, during the Dissolution, he was appointed to dispose of religious property in the district, he took the opportunity to secure lands and property to add to his foundation for the education of poor boys, endowed with his own

Berkhamsted property in 1523. This was the start of the Berkhamsted Schools.

At first Dr Incent's school flourished, having nearly a hundred pupils at the end of the sixteenth century, but during the succeeding two hundred years it fell upon hard times and waned almost away. When in the middle of the nineteenth century the school was revitalized and Dean Incent's projected number of 140 scholars was at last reached, these scholars, with a few exceptions, were fee-payers, and Berkhamsted joined the long list of medieval foundations for poor scholars that today educate the children of the better-off middle class. Later the school became grant-aided and places for clever boys were paid for by the county, but when the 1944 Education Act was passed the governors opted for independence as a public school.

The lovely old buildings of the Boys' School, and some very creditable modern ones, take up most of the west side of Castle Street and stretch back to Mill Street, where Newcroft, the new building, was opened in 1958 by the Queen Mother. Berkhamsted Girls' School operates under substantially the same Board of Governors, and occupies premises in Upper Kings Road specially built for the school in 1902, though much enlarged over the years. This unremarkable building is rivalled by Dacorum's Ashlyns School, built higher up the hill in Chesham Road. Ashlyns Estate has occupied its hilltop site since the fourteenth century, remaining in private hands until the 1920s when it was bought by the Thomas Coram Foundation to build a new Foundling Hospital to replace their London Home. It was the building and lands of this 'Hospital' that Hertfordshire County Council acquired for Ashlyns School in the 1960s when it was decided to make it the county's first comprehensive school. It is a showplace, with substantial buildings set in smooth green lawns, and an imposing chapel fronting the road.

The town has its literary associations: the publisher William Longman, founder of the now enormous Longman publishing house which, among other companies, owns Penguin Books, lived at Ashlyns Hall when he published Macaulay's *History of England*. The sales of this book exceeded all hopes, 140,000 being sold and one of the cheques to Macaulay on account being for £20,000. In the 1940s one of the historian's descendants, Professor George Macaulay Trevelyan, came to Berkhamsted to write his *English Social History*, another book whose sales were unprecedented and one which the author was to see attain the prestige of a standard work in his lifetime. G. M. Trevelyan was also Founder Chairman of the Youth Hostels Association. Another literary family, J.H.B. and Marjorie Quennell and their son Peter Quennell, the biographer, lived at Berkhamsted at this time, as did the novelist Graham Greene, whose father was Headmaster of Berkhamsted School. In 1980 Mr Greene's novel *The Human Factor* was filmed in the town and on the nearby Ashridge Estate. Probably Berkhamsted's most famous literary figure, though, is the poet William Cowper, born in 1731 at the old rectory of Berkhamsted St Mary's, though it seems a little unjust that Cowper should always be thought of immediately in connection with Berkhamsted, while the more recent literary figures, whose output was enormous by contrast, have to be discovered by research.

The church of St Mary at Berkhamsted dates back to Saxon times, and except for Wing is easily the oldest church in this area of old churches. There is some lovely old glass, and a seventeenth-century painting of the Madonna and child in the north aisle. St Mary's is the centre of the original settlement of Berkhamsted, standing to the north of the present town. After St Peter's had been built in the 'newer' part of the town centred on the coaching road, St Mary's became known as the North Church; as so often, the description became a name, and it is as Northchurch that the village is now known. At the Northchurch end of the High Street is a row of single-storey almshouses, 'The Guift of John Sayer Esq. 1684'. John Sayer was head cook to Charles II, following him faithfully in good times and bad. He had family connections with Berkhamsted, and bequeathed £1,000 in his will, no small sum at that time, to provide accommodation for six poor widows. This sum was added to by his wife, who had the almshouses built after his death. In all £269 was spent on the terrace of six houses, the remainder of the bequest being invested for their upkeep. The almshouses have been remodelled recently, keeping the same exterior, and now provide homes for only four old ladies, who are no longer required to walk to church on Sundays two and two, all dressed alike and with the oldest bringing up the rear!

I expect the old ladies of Northchurch were, in their time, among those disturbed by Peter the Wild boy of Berkhamsted who was frequently to be seen wandering about the district during the second half of the eighteenth century. George I, on a visit to Hanover, 'found' the boy sleeping in byres and under hedges, living with animals and eating the fruits of the fields, brought him to England (on whose authority, one wonders?) and boarded him out at Northchurch where he lived out his years and was buried in the churchyard when he died in 1785. Never violent or difficult, he readily performed such small tasks as were given to him, but all efforts to teach him to speak were in vain. He loved the woods and the countryside, and was so often found wandering abroad that his 'keeper' fitted him with a dog collar giving his name and address, and promising a reward for his return. A contemporary portrait shows a heavily bearded, rather puzzled-looking fellow, and my own theory is that the poor chap was deaf. One can only glimpse his bewilderment at being removed willy-nilly from familiar surroundings and shipped across the sea to be dumped among strangers. His gravestone is still to be seen in St Mary's churchyard, inscribed with the only name he ever knew: 'Peter the Wild Boy'.

7

Ashridge, Aldbury and the Gaddesdens

The Ashridge Estate lies to the north-east of Berkhamsted, on the far side of Berkhamsted Common. Today it is in the care of the National Trust, as so much of our best countryside is, miles of free green playground preserved for our delight. With stretches of broad heath, beechwoods and quiet glades, it is a favourite spot for winter walks and summer picnics, only the area belonging to the Management College on the eastern edge being excluded.

Its history goes back to 1283 when Edmund son of the Earl of Cornwall, who at that time held the manor, founded a monastery on the site to guard his precious Holy Relic, a phial said to contain the blood of Christ, given to him by the Patriarch of Jerusalem. The monastery flourished, bringing many pilgrims to worship at its shrine, and at the Dissolution it was taken over by Henry VIII as a royal residence in place of Berkhamsted Castle, which had become too old-fashioned and uncomfortable. Queen Elizabeth spent much of her childhood there, inheriting the house under King Henry's will and later selling it to her Lord Keeper of the Seal, Sir Thomas Egerton. He it was who combined Ashridge with the manors of Frithsden and Little Gaddesden into a considerable estate. His descendants became the Dukes and Earls of Bridgewater, and the estate remained in the hands of the Bridgewater family, though not in direct line, until the last Earl died in 1921. It was then that the estate, excepting the mansion and 230 acres of garden, was bought by public subscription and given to the National Trust.

The Trust's holding extends over some of the finest stands of beechwood and stretches of chalk downland in England: Ivinghoe Beacon, Pitstone Hill, Steps Hill, Clipper Down, and Ringshall Coppice, running down to Aldbury, Berkhamsted and Northchurch Commons. These commons extend to more than 1,000 acres, the largest single stretch of common land in England. Berkhamsted Common in particular serves to illustrate a remark made by Dr Dudley Stamp in the Introduction to his *Common Lands of England and Wales*, to the effect that there are over 500,000 acres of common land in Great Britain, most of which we owe to some obstinate old man who refused to agree to what everyone else thought was for the best at the time. In 1865 Lord Brownlow, then owner of Ashridge, sought to enclose Berkhamsted Common, but one old man with rights of commonage went to law to prevent him, and won. A truly English victory.

The mansion that Queen Elizabeth knew, much changed and added to over the years, was so neglected by the third Duke of Bridgewater that it had to be pulled down after his death. The third Duke was one of those eccentric Englishmen that made the eighteenth century what it was. Bigoted, cruel and enormously wealthy, a misogynist crossed in love who would allow not so much as a washerwoman to cross his threshold, he held to his whim in all things and would hear reason from none. Yet one man captured his imagination, and between them they changed the face of Britain. James Brindley was born at Chapel-en-le-Frith to poor parents, and it was not until his middle thirties that his great gift for engineering became plain. Among his inventions was a water engine for pumping out mine shafts, which so impressed the Duke that he employed Brindley to build a canal from Worsley to Manchester, carrying coal from his mines at negligible cost right into the heart of the Midlands. The canal was a great success, and heralded a new era of cheap water transport, without which the Industrial Revolution could have been delayed another hundred years.

Brindley, who was completely unlettered and could neither write nor draw, solved all his problems on the spot by rule of thumb and the application of his particular genius, and he always succeeded. Yet it was the Duke who was hailed as the Father of Inland Navigation, and who is commemorated as such by a great Doric column at Ashridge on the National Trust land. (There is a small charge for the privilege of climbing this monument, but once at the top the views are breath-taking.) With so much to occupy him in the North, it is not surprising that the third Duke had no time for Ashridge; the mansion mouldered and decayed beyond repair and all that remained after its demolition was the vaulted undercroft or crypt which had once been the monks' dining-room; the Monks' Barn, and the deep well shaft.

The rebuilding of Ashridge was entrusted to the architect James Wyatt, who also built Fonthill Abbey. With unlimited funds at his disposal he designed and built a truly fantastic neo-Gothic pile in Totternhoe stone, from which almost nothing seems omitted. Turrets and towers and pinnacles, battlemented walls, gatehouses, courtyards and keeps, Ashridge has them all. H. J. Massingham described it as a 'wedding cake', yet it has elegance; beauty even, when the summer sun touches its mellow stone to gold. After James Wyatt's untimely death his kinsman and fellow-architect, Matthew Digby Wyatt was commissioned by Lady Marian Alford, mother of the then Earl, to redecorate much of the interior in the Italian style. The gorgeous painted ceiling and marble columns of the present conference room were done to his order, though the delicate cantilevered staircase and fan-vaulted roof to the main hall were wrought before his time. In 1969 the spire to the chapel was found to be unsafe; it was removed, and a replica made from fibreglass was lowered into position by helicopter. Great are the marvels of science.

When the Ashridge Estate was sold off in 1921, the mansion and surrounding gardens were bought for the Conservative Party by Mr Urban Broughton, a gentleman who had made a fortune in the U.S. before returning to England to enter Parliament as M.P. for Preston. An endowment fund of £200,000 was raised from other sources, and as the Bonar Law Memorial Trust the foundation opened a residential College of Citizenship at Ashridge in 1929, to give instruction on civics, politics and current affairs. After ten years the war put a stop to these activities and in 1954, after the mansion had been used in turn as a war emergency hospital, a teacher training college and a finishing school for young ladies, the Trust was wound up and reformed by Act of Parliament as the Ashridge (Bonar Law Memorial) Trust with full charity status, and the obligation that in future it should be free from all political bias. Gradually Ashridge became known as a foundation for management training, and as the Ashridge Management College it now has an international reputation, passing some 3,500 industrial, commercial and public sector managers through its courses every year. To suit its purpose as a management college many changes have been made since the 1950s. The Monks' Barn has been altered to provide study-bedrooms, and two new bedroom blocks have been built with hotel-type accommodation almost to the standard of the London Hilton.

For all this magnificence, Ashridge's greatest glories are to be seen in its gardens. The sight of massed rhododendrons and azaleas blooming in June against their dark background of Wellingtonias is unforgettable, and it would be a sin to miss the evocatively named Liquidamber Walk when it is aflame with the red-gold colours of autumn. Capability Brown is said to have had a hand in the lay-out of the park at Ashridge, but the design of these gardens is largely the work of Humphry Repton, and it was his idea that several small gardens should complement each other to form the whole. The present Superintendent, Mr Malcolm Lingard, laid out the Lazell-block garden, planting it with winter-flowering heathers so suitable to the chalky soil. The Ashridge gardens have been described as the finest in Hertfordshire, and they cannot have bloomed more gloriously for kings and nobles than they do for us today. Though the mansion is closed to the public except for Easter and Spring Bank Holiday weekends and for five days in August, these gardens may be seen every weekend from April to October, and are worth driving miles to see.

The first houses of Little Gaddesden village were built at the north gates of the Ashridge estate in Elizabethan days for the more important servants of the estate, and this altogether delightful little hamlet has been associated with the Bridge-water family ever since. Not one modern house intrudes today along its broad main street, where the verges are soft and green and even the smallest dwellings are set back behind long gardens. The only 'new' building is the Little Gaddesden Post Office and Stores, a flat-roofed, single-storey shop of the type often seen in seaside settlements; a blue and white enamelled sign attached to the wall announces it as 'Post Office, Money Order Office, Savings Bank, Insurance and Annuity Office'. Clearly a place of great importance.

The series of 'No Through Roads' on the Ashridge side of the main street lead to closes of modern houses; here are very desirable residences indeed, all individually designed and gracefully set in well-kept gardens. On a corner of the green is the Manor House, hidden behind a yew hedge. It is certainly Elizabethan, and before the death of its former owner, a Miss Ehrhart, it was open to the public. Miss Ehrhart was a musician; she was delighted to show off her collection of spinets and harpsichords and to entertain visitors with gruesome stories of a former owner who, crossed in love, directed in his will that his coffin should be placed on the roof of the house in full view of his perfidious lady-love, who lived next door.

On the corner by the War Memorial is John of Gaddesden's house. John was physician to Edward III as a young man, and made his reputation by the lucky fact that under his care the King's son recovered from the smallpox. He wrote a book on medicine called *Rosa Angelica*, subtitled *How to make money from Medicine*. Money was clearly much on his mind, one of the chapters being headed 'Disagreeable Diseases which the Doctor can Seldom Make Money By'. He lived to a ripe old age, treating his patients with remedies such as 'an ointment of dove's dung or weasel's blood', or 'a concoction of boar's bladder, mistletoe and extract of cuckoo', and saw his *Rosa Angelica* run to four editions.

Another Little Gaddesden man to make money from his pen was William Ellis, who bought Church Farm in the eighteenth century and proceeded to churn out books, treatises and pamphlets on farming and husbandry whilst his own lands fell into ruin. A most prolific writer, his work was an indiscriminate hodge-podge of recipes, cures, warnings, anecdotes and farming hints, unproven and unsubstantiated, sometimes scandalous and often plainly absurd, but always readable. He achieved great fame both at home and overseas as an agricultural expert, before dying in 1758 broke, and with his lands a wilderness.

A room in the Bridgewater Arms, further along the main road, was used as a schoolroom in the 1850s. This inn is in the centre of the village, unlike the church of St Peter and St Paul which is isolated at the end of a long drive half a mile to the north-west, and sits among yews and cedars in the middle of park-like farmland with lovely views all around. Although it seems so alone it is still very much a part of Little Gaddesden, as the notices about the church and in the porch attest. There is a fine East window, and numerous memorials to the Bridgewater family, very lavish and imposing, but what most impresses is the wonderfully well-cared-for air of this little church; the highly polished floor and pews and bright brasses show how greatly it is loved. Altogether, the whole aspect and structure is so fresh and bright as to belie its seven-hundred-year heritage.

W. Branch Johnson described Little Gaddesden as 'posh', and I suppose he was right. But posh or not, it is a pleasure to the eye and worth a visit. Its neighbour, Great Gaddesden, lies on the River Gade, from which both villages take their name, two miles away by footpath and lane to the south-east, two miles nearer the A41, Hemel Hempstead, rush, bustle and all that is urban. Great Gaddesden is not at all posh; its great attraction is the river and the waterbirds attracted there. Waterend, where the Gade becomes wide and shallow and is spanned by a dainty bridge, is a much-photographed beauty spot.

Tucked away at the foot of the scarp on the other side of Berkhamsted, towards Tring, is the picture-postcard village of Aldbury, a classic tourist attraction with its Tudor houses, ducks on the pond and well-weathered, genuine stocks. It is a pity that part of the old village green has been paved to make a car-park, but that is the price of fame, and Aldbury is without doubt famous.

Village records go back to the fourteenth century, and by the beginning of the sixteenth the Tudor cottages were already being lived in. Stocks House, to the north of the village, was not built until 1773, and was remodelled in the late nineteenth century when the house was bought by Thomas Humphry Ward, a tutor of Brasenose College, and his famous wife. Mrs Humphry Ward was a popular Victorian novelist of the romantic kind, but her novels are little regarded today. She did much good work among the poor of London, inspiring the philanthropist Passmore Edwards to endow a settlement in her name in Tavistock Square for poor relief, but she was very conventional in her beliefs and refused to associate herself with the cause of Women's Suffrage. Her daughter Julia married the historian G. M. Trevelyan, and subsequently lived at Berkhamsted.

The slender tower of the church of St John the Baptist rises to the west of Aldbury village. It is part thirteenth century, but only vestiges of this early period remain. The most notable item is the Pendley Chapel, divided from the body of the church by a Perpendicular screen. It holds the monument to Sir Robert Whittingham and his wife dated 1452, which was originally at Ashridge and was brought from there to Aldbury in 1575. The Verney Memorial also came from Ashridge. The home of the Whittingham family was Pendley Manor, to the west of Aldbury on the road to Tring. There was once a thriving village at Pendley, but in 1440 Sir Robert was granted a licence to 'empark 200 acres', and he cleared the whole village. A record of 1506 states:

About eighty years before, Pendley was a great town whereof part lay in the parish of Tring and part in the parish of Aldbury. There were in the town above 13 ploughs, beside divers handicraftsmen, as tailors, shoemakers and candlemakers with divers others. The town was afterwards cast down and laid to pasture by Sir Robert Whittingham who built the said place [Pendley Manor] at the west end there as the town sometime stood, for the town was in the east and south part of the said place.*

Pendley Manor is now an Arts Centre and a centre for adult education under the direction of Mr Dorian Williams, the famous rider, whose family were formerly Lords of the Manor.

* *Lost Villages of England*, Maurice Beresford, Lutterworth Press, 1971.

8

Tring, Wigginton and Grimsditch

In the days when Robert of Mortain was driving the men of Berkhamsted to build his castle, Tring was no more than a few huts at the gap in the hills where the Icknield Way crossed Akeman Street, and these two Roman roads still cross at Tring today. 'Tring' itself is a Saxon name, meaning 'hanging trees on a slope', but there has been a settlement of some sort at this sheltered crossing place since pre-history, though history has largely passed it by leaving a quiet, unspoiled, truly English little town. From a population of between 1,500 and 2,000 in the year 1800, it has grown to between 10 and 11,000 today. There has not been much industry; milling and brewing, a little straw-plaiting for the Luton hat trade, and lace making, but until the Rothschild family bought Tring Park in 1872 and injected money into the neighbourhood, Tring was supported mainly by its services as a market town and by the coaching trade. There is some light industry in Tring today, but it is still very much a country town, and its people are country people.

Everywhere one meets friendliness and courtesy, and it is a pleasure to shop in this quiet town where the shops along the High Street seem more useful than fashionable, housed not in long, modern parades but in individual buildings, most of which retain their elegant nineteenth- and early twentieth-century shop-fronts. Before the Tring bypass was opened in 1977 to take through-traffic away from the narrow High Street, congestion made life a misery for residents and shoppers alike. But with most of the heavies now using the bypass, Tring has returned to the peace of earlier years.

The open market-place and bus station in front of the parish church of St Peter and St Paul leaves this late Perpendicular building on view from the High Street in all its splendour. Though dating from the thirteenth century, the church was much restored in the 1800s and the glass is Victorian, as are the rood-screen and choir stalls and the painting on the chancel roof. Hemmed about with trees and flowers, the church is a truly pretty sight; even in winter it seems to dwell in greenery, while the delicate stone tracery of its windows and the chequered stonework about its battlemented tower and nave lend a dainty air. Together with the spread of the neo-Tudor Rose and Crown on the other side of the High Street, rebuilt in 1906 as a 'hunting lodge' for the Rothschilds, it sets the character of the town as solid, respectable and a place to be reckoned with. 'Here I am and here I stay,' says Tring.

Sadly, one sniffs the wind of change in the boarded-up cottages along Akeman Street, and many of the intriguing old alleyways off both sides of the High Street now lead to groups and closes of modern houses. The bulk of the post-war development, though, is to the north of the town in the flat country towards Marsworth, where there are rows of pleasant, modest houses adjoining farmland.

In the centre of the town a notable new development is the Sutton Housing Trust's design on the old vicarage site behind St Peter and St Paul. The large, old-fashioned vicarage, built when the church was restored in 1828, has been retained together with its impressive gateway as part of a modern complex of new vicarage, parish hall, and offices for the Housing Trust, called Sutton Court. A most pleasing and practical arrangement that received an R.I.B.A. Architectural Award in 1973.

Beyond Marsworth village is the site of the famous Tring Reservoirs and Nature Trail. The four reservoirs of Marsworth, Tringford, Wilstone and Startopsend were excavated at the beginning of the nineteenth century to store reserve water for the Grand Union Canal. They are Marl lakes, fed and freshened by natural springs, and over the years they have become an important wetlands habitat. Walking here one day I was lucky enough to meet a great naturalist, scanning the sky with his binoculars and asking if I could see a hawk. There was often one up there, he said, hiding among the gulls. He took me round the nature trail, showing me Jew's Ear fungus on the elder trees and pointing out the different grasses and rushes, and as we walked he talked a little about himself. He was a City worker, travelling daily to Euston from Tring station, but his dreams were of these wetlands, and his day only started when he could get out there with his binoculars. The grey shrike was to be seen, he said, and the little ringed plover that makes its nest in a scrape in the shingle, also the greenshank and the sandpiper, and very occasionally, if you knew what you were looking for, the water pipit.

There is a heronry on the far bank of Startopsend, well away from the road, and these great birds can be seen during the first half of the year flapping across the lake to settle in the surrounding farmland, trailing their long legs almost in the water. About the banks and water-margins are warblers and wagtails; chiffchaffs and blackcaps sing in the trees, and on the water are dabchicks, coots, and any number of ducks—tufted duck, mallard, pochard and shoveller are common, and they are joined occasionally by the rarer teal and widgeon and the spectacular goosander. Further out on the lake pairs of great crested grebe, handsome relatives of the little brown dabchick, with shiny white breast and chestnut neck-ruff, dance and bow and 'walk' together on the water in their elaborate mating rituals.

The British Trust for Ornithology has conducted a ringing survey on the reed and sedge warblers that nest among the reed-beds, and has found that after an 8,000-mile round-trip to Africa and back these birds return not only to Tring and the reservoirs, not only to the same clump of reeds, but to the exact spot in the reed-beds where they were hatched and reared. A most remarkable feat, by any reckoning.

On weekdays in summer, when trees in full leaf hang heavy over the water and the banks are bright with great clumps of yellow flag iris and patches of orange balsam, these man-made lakes are lonely and peaceful. Nothing falls upon the ear but bird-song, the small sounds fishermen make as they gentle their bait into the water, and that friendly little noise the coots are so good at. This is the best time to wander the nature trail, seeking out the water figwort, and the dark runners and small pinkish flowers of mudwort that rates two stars for rarity in the Collins guide.

But quiet little Tring has an international claim to fame in the natural history world far greater than that of its reservoirs and nature trail. Housed in a solid, red-brick building at the junction of Akeman Street and Park Street is a world of wonder—the Museum of Natural History founded at the turn of the century by the second Lord Rothschild. Now under the care of London's Natural History Museum, it is world-famous for a collection of over a million bird-skins, including one of the Great Auk, extinct since 1840. These 'skins', which are partially stuffed to bird-shape and stored in long trays, are not conveniently housed for display so the ornithology wing is not open to the public, but even without this wing the Museum is a marvellous and fascinating place.

First on view as one comes through the turnstile are the cases of life-size bears and big cats. The tiger from Northern China must be seven or eight feet from nose to rump (not tail-tip), yet the tiny cub beside it is only the size of a half-grown kitten. Lord Rothschild sent collectors all over the world for specimens, and accepted only the very best for his museum. There are twenty-six different African monkeys, and twenty more in the next case from Central and South America, together with the small chimpanzees and baboons, and across the aisle the man-size gorillas have a case of their own. Here too are curiously marked and brightly coloured birds from all lands, their plumage still clean and fresh for all that they have been dead and stuffed for eighty years.

Upstairs are crocodiles, fishes, humming-birds; skeletal casts of a giant sloth and a giant armadillo fossilized in the last Ice Age, and in this same gallery are the great creatures, hippo, rhino, camel, elephant, all fine examples of the taxidermist's art. Also the sea creatures and sea-shells, and case after case of bugs, beetles, insects, moths and butterflies. If you think you can't stand beetles, go to Tring and see the chubby, friendly fellows they have there, in the same gallery as the foreign butterflies whose glowing colours no artist's palette could match. The trays of British butterflies and moths next to the zebra hall are the prize, though, for these you might actually see on your travels about the countryside. As a curiosity, in one of the trays is a giant cat-flea, nearly a quarter of an inch long, taken from a vole in Hertfordshire. For the poor vole, not much larger than a good-sized mouse, it must have been like carrying a giant, blood-sucking rabbit around all the time. No wonder the creature died.

Only a very rich and eccentric person could have gathered together, mounted and housed a collection such as this, and the second Lord Rothschild was undoubtedly both. He used to ride about the family estate in a little cart hitched up to a pair of cassowaries, a bird slightly smaller than an ostrich, till one of them unwisely bit his father, when they were banished from the shafts and replaced by three zebras and a pony. This latter equipage he drove regularly through the streets of Tring, in older, quieter days. Thanks to his generosity in leaving this museum to the nation, today we can all enjoy the fruits of his enquiring mind.

A footpath beside the museum leads through to Tring Park, described by Daniel Defoe, writing of the Chilterns in 1778, as 'a

park of 300 acres with a beautiful wood inclosed'. Tring Park
was bought by Hertfordshire County Council for public use in
1938, when death duties forced the sale of this Rothschild
estate. Also in the care of the Council are Stubbing and Grove
Woods, some of the most beautiful small beechwoods in all
Hertfordshire, and much loved and used by the people of Tring.
Oddy Hill, near Wigginton, where many lovely chalk grassland
flowers grow, is also favoured for walks and picnics.

Save that it is set idyllically among beechwoods, Wigginton is
an unremarkable village, much favoured by commuters for its
nearness to Tring station, a mile or so away to the north-east.
The villagers managed to preserve their common from the
efforts of Sir Henry Guy, then owner of Tring Park, to enclose it
at the turn of the seventeenth century, and during the Civil War
Cromwell's Ironsides rallied on this common before attacking
the Royalist stronghold at Berkhamsted. Legend has it that at
evening on the anniversary of this battle, bird-song on the
common is silenced by the jingle of spurs and the rattle of
caissons as a phantom army in Puritan garb forms and wheels
and clatters away once more to besiege the waiting town.

A mile to the south of Wigginton, and worth remark, is the
170-acre estate of Champneys. Britain's first ever health farm
and naturist resort was started at Champneys in 1925, when
people who took their health seriously and bothered about their
diet were regarded as harmless cranks. Today we all watch our
diet and worry about cholesterol, and the new Champneys with
its exercise, massage and treatment rooms and its emphasis on
health foods is there to point the way to the body beautiful. The
sheer, gorgeous luxury of the place would raise an eyebrow or
two among those first club members who dedicated themselves
to nature and the simple life, fifty years ago.

Between Wigginton village and the Champneys estate,
hidden in the woods and disguised along the fields and
meadows, is one of the Chilterns' great mysteries: the ancient
earthworks known as Grimsditch or Grim's Dyke. Stretches of
this huge earthworks can be traced in all three Chiltern
counties, and its purpose has exercised the imaginations of
writers and historians for many years. Of vast proportions,
often as great as forty feet wide and thirty feet deep, the ditch is
traceable here in a nine-mile semi-circle from Northchurch to
Cock's Hill, passing close to Wigginton Bottom and Hastoe.
Below Wendover, a piece runs in a north-west-south-west

dog-leg hard by John Hampden's house, and there is another notable piece in the Oxfordshire Chilterns where a three-mile stretch from above Henley takes course to Mongewell, passing below Nuffield and above Rotherfield Greys. Speculation has placed it in many periods from pre-history to Roman times, but with the more accurate dating methods available today we are now able to say with some precision that it was constructed around A.D. 800, give or take a few hundred years. As to its purpose, it seems to be a question of you pays your money and you takes your choice; it has been variously described as a defensive earthworks, an elaborate boundary marker, a device to keep livestock from straying, and more recently, by Brian Bailey* as a fire-break, dug when the beechwoods were being cleared.

If we look at the facts and set the ditch in its proper period, however, the most probable explanation clearly emerges. We know that the ditch is post-Roman, that it was laboriously dug by well-organized labour, that it was built piecemeal, and that only part of it survives. Cast about for parallels and one comes instantly to mind—Offa's Dyke. This great defensive boundary was also built piecemeal, in places 25 feet deep and 60 feet wide, and like Grimsditch is a plain dyke with the earth thrown up on one side to form a bank. No one doubts the purpose of Offa's Dyke, since it defines a still-recognized boundary between England and Wales. King Offa was active in the Chilterns; he had a hunting lodge at Moor Park and kept court at Berkhamsted, and the *Anglo-Saxon Chronicle* makes it plain that there were battles and skirmishes up and down the Chilterns throughout the whole of his reign, and after. 'In this year [779] Cynewulf and Offa contended around Benson and Offa took the village.' Yes, I would come down heavily on the side of those who think of Grim's Dyke as defensive boundary ditch, and place the responsibility for it firmly at King Offa's door.

* *View of the Chilterns*, Brian Bailey, Robert Hale, 1979.

9

A Walk Along the Ridge

As you and I set off on fresh spring mornings unwillingly to work, a certain ex-Civil Servant dons his walking boots and shoulders his rucksack for another day's meander along the Chiltern footpaths. Retired in the early 1970s, he announced a resolve at one of those little office parties we all indulge in when our chains are struck off to use his years of freedom walking every single footpath in the Chilterns. It would take ten years, he thought, for there were hundreds of footpaths, and some of them he would cover many times. It was from him I learned, through a mutual friend, the correct route of the Ridgeway Long Distance Footpath in the tricky section that crosses Tring Park and winds on through Halton Woods towards Wendover, and I never set foot on the rich pattern of Buckinghamshire byways without expecting to see him, suitably grey and weatherworn in his faded anorak, tramping the hills with his face towards the sunset, like Matthew Arnold's Scholar Gipsy.

Anyone wishing to acquaint himself with the Chiltern Hills could do worse than take a British Rail ticket from Euston to Tring station and walk the Ridgeway from Ivinghoe Beacon to Princes Risborough, making the return journey from the station there. It might be done as a marathon in the course of one long summer day, though a better plan would be to take it easy, explore a little, and spend a night somewhere along the way. It would be a pity to rush the bird's-eye views of historic towns and hamlets and the glories of the Chiltern countryside to be seen from the Ridge.

At just short of eight hundred feet, Ivinghoe Beacon is not the highest of the Chiltern Hills; that distinction goes to Coombe Hill above Wendover, but it seems steep enough to the walker until the view begins to work its magic. On the left is the green swell of the National Trust's Ashridge beechwoods, hiding roe and fallow deer in their perfect cover, and ahead is the rise of the hill. Underfoot only the sparsest layer of turf covers the unyielding chalk, turf which in too many places is worn away by the thousands of pairs of feet that tramp it every year.

The summit of Ivinghoe Beacon is crowned today with nothing more romantic than an Ordnance Survey triangulation point, but it is easy to call up the past as one stands at the top, to picture great warning fires burning and to recreate the grassy banks and earthworks of the hill-fort that was here in the Iron Age. Across the valley to the east a bold white lion carved into the chalk face of the hill above the B4506 marks the Zoological Park at Whipsnade, but the best views lie on the other side of the plateau. Here at the foot of the hill is Ivinghoe village, with Pitstone village and windmill beyond. The windmill is dated 1627 and thought to be the oldest surviving post mill in England. The significance of these 'post' mills is that the body of the mill was built on a stout post separated from the base, so that the whole structure, not just the head or 'bonnet', could be turned to bring the sails into the wind. Now owned by the National Trust, this mill was recently restored to working order by keen members of the Chiltern Society.

Ivinghoe village is quiet and attractive, with dignified houses of mixed style and period, apt to burst into life on Friday and Saturday evenings when the Youth Hostel is full of walkers and cyclists enjoying a weekend in the country. The manor of Ivinghoe was possessed from Saxon times until the Dissolution by the See of Winchester, which owned vast estates all over the country including a Bishop's Palace, still to be seen, on the south bank of the Thames at Southwark. The fine decorations and elaborate carvings in the great thirteenth-century church of St Mary bear witness to Ivinghoe's grand associations.

Due north of Ivinghoe lies the village of Wing, where the Saxon church of All Saints is famous for its most unusual polygonal apse, one of only four such apses in the country. There has been a church on the site of All Saints' since the seventh century, and this apse is known to have been rebuilt in the tenth century on existing foundations. The church is pure Saxon in form: it has the largest Saxon chancel arch in England, and the crypt below the apse, once used as a charnel house, also predates the existing church. At Cheddington village, on a direct line between Ivinghoe and Wing, the church has a post-Reformation wooden pulpit very pleasing to the eye, and around the hillside to the south of the village are a series of terraces and lynchets, the work of Celtic man. Further along the Ridgeway beyond Wendover, All Saints' at Little Kimble dates from the eleventh century; and further on still, beyond Chinnor, is Aston Rowant's little tenth-century church.

It is no coincidence that so many ancient churches are to be found along the route of this oldest road. Those nomads who were the first to feel the longing for permanency and a home of their own naturally chose sites within easy reach of the main lines of communication, and even the smallest settlement would have had its holy place or shrine, and its burial-place for the dead. As this island was converted, Christian churches and churchyards took the place of those pagan shrines, sometimes using not only the site but the very building. The polygonal apse at Wing, for instance, is said to be based on a triangle of three by four by five megalithic yards (2.72 feet), indicating that a far older structure previously occupied the site. Speaking on the subject in 1969 in a B.B.C. radio broadcast, Mr Ian Rodger suggested that Wing was probably the oldest continually used religious site in Britain.

> This particular three by four by five triangle produces the egg-shaped oval which Thom classifies as Type One. The oval shape is created by describing arcs from the point of the triangle, which is projected astride the axis line, the line of stellar observation. It commemorated, as it were, the observation point and provided a sanctuary around it, which was then marked by tree stumps or stones. Borst considers that the points of the polygon at Wing mark the sites of the original pillars. The wood henge at Arminghall in Norfolk, which was composed of eight wooden pillars, employs the same geometry but at twice the scale. Borst considers that the two structures are near contemporaries, and as the wood at Arminghall has been dated at 2500 B.C. he presumes a similar date for Wing.*

From Ivinghoe the Ridgeway goes on over Pitstone Hill, where the tall, shining chimneys of Pitstone Cement Works can be seen below in the valley, with the great chalk pans showing white beside them. Cement has been worked in patches all along this ridge since Roman times, but today it is big business and these cement works are one of the largest in Europe. Mercifully distance lends enchantment to the view, and from the hilltop all is calm and remote, neither the noise and dust nor the scale of the workings impinges upon the view, though a different story might be told at Chinnor where the workings are right beside the path.

Pitstone Hill, Steps Hill and Clipper Down are among the

---

* Talk entitled 'Megalithic Mathematics' can be read in its entirety in *The Listener*, November 1969.

finest examples of chalk grassland in England. Spring gentians flower at Ivinghoe, and at Pitstone the pasque-flower grows. This beautiful little anemone of deep cerise colour used to be common on Pitstone Hill, but only a few plants now remain and sharp eyes are needed to see them in the grass. Wild orchids, too, flourish on these airy uplands, together with the vetches that feed the caterpillars of the Chalkhill Blue butterfly. In 1980 Pitstone was the scene of a massive effort in conservation as groups of members from the Youth Hostels Association laboured to clear the scrub and undergrowth that has been choking the grasslands in recent years. Forty acres of hawthorn scrub was cleared and burned between October 1979 and March 1980. This scrub encourages lank grass, and smothers out the downland flora which needs clean, close-cropped turf in order to flourish. If the scrub is not cleared, taller flowers like foxglove and rosebay willowherb take hold, seedling trees thrive, and within a few generations the chalk grasslands revert to woodland once more. Much of this valuable clearing work is done throughout the Chilterns by members of such organizations as the Chiltern Society, the Berks, Bucks and Oxfordshire Naturalists' Trust, and by members of local amenity societies. Every walker on the hills owes them a debt of gratitude.

From Tring to Wendover the old green road has disappeared under modern development; we shall not see it again before Coombe Hill, beyond Wendover. In its place the Countryside Commission have waymarked the modern Ridgeway Long Distance Footpath across Tring Park and through Halton Woods, a stretch that is an intriguing mixture of urban and rural. It is patched in piecemeal along roadways, across meadows and through woods and even, in one place, hacked through the middle of a hedge, wherever the Commission could find a few yards of route making in the right direction. From Halton Woods, which were felled by German prisoners of war during the First World War and replanted, the footpath runs through the middle of Wendover before climbing back on to the ridge at Bacombe Hill.

No more euphonious name than 'Wendover' could be found for this quiet Buckinghamshire town, whose roots go back to the beginning of recorded history. Robert Louis Stevenson described it in his *Essays on Travel* as lying 'well down in the midst [of the plain] with mountains and foliage about it', and so it is today. The broad High Street is flanked by the modern shops of

any such small town, but where the A413 goes off towards Great
Missenden antiquity asserts itself; the cottages here in South
Street and along Pound Street are old and timbered, and are
mentioned in accounts of the town as far back as 1461.

There are several old inns: The Red Lion, half-timbered and
with brick nogging but restored towards the end of the nineteenth century; The Kings Head, formerly an Elizabethan
house; The Two Brewers, whose wavy seventeenth-century
roof still has tiles of the period; The King and Queen in London
Road, also seventeenth century, but much altered; and the
Temperance Hotel in Aylesbury Road, part sixteenth century.
All Wendover's main streets are broad and gracious, but particularly Aylesbury Road, a tree-lined concourse distinguished
by rows of attractive old houses of varying dates and styles on
both sides. Pevsner devotes two whole pages to this small,
unspoiled town in his *Buildings of England* series, and not
without justification.

St Mary's Church is situated well away from the town centre
at The Hale, a pretty situation with many trees and a little
stream running nearby. This is probably the original site of the
town, since the name 'Wendover' does not, as it sounds, have to
do with wending or wayfaring but is an Old English word
meaning 'a white (chalky) place by a stream'. It was an
important place in the Middle Ages, with pilgrims coming from
all around to be blessed at St Mary's Rood Cross. In 1506 a
number of Chesham people who had spoken out against idolatry
were sentenced to make pilgrimage to Wendover, including
Thomas Harding.

The Chiltern men have ever been plain men, and Dissenters.
In the steps of such as these Chesham pilgrims followed Wyclif's
Amersham Martyrs and other Lollards and Levellers in con-
gregations all over the Chilterns. Sir Thomas Cheyne, of
Chenies Manor, was among those imprisoned for the cause,
though in general Lollardry was found among men of humbler
origins, as Quakerism was in the following century. Wendover
was sending two burgesses to Parliament as early as the fourteenth century, and was represented in its time by such famous
free-thinkers as Edmund Burke, Richard Steele (who founded
the *Tatler* with Addison), and the best-known Dissenter of them
all, Ship-Money Hampden.

When discontent stalks the land it falls always to one person
or group to make a focus, a rallying point; to fire, as it were, the

first gun. John Hampden performed this function at the start of the Civil War. Parliament, which in those days assembled only at the King's behest, had been adjourned for two years, and when the Members, Hampden among them, were finally called to Westminster it was but to rubber stamp the King's demands for more money. Among other taxes, he proposed to levy Ship Money on all estates throughout the kingdom. This ancient tax had long fallen into disuse; it was traditionally levied in times of war on maritime towns and ports only, to provide ships for the King's service. Hampden was among many who refused to pay, declaring the tax to be unconstitutional, and together with various of his neighbours he drew up and signed a formal Refusal, a copy of which hangs today in St Nicholas's Church, Great Kimble.

Carlyle gives an account of the scene in his *Cromwell Letters*:

Two obscure individuals, Peter Aldridge and Thomas Lane, Assessors of Ship Money over in Buckinghamshire, have assembled a Parish meeting in the church of Great Kimble, to assess the rate of Ship Money of the said parish; there in the cold at the foot of the Chiltern Hills, '11th January, 1635' the Parish did attend, John Hampden Esq. at the head of them, and by a Petition still extant, refused to pay the same, or any part thereof—witness the above Assessors, also the Parish Constables ... John Hampden's share for this Parish is twenty-one shillings and sixpence; for another Parish it is twenty shillings; on which latter sum, not the former, John Hampden was tried.

The piece of land in question was an estate in Prestwood, at Honor End. In 1863 a memorial was erected at Honor End Farm with the inscription: 'For these lands in Stoke Mandeville John Hampden was assessed 20s. Ship Money, levied by command of the King without authority of Law, 4 August 1635. By resisting this claim of the King in legal strife, he upheld the rights of the people under the law, and became entitled to grateful remembrance. His work on earth ended after the conflict in Chalgrove Field, the 18th June, 1643. And he rests in Great Hampden Church.' Prestwood was at that time attached to Stoke Mandeville.

It is true that Hampden did 'resist the claim of the King in legal strife', but he lost his case in the courts, and was ordered to pay up. This he consistently refused to do, and the King rode to Westminster to demand of the Commons that Hampden be surrendered to him together with others who had refused to pay, Jonathan Pym, Denzil Holles, William Strode and Arthur Hazelrigg. The Commons would have none of it, and while the King's men were arguing at the front with the Sergeant-at-Arms, John Hampden and his friends rode out at the back!

As Edmund Burke said later: 'Would twenty shillings have ruined Mr Hampden's fortune? No, but the payment of half twenty shillings, on the principle it was demanded, would have made him a slave.'

There is a story that some years before all this John Hampden and his brother-in-law, Oliver Cromwell, disillusioned with life in England, decided to take ship for the New World. They were actually on board and ready to sail when the King had them arrested and brought back. An unwise move, to say the least; it cost him his head.

Wendover must be the only town in England with an official Footpath running through its main street. It is certainly the only place along the way where walkers on the Ridgeway Long Distance Footpath can pop in for a cup of tea and a bun, or even spend the night in a comfortable bed, without deviating from their route. The old green road, the Roman road and the new Long Distance Footpath all run together along Wendover High Street to where the Shoulder of Mutton Hotel stands beside the railway station. There the old road and the new footpath go off left behind the substantial modern houses of Ellesborough Road to climb Bacombe Hill and attain the ridge once more. From this ridge there are superb views northwards across the Vale of Aylesbury, five or six miles away as the crow flies but seeming so close in the clear air that you might think to shout out and be heard there. The prosperous, peaceful farming country shows to its best from here. To quote R.L.S. again: 'The great plain stretches away to northward, variegated near at hand with the quaint pattern of the fields, but growing ever more and more indistinct until it becomes a mere hurly-burly of trees and bright crescents of river and snatches of slanting road, finally melting away into the ambiguous cloud-land over the horizon.'

A stile, a few posts and a little copse, and you've left Bacombe Hill for Coombe Hill, at 832 feet the highest point in the Chilterns. Like Ashridge and Ivinghoe Beacon, now a dozen miles away, Coombe Hill is National Trust land, here donated by Lord Lee of Fareham who also gave Chequers to the nation. It is easy to forget as we wander through this countryside that our right to do so is a comparatively recent one. Once all this land would have been in private hands, fenced and guarded and sewn with man-traps. And long before that we would have had rights, such as they were, over only a very small piece of land, and held those rights, most of us, at the price of serfdom. Even a villein, or copyholder, might not sell his house nor lease his land without permission from the lord of the manor, neither could his son be clerked nor his daughter married without the lord's consent. It behoves us to remember, too, as we tramp the woods and hills, that all this land has to be 'managed' by someone, whether National Trust, local authority or private landlord, and such management is expensive. On National Trust land there is usually a collecting box for help towards this expense, and it is a pleasure to cross the Trust's palm with silver after a day spent as its guest.

On the summit of Coombe Hill is the Boer War Monument, commemorating 148 men of the Chilterns dead in their country's service. Almost in view from the monument is Chequers Court, country home of the prime ministers of England; the way there on foot lies through mature Buckinghamshire beechwoods, a way so peaceful, so padded with the leafy harvest of years, so enclosed above with the tracery of branches, that not the most troubled soul could fail to find rest here nor the most weary to find refreshment. On weekdays one might walk the whole way and see neither man nor horse nor dog, and in winter the weekends are as quiet. Only in summer, when the paths are bordered with wood sorrel, white wood anemones and deep-pink herb robert, does one meet a few walkers and riders.

The peace of these woods has so captivated our prime ministers and other politicians since Lord Lee gave them Chequers in 1922 as a retreat from the cares of State, that more than one of them subsequently retired to the Chilterns. Ramsey Macdonald was the first to form links here, with his daughter Ishbel keeping The Plow at Speen. Then after the war Clement Attlee settled at Prestwood, Aneurin Bevan and Jenny Lee bought a Chiltern farm, and Harold Wilson settled down to write his memoirs in the farmhouse near Great Missenden where Herbert Austin, father of the Austin Seven, was born.

Chequers was restored and refurnished in its original Elizabethan style by Lord Lee and his American wife during their years of residence there. The estate is thought to go back to the thirteenth century, though its exact origins seem not to be known. The house which Lord Lee bought and renovated was built in the sixteenth century by William Hawtrey, who was gaoler to Lady Jane Grey during her years of imprisonment there. Ellesborough church of St Peter and St Paul, that splendid church set on a hill, where a succession of prime ministers and their guests have worshipped over the years, has many memorials to the Hawtrey family.

10

Hampden Country

Once past Chequers the country opens out briefly into cornfields before rising to Pulpit Hill, where the map shows an Iron Age fort beside the Old Road. This is reported to be the site of Cymbeline's Castle, where Cunobelinus, King of the Britons, is said to have fought the Romans in the first century A.D. Apparently he lost, but only temporarily; a little matter of a few hundred years.

The high down here is scrubbier than the rich grasslands above Tring, altogether rougher and humpier. Over to the right is the famous spread of box trees known as the Kimble Boxes, one of only four such large areas of box in England. A little way further on, at a sharp dip, a broad pathway crosses the ancient track leading north to Great and Little Kimble and south to Longdown Hill, where it emerges on to a winding country road bisecting some of the prettiest country in Buckinghamshire. It is my belief that this path, bordered by trees hung about with fluffy grew whirligigs of Traveller's Joy, is the route once taken by John Hampden from his house at Great Hampden to Great Kimble church, on the rare occasions when he went. Being a Dissenter, he was more than once fined for non-attendance and warned to mend his ways.

Here on the dip-slope of the hills, in the triangle bounded roughly by Wendover, High Wycombe and Princes Risborough, are the villages of Great and Little Hampden, Dunsmore, Speen, Hughenden Valley, Lacey Green and Loosley Row, set among tiny hills with here and there a white-washed farmhouse, here and there a wood or coppice. Little lanes wind up and down beside cornfields from Longdown Farm to Rignall Farm, by Hampden Bottom and King's Beech; from Hotley Bottom to Bryants Bottom and from Buckmoorend to Little Hampden. This triangle of country occupies hardly more space on a one-in-fifty-thousand O.S. map than can be covered by a child's hand, yet it is so interconnected with lanes and footpaths and so well supplied with inns for lodging and refreshment that one could tramp the beechwoods and byways for a week without becoming bored.

Tucked away along these lanes is the village of North Dean,

where the sculptor Eric Gill and his little band of stone-masons settled in the 1930s, dedicating themselves to Art and the Simple Life. Eric Gill says in his autobiography that if he had sent out a circular to the estate agents setting out his exact requirements he could have been offered nowhere more suitable to his purpose than the seventeenth-century farmhouse at the top of Pigotts Hill that he came upon by chance. Here where the lane end runs into woodland he found a home for his family, a brick barn for his stone room, and a stable block to convert to family living units for his masons, all joined in one continuous building round three sides of a grassy quadrangle. With a low wooden hut built along the fourth side to provide a schoolroom for the many children that lived on the place, the orchard and vegetable gardens and the sty to house a couple of pigs, Pigotts supplied most of their simple needs. It even supplied the room, a brick-floored Buckinghamshire half-dairy set half a storey down against the north wall of the house, which Eric Gill converted to his private chapel. The chapel bell hangs yet against the wall of the stone room, and is a feature of the place. One can imagine it telling the monastic hours, prime, terce, sext, while inside Gill's 'band of medieval craftsmen' smoothed their stone and chipped out their memorials.

Today Pigotts resounds to a sweeter sound than the knock of steel on stone, for the present owner, who bought the establishment after Eric Gill's death, is a musician, and in the school-house and stone room he makes music with his many friends. I set out to find Pigotts one crisp January day when a pale winter sun filtered through the trees and sudden showers came and went so rapidly that one was hard put to decide whether hail, rain or snow was their main constituent, and found instead the Pink and Lily, that inn with the curious name that one hears always associated with the poet Rupert Brooke.

The journey started at Dunsmore, a short step from the parking area at the back of Coombe Hill. A handful of houses, a village pond, and two inns, Dunsmore is tidy, leafy and chic. It was busy, too, with people trotting up and down the steps of the Bucks County Library van parked beside the village hall. From the Black Horse at Dunsmore a bridle path through Hampden-leaf Wood leads direct to the Rising Sun at Little Hampden, a matter of a mile or so away. From Dunsmore to Little Hampden by road was five times as far. The Rising Sun at Little Hampden is much favoured by local people, who traditionally turn up in fancy dress on Christmas Eve, when the place is so packed you can hardly get in at the door. 'Little' the village is, indeed, a scattering of old farms, old church and old cottages dotted about among trees where the lane ends and the beechwood begins. On sunny days the hamlet is idyllic; on days when all the world is grey, rain drips from the eaves and the woods are dank and still, it must seem like the last place on earth. In the tiny thirteenth-century church is a wall-painting believed to date from the time of Henry III, of the Weighing of Souls; St Michael stands with the scales, the Devil on one side of him, Our Lady on the other.

The only lane from the village leads to its 'big' brother, Great Hampden. This village is marked on the map as Hampden Row, but the sign as you enter clearly says 'Great Hampden'. Here John Masefield lived for a while in the 1920s, and was inspired to write his famous poem 'The Everlasting Mercy'. Both the Hampdens have the air of working villages, with houses that look as though they are actually occupied by country people. They are among the few villages in this part of Buckingham-shire to have escaped the attentions of the developer. So many of the villages north of Great Missenden, and almost all of those to the south, now house more commuters than local workers, and property prices reflect this. At Great Hampden one is met by thatch, proceeds to brick and flint, and finishes at a row of modern semi-detached council houses. Cricket is played on the green, tucked away behind the Hampden Arms, and until recently the village housed one of the last working smithies in South Buckinghamshire. But the village is diminutive, even smaller than its 'Little' brother.

Great Hampden's Perpendicular church of St Mary Mag-dalene is sited within the grounds of Hampden House, a small church, befitting the small parish it serves, but evidently much used and much loved. Every other year the ladies of the parish hold a Flower Festival to celebrate the Feast of St Mary Mag-dalene, 22nd July. They transform the little church into a bower of flowers, their efforts varying from the elegant, professional-looking arrangements of lilies and long-stemmed roses in the window embrasures to the simple posies of garden flowers that decorate the ends of the Tudor box pews, and the scent of this mass of sweet blossom combines with the musky, centuries-old church smell of incense and old hymn books into a memorable aroma. The church houses the Hampden memorials and has some very pretty stained glass, including a Victorian window depicting the Agony in the Garden at Gethsemane, and a modern memorial window in the side chapel to a soldier killed in India in 1946. Beneath this window is Great Hampden's War Memorial, showing that even this tiny village lost six men in the First World War and seven men in the Second.

A mile along the lane from Great Hampden is Speen, largest of this group of villages and one of the most attractive. Along the broad main street handsome Georgian-style houses are interspersed with traditional brick and flint, while neatly disposed groups of modern semis and well-set up houses of the between-wars period prove that a village does not have to be all timber and thatch to please the eye. Set compactly about a junction of three lanes, Speen has not been visited by the fate of Hughenden Valley, Naphill and Walter's Ash which run together along a by-road in a classic example of ribbon development. The accommodation units and married quarters of R.A.F. Strike Command don't help them, and though some thatch is still to be seen and some brick and flint, the modern in-filling is more obtrusive than at Speen. At Hughenden Valley in particular some of the modern houses, though doubtless architecturally satisfying in another setting, sit ill in a rural area.

Lacey Green, separated by fields from Naphill and Walter's Ash, has its grouping of church, inn and church-school in traditional flint, and some thatched cottages. Where the road forks downhill to Loosley Row on the left at a fierce hairpin bend, the eye is drawn to a patchwork of tidy fields beyond the High Wycombe to Princes Risborough Road, and the finger of Stokenchurch radio beacon dominating the skyline. Beyond those fields and that beacon is Oxfordshire. Lacey Green's lovely smock mill was moved to its present site from Chesham in 1821. Like the post mill at Pitstone, it has been lovingly restored to working order by members of the Chiltern Society.

As the lane snakes out of Lacey Green going north it runs downhill to pass Wardrobes, where there has been a house of that name since early in the fourteenth century. It is just past Wardrobes, at the junction of Pink Hill and Lily Bottom Lane, that one comes upon the Pink and Lily, a small, square, disappointingly ordinary-looking building, painted bright pink. Its inn sign shows Mr Pink and his Lily in a style of dress such as Jane Austen's characters might have worn. Mr Pink was butler at Hampden House, before marrying Miss Lily, the parlourmaid, and setting up his own house. The inn is older than it appears, with windows blocked up to avoid the seventeenth-century Window Tax. Its walls are solid 13-inch brick, and the vast cellar below changes its temperature, the landlady says, by not so much as a degree summer or winter.

The diminutive bar parlour is almost a shrine to Rupert Brooke, who came to the Pink and Lily on his walks in Chiltern country in the carefree days before 1914. On one occasion, half-drunk with Buckinghamshire air and beechwoods, good food, good company, drink and a warm fire, he tossed off a cheerful, zany, tipsy verse about his walk and the Pink and Lily and all, and left it behind for a keepsake:

> Never came there to the Pink
> Two such men as we, I think.
> Never came here to the Lily
> Two men quite so richly silly.

The whole poem now stands framed on the lintel between two photographs of the writer in which he looks soulful, citified and poetical, not at all as he must have been on his happy days outdoors in the country. His much-quoted poem 'Chilterns', written about the same time, reflects a more sober mood:

> I shall desire and I shall find
> The best of my desires;
> The autumn road, the mellow wind
> That soothes the darkening shires,
> And laughter, and inn fires.
>
> White mist about the black hedgerows,
> The slumbering midland plain,
> The silence where the clover grows,
> And the dead leaves in the lane,
> Certainly, these remain.
>
> And I shall find another girl,
> A better one than you;
> With eyes as bright, but kindly,
> And lips as soft, but true.
> And I dare say she will do.

That poem is dated 1913, two years before he died at Skyros, that 'corner of a foreign field that is forever England', leaving behind forever the massed woods that show dark against the rolling Buckinghamshire hillside and the friendly lights of the villages twinkling at dusk to show the weary traveller home.

11

The Hambleden Valley

Any hamlet or suburb may describe itself as a 'village', but there is no mistaking the genuine article when you come upon it. Be the houses of rosy red Tudor bricks, timber and thatch, Buckinghamshire brick and flint, mellow stone or grey, the true English village speaks antiquity in a way that mere clusters of houses cannot aspire to. Like the patina on old oak panels, the village grows with time and use, with land passing from father to son down the generations, in places where the same old church and the same old inn have stood for centuries hand in hand.

A richness of such villages lies to the west of High Wycombe in the Hambleden Valley, between the Oxford road and the Thames. They hide along lanes where pheasants tread in a secret country of hanging woods and quiet coombs, and the finger of time has touched them but lightly. The lanes that serve them are winding, single-track pathways leading through the woods from nowhere-much to nowhere-in-particular, and the 20 m.p.h. patience required to negotiate their bends and twists in any modern vehicle, with the obligatory backing and squeezing into the trees when it meets another, deters all but the true country-lover. Fingest, Turville, Skirmett, Frieth; even their names suggest a time long gone, a language forgotten; and if fame has passed these villages by, that is their fortune. Only the wanderer in the autumn woods sees their real beauty, looks down from the hills upon the houses clustered around the tiny, mortar-faced churches, sees the wisps of smoke drifting up lazily from old, twisted chimneys, and pauses to wonder.

At Fingest the 'strange and lovely Parish Church of St Bartholomew', as the church guide describes it, is worthy of wonder. The massive tower is Norman, with walls 60 feet high and 4 feet thick, built so true that each inside diagonal measures the same 27 feet 4½ inches throughout its height. The curious twin saddle-back roof to the bell-chamber that so takes the eye was added comparatively late in the church's history, and the bell-chamber itself is of more delicate construction than the tower it tops, the rounded arches to its eight windows marking it as medieval. The chamber now houses only one bell, the others having been lost to Hambleden in a wager by an eighteenth-century incumbent, and the one poor bell remaining seems hardly enough reminder that the original purpose of this great tower, as of all church towers, was to house the bells, those messengers whose iron tongues cried out across the land, not only calling to worship but counting the hours of the passing day and telling the news of man's mortality. Nine times they tolled to tell the death of a man, six for a woman, followed by one slow stroke for each year of the dead person's age.

As for the rest of the church, the buttressed nave with its beautiful brackets and beams is twelfth century, the chancel thirteenth, the two north windows Early English, and the south windows Perpendicular; church records tell of major work done in the 1800s, the 1930s and the 1960s, a reminder that only the constant devoted attention of incumbents and worshippers alike has preserved this church for close on a thousand years. A note in the Record Book under the list of Donations testifies to this; between the names of cash donors a firm hand has written, probably to the embarrassment of the lady concerned: 'Mrs Boddy—Many years of devoted and unpaid work to keep the Church clean and tidy'.

A writer of the 1940s described Fingest as 'going round the edges like a leaf in October'. 'Let it go,' he said, 'as long as we can keep Turville.'* He would be pleased to learn, were he still with us today, that Fingest has 'gone' no further since his time, rather has the village been restored and preserved with loving care, even as its church has. But one can understand his enthusiasm for Turville, lying hardly a stone's throw from Fingest along the lane to the west. Here the cluster of pretty cottages snuggles around the tiniest of village greens, with the seventeenth-century Bull and Butcher Inn to serve their needs. This inn owes its licence to St Mary's Church at Turville, for masons carrying out restorations there refused to continue working until beer and victuals were supplied, one of the earliest recorded tea-break strikes! A local householder promptly applied for a licence and the village inn was born.

Turville's unobtrusive church of St Mary the Virgin with its squat, sturdy flint tower, flanked as at Fingest by a small nave and smaller chancel, is part fourteenth century. It is separated by no more than a pathway from the village green which seems

* *Chiltern Country*, H. J. Massingham, B. T. Batsford, 1940.

to be an extension, almost, of the big, grassy churchyard, a churchyard that was enlarged in 1970 by a piece taken from the church glebe. A row of old spruce trees was felled at the same time and the area replanted with beech, whitebeam, yew and wayfaring trees. One of the advantages of living in villages such as these is that there might actually be room for you in the churchyard when your time comes. Try as they may to be reassuring, with trees hiding their chimneys and flower gardens where fountains play, the modern crematoria where most of us will meet our end do little to convince us that our souls are Heaven-bound, and few of us in this overcrowded island can rely on the traditional six feet of ground where it is so much easier to believe that 'though worms destroy this body, yet in my flesh shall I see God'.

The same centuries of loving care show in Turville's church as at Fingest, though some of the restorations were less than kind. ('All the old box pews were thrown out, together with the three-decker pulpit'; see the booklet on church history.) In this century the parishioners have added a modern stained-glass window designed by John Piper, who designed the glass for Coventry Cathedral, and made in the Chiltern studios of Patrick Reyntiens, the stained-glass artist.

Turville was the home of many Buckinghamshire bodgers before High Wycombe industrialized the furniture industry. Now their descendants assemble factory-made chairs on the new industrial estates at Sands and Lane End and the beech-woods know them no more, but until the last war it was still possible for the solitary bodger to build his bothy in the woods and set up his pole-lathe, bedding down at night among the wood-shavings and cooking his food over an open fire. Within living memory one such, who worked near Stokenchurch, was found dead beside his bothy, killed off, as an old animal might have been, by a hard winter. Most of the bodgers were entrepreneurs as well as craftsmen, bidding at auction for a small stand of timber, twenty or a dozen trees, which they then felled or coppiced and worked on the spot into parts for the Windsor chairs for which the district was famous. Chair legs, rails and splats were turned from beech while the wood was still green, and left to season after turning. If the wood was properly split along the grain the turned parts always dried straight. Chair seats were carved separately from a close-grained wood such as elm or fruitwood, and the parts were then sold to chair-framers whose job it was to fit the legs, rails and bows into the seat ready for the polisher.

Bodgers worked the timber all along the Chiltern ridge, and the High Wycombe chairmasters would go out with their wagons to the villages to buy up the product of their labour. The different villages had their specialities; those around Chinnor, for example, were known for rush-seated ecclesiastical chairs. But the greatest demand was for legs and rails for Windsor chairs, of which vast numbers were made in the nineteenth century. The records of one factory show that at one time it was turning out 9,000 chairs a week, and a contemporary account tells of piles of turned chair legs stacked up outside the cottages in Turville to season.

Skirmett makes a triangle with Fingest and Turville, along the lane towards Hambleden. The seventeenth- , eighteenth- , nineteenth- and twentieth-century houses there include an old chapel, a redundant church, and 'The Old Post Office', all now converted into dwellings. Lacking any noticeable centre apart from the King's Arms and strung out in one long row between cornfields, Skirmett yet has the air of a true village. So far it has escaped the fate of Lane End and Cadmore End, nearer to High Wycombe, both invaded by busy B-roads and losing their character thereby. Lane End is an attractive suburb of High Wycombe, but it can no longer be called a village, though a handful of ducks on each of the ponds show how things were in the days when Fingest's one remaining church bell was re-cast in the foundry there. Carters no longer stop their patient horses for a drink at the pond before breasting the hill into Wycombe, and the Chairmakers' Arms now takes more custom from week-end motorists than from drovers and farmers.

At Flint Farm between Skirmett and Hambleden, where the lane goes off towards Frieth, there is a rare survival, a cruck-framed cottage. Such cottages take their name from the forks or 'crucks' of curved uprights that were used as supports in the end walls of the cottages. Together with the connecting roof-tie, these crucks formed the framework of the cottage, which was then filled in with brick or wattle and daub. The standard measurement between crucks was 16½ feet or 5½ yards, one rod, pole or perch, the Old English measure based on the amount of space needed to house two pairs of oxen.*

* G. Eland, *In Bucks*, 1923: quoted in *Country Like This*, 1972.

Hambleden, at the foot of the valley, has been described as one of the prettiest villages in England, and its church as a mini-cathedral. It is near enough to the river to be called a Thames-side village, and but for the A4155 Marlow to Henley road which cuts off all save the mill from the water, a Thames-side village it might well have become. But the road has preserved it, and in character Hambleden still belongs to the hills. Like Bradenham in the Hampden country, this 'village on a slope', as the name signifies, is a National Trust village. Several lovely chestnut trees shade the village green, and there is every other attribute of picturesque beauty: Jacobean manor house, village green with pump, cricket ground, and charming old cottages with a stream before their doors. The parish register of 1640 lists Hambleden's householders at that date: '10 yeomen, a glover, a bargeman, a weaver, a bricklayer, a carpenter, a lath-shaver, a miller, a wharfinger, a mason, a smith, a wheelwright, a flour-maker, a hemp-dresser, a shoemaker, a joiner.' Only the whar-finger signifies that the great Thames flows scarce a mile away.

The church of St Mary with its gabled lych-gate is grand indeed for so small a place. It was started in Norman times and still has its Norman font, but many alterations and additions have been made over the years. In 1721 a new tower was built to replace the Norman central tower that had fallen in 1703, and as at Fingest and Turville, most generations have added some-thing to their church. Pevsner cites examples of thirteenth-, fourteenth-, fifteenth- and sixteenth-century work. But more famous than the church is Hambleden's old weather-boarded mill beside the Thames, now used as headquarters for a yacht basin. Hambleden Lock was built in 1376, at a time when the London bargemen were making complaints about the number of locks on the Thames and the tolls they had to pay, contrary to their franchise. In those days the Thames was a busy thorough-fare, and Hambleden's broad mill pool would have made good overnight moorings along the way.

At nearby Yewden Manor excavations in 1911 revealed a Roman villa and an Iron Age settlement in layers on the same site. Fourth-century coins were found, a mosaic floor, and ninety-seven infant burials. There is an avenue of yews here of great age, perfectly complementing the old Manor House to which they gave a name. These yews probably saw Thomas of Cantelupe, friend of Simon de Montfort. Thomas acquired the 'Cantelupe' on his travels. The house where he was born stood on the site of Yewden Manor, and he was the last Englishman to be canonized until this century, when the Jesuit Edmund Campion was sainted. Thomas is not the only famous man connected with this tiny village. W. H. Smith, bookstall magnate and cabinet minister, is buried in the churchyard, having lived out his last years at Greenlands, a Victorian mansion on the Thames. Sharing his country resting-place is Major George Howson, who started the tradition of wearing Flanders poppies on Armistice Day. Arthur Mee wrote of him:*

There lies in Hambleden churchyard one of the bravest men of the Great War, and one of the most effective benefactors of the men who were disabled by it. He was Major George Howson, who organized the Poppy Factory run by the British Legion at Richmond. Nowhere is there a happier family than these 360 men who live in a delightful row of flats by their factory, and they owe their happiness to the inspiration of Major Howson, a soldier of the noblest type.

Himself disabled in the war, where he won the Military Cross, he was eager to help when it was over, and he founded the Disabled Society, out of which grew the idea that the men might be set to work making things. He set them to work making flowers, and the first beginnings of poppy-making were in a room he hired off the Old Kent Road. Now this factory at Richmond, the House of Remembrance that never forgets the men who won the war, produces over forty million poppies in a year. The Major is no longer among his men, for at Armistice time in 1936 he lay dying on a bed of pain and would not be denied his longing to see once again the Field of Remembrance at the Abbey. The inspiration for it had come to him in a dream, and they laid him in the ambulance and drove him there, and, as he lay watching the pilgrimage to this little garden of crosses and poppies, the King came to the ambulance and talked to him. It was his last sight of the Garden of Remembrance. He went back to Richmond, and his last words at the factory, spoken to one of the original five members of the staff, were: 'Remember, if I peg out I go in the factory van.' As the ambulance left he led the singing of 'Are We Down-hearted?' and that is how his men remember him.

* *The King's England—Buckinghamshire*, Arthur Mee, Hodder & Stoughton, 1940.

12

High Wycombe

When the first bricks were laid to Yewden Manor beside that avenue of ancient yews at Hambleden, High Wycombe, at the head of the Hambleden Valley, was already a thriving market town. The age of the parish church of All Saints is told in its consecration by Wulfstan, who was Bishop of Worcester from 1062 to 1095; the original home of the Royal Grammar School was twelfth century; there are references to a Guildhall on the present site as early as 1380; it is an old, old town, though on first sight one might not think so today. Standing at a junction of valleys on the main route from London to Oxford, High Wycombe was ideally situated to grow and prosper over the years, and now it is the largest of the Chiltern towns, larger far than the county town of Aylesbury, with a District Council that serves a population nearing 150,000 spread over twenty-three parishes.

One of the keys to the town's development is to be found in the beechwoods that grow in such profusion on the sides of the surrounding hills, for they and the men that worked them led to the development of the furniture trade for which High Wycombe is now known the world over. As early as 1700 the bodgers were bringing in their turned legs and rails to sell in the market, and all over the town in sheds and backyard workshops seats were made, bows bent, rails glued and the finished chairs turned out. A High Sheriff's report of 1798 lists thirty-three chairmakers in the town, and a century later there were over a hundred factories 'mainly producing chairs'. Between 1801 and 1960 more chairs were made in High Wycombe than by all the London manufacturers put together, and when the American evangelists Moody and Sankey called for a rush order of chairs for one of their Revival meetings the town had capacity to complete 19,200 of them in a few weeks. There are well over a hundred furniture factories in and around High Wycombe today, some of them still bearing the names of eighteenth- and nineteenth-century chairmasters, and between them they produce over eighty per cent of the chairs made in Britain.

The old chairmasters were doughty men, out with their wagons early and late, up and down the hills and around the muddy, rutted lanes to the villages, first collecting from the bodgers and then delivering their finished chairs. James Gomme was making furniture on the site of the present G-Plan factory in 1798, though High Wycombe's first furniture factory was founded some years earlier by Samuel Treacher and Thomas Widgington, who are credited with having evolved the Windsor chair. Another familiar name is that of Frederick Parker, awarded a gold medal at the Crystal Palace in 1884 for one of his couches.

Among the exhibits in the Chair Museum at High Wycombe are coins struck by James Gomme for issue to his workmen, before the practice became illegal; copper coins, marked on one side 'James Gomme' with the date, together with a picture of the Wycombe Guildhall, and on the reverse with the legend 'High Wycombe, Buckinghamshire, Token . . . pence'. The issue of such tokens was common in the nineteenth century and is said to have arisen from a shortage of copper coin, but it was abused, and the tokens came to be used to pay workmen who could then use them only at the issuer's own shops or take a discount for them elsewhere, sometimes receiving no more than two-thirds or three-quarters of their face value. It was to eliminate such frauds that the Truck Acts were passed in 1831 making it illegal to pay workmen other than in coin of the realm, and forbidding any deductions from wages other than those authorized by statute.

Windsor-style chairs were first recorded in the 1650s, substantial articles, usually of beech with elm seats. Later they were taken up by Chippendale, who lightened and softened the design, taking the Windsor out of the kitchen and planting it firmly in the dining-room or salon. In the eighteenth century rush-seated, ladder-backed chairs came into fashion, followed by a cane-seated spoon-backed style, both very light-weight and elegant beside the heavier, wooden-seated Windsors. The seats for these cane and rush chairs were 'put out' to be worked by the cottagers. There was some skill to the task, particularly with the more intricate patterns, though often the simpler work was done by quite small children. The cane-workers were the élite, rush being very clumsy and messy to work, often muddy from the river, dusty when dry and giving off an evil smell when damped down ready for working. Women were still taking in seats for caning as late as the 1930s, when it was the custom for children to pick up half a dozen seat frames on their way home from school and return them completed on their way back next morning.

This outwork was a very necessary addition to the family budget, particularly in the late nineteenth century when a man would be required to make up a dozen plain chairs for his day's work at one shilling the dozen, sometimes working on in the evenings cutting wedges at a penny a gross. The Windsor chair framer would receive a piecework rate of as much as 5s. for his dozen chairs, but for this he would have to cut the joints, make and fit tenons, drill the necessary holes and frame up legs, arms and back on to the seat, with all the laths, rails, stretchers and splats, a formidable day's work which lasted from six in the morning until eight at night, six days a week. Out of his wages a workman supplied his own tools and glue, and paid twopence a week for use of the grindstone and a halfpenny towards the wages of the boy who fetched and carried and cleaned the place up. One of his few privileges was the right to choose free wood for his marriage chair. Some of these chairs are still in the possession of old chairmakers' families, beautifully made of fruitwood and elm, and greatly treasured. The Chair Museum, housed in a lovely old eighteenth-century building on Castle Hill, has examples of chairs, workman's tools, etc., from the early days of furniture making, as well as a reconstruction of a bodger's workshop.

A good Windsor chair fetched about 6s. in the market in 1800; in 1874 an order for rush-seated chairs for St Paul's Cathedral was filled at 4s. the chair, and when the factories started to turn out their new designs after the 1939–45 war an Ercol Windsor carver sold for £5.15s. The furniture trade is a long way from these prices today, with operatives in the new factories on the trading estate at Cressex earning upwards of £5,000 a year. The old cottages where much of the outwork was done were swept away in the post-war town centre development, and today's furniture workers live in the new estates built on the hills around the edges of the town. Sixty thousand people now dwell where in the 1930s there were but 17,000, and even at that time H. J. Massingham was rueing the inevitable modernization, describing High Wycombe as a 'vast dustbin of houses', though in his time the River Wye still ran through the centre of the town and cattle still grazed on The Rye. If he had asked the opinion of those who dwelt in the 'vast dustbin' I expect he would have been told that *they* found their new houses comfortable and commodious and much to be preferred to the jumble of old cottages they had left behind, which tended to be more picturesque than comfortable.

The old roads around St Mary's Street and Newlands where half the working-class population of the borough lived during the growth of the furniture industry have all been redeveloped since the war. Now the river is culverted for the best part of a mile under the town, and where it once flowed under the bridge at St Mary's Street there is a new bus station, multi-storey car park, 100,000 square foot superstore, and Octagon Shopping Centre, a two-tier indoor shopping complex with larger stores on the ground floor and smaller units in the galleried upper row, similar to London's Brent Cross Centre which it pre-dates by several years.

This new development rubs shoulders with the broad Georgian High Street that leads from the municipal buildings in Queen Victoria Road to the church and Guildhall. The old houses in the High Street have been cleverly adapted to modern use without losing too much of their charm, and prominent among them is the Woolworth store occupying a building that previously housed the Red Lion Hotel, a hostelry that could trace its history back to 1312. The building was remodelled and reconstructed for Woolworth's, but the long, classical façade remains, with the lower storey built into a series of brick arches to complement the Guildhall. This façade is unique in a company that by tradition keeps its shop-fronts in uniform red and gold, instantly recognizable in whatever town they may be situated. The bold red lion on the portico is a memento of the old hotel, though it is not the one on which Disraeli sat to make a speech after one of his Parliamentary elections; that lion is in the entrance hall at Hughenden Manor. The one in the town is a replica, carved by Frank Hudson, a resident of High Wycombe.

The present Guildhall, last of many such to occupy the site, was designed by Henry Keene for the Earl of Shelburne, who presented it to the town in 1757. The Earl, who has a large and ornate memorial tucked away in a side chapel in All Saints' Church, also built Wycombe Abbey at the foot of Marlow Hill, commissioning the design from James Wyatt in 1795. The building was never an abbey, and was sold for a Girls' Public School in 1896 by a later owner, Lord Carrington, who moved out and built himself a new house on Daws Hill. Lord Carrington was a great influence in the development of High Wycombe, for he built Queen Victoria Road in the old Queen's memory, subsequently presenting the road and its adjoining land to the town for new civic buildings. The Town Hall was built there in the early years of this century, and the Municipal Offices, Public Library, Police Station and Post Office, all fine examples of between-wars architecture, in the 1930s. Nearby are the modern Law Courts designed by Fred Pooley, one-time Chief Architect to the Buckinghamshire County Council and subsequently President of the R.I.B.A.

At the top of the High Street opposite the Guildhall is the Little Market House. Built in 1761 to the design of Robert Adam, this is a jolly little multi-arched octagonal building with a lantern roof, known locally as the Pepperpot. My guess is that its old red brick and well-wrought arches will still stand when that other Octagon, the modern shopping precinct across the way, is a crumbling ruin, its galleries gutted and the concrete scaling from its rusting iron bones. Unless, of course, the Little Market House is so unfortunate as to be knocked down in a traffic accident as the old Toll House was. For the car is the curse of High Wycombe. Though the Inner Relief Road gained a Civic Trust Award for the Authority in 1968, the remaining narrow medieval streets around the church and Guildhall are still heavily congested with traffic. Mostly, one suspects, with desperate shoppers who haven't obeyed the notices, driving round and round trying to find their way into one of the car parks.

Before the Relief Road was built it was possible for visitors to the town to park near The Rye and enjoy a walk along the river. Indeed, this comely stretch of green with the water running through positively lured one from the car to enjoy it at close quarters. Today the raised carriageway hides it all from view, and the stranger drives through the town on the A40 never knowing that either the river or The Rye exists. Yet it is all still there, river, mills, dyke, back-stream and cricket ground; the High Wycombe Society have worked out a two-mile Water Trail around The Rye, passing the municipal swimming pool, which is built where yet another Roman villa and traces of a Neolithic settlement have been excavated in layers, and four of the forty-three water mills that at one time were turned by the River Wye on its journey from its source at Chorley Farm, near West Wycombe, to the all-embracing Thames.

The ruins of Pann Mill are nearest to the road. Little more now than a shed beside an iron water-wheel, Pann Mill was a working corn-mill in Saxon times and continued so until the last family moved out in the 1960s; the wheel still turns when the sluice is opened. Bassetsbury and Marsh Green Mills, which have been corn-mills and paper-mills by turns, have both been converted for housing. At Bassetsbury in particular the character of the old mill has been retained, the millstream flowing under the house can be viewed through a glass panel in one of the rooms and the great water-wheel still stands against the back wall of the building. At Rye Mill the old paper mill has become a garage, where once again the millstream passes under the building. Many of these old converted mills make a feature of the water they stand over. The Millstream at Old Amersham, formerly a restaurant and now a high-class couturier's, is another building where the millstream can be seen through glass where it rushes along under the building, though no water is apparent from outside the building, a fact which gives one an uneasy feeling that any minute the floor might give way and house and contents be swept away underground along the stream.

The roads from High Wycombe lead north to Hughenden Valley, east to Amersham, south to Marlow and west towards Oxford. The road west, the A40 to Stokenchurch, passes the historic villages of West Wycombe, Bradenham and Radnage. Previous writers on the Chilterns have been lyrical about Radnage, but today it is a village that has lost its charm; separated into three hamlets of Town End, Bennett End (formerly Bennit End) and The City, it seems at first sight to be all lanes and modern bungalows. But antiquity is there: at Bennett End the Three Horseshoes, all chimneys and Georgian brick, was built in 1745, and a similar date can be presumed for the nearby cottages, while at Town End the lovely little Decorated church with its Saxon font sits sweetly in the landscape. It cannot compare, though, with West Wycombe. Nothing compares with West Wycombe, where the main street shows every nuance of English architecture from the fifteenth century to the nineteenth. Queen Anne windows, Regency stucco, oriels and timbered gable ends, jutting upper storeys, a wealth of exposed beams, and even some wattle and daub; old inns, dower house, fifteenth-century church loft with weather vane and clock, West Wycombe has them all. There have been only two new houses built in the village this century, and one of those is the rectory built in 1967.

West Wycombe was purchased from Sir John Dashwood by the Royal Society of Arts in 1929, to be preserved as 'a fine picture of English life and history'. The Society passed on the village to the National Trust in 1934, and at the same time Sir John donated fifty-nine acres on Church Hill and the Dashwood Mausoleum. The gift to the Trust was completed in 1943 by the present Sir Francis Dashwood with West Wycombe House and Park. The house was rebuilt in the late 1700s by a previous Sir Francis, 'Hellfire' Dashwood, Lord le Despencer, a cultivated and much-travelled man with an interest in classical architecture. He had the house rebuilt in the Palladian style (yet another rival to Stowe), dammed the River Wye to form an ornamental lake, and employed Humphry Repton to lay out the park. Pevsner gives four whole pages to this property; to the description of the house and grounds, the island temple below the cascade, the lodges with their Ionic columns, the Temple of the Four Winds copied from the Temple of the Winds at Athens, the tall arch with the Apollo Belvedere which screens the stables and offices, and countless other beauties.

In his time Sir Francis held Cabinet posts as Chancellor of the Exchequer and Postmaster General, rewrote the Book of Common Prayer into everyday English, and built a new road into High Wycombe to provide work locally, yet his popular reputation today is only concerned with the Hellfire Club, supposedly founded for the practice of black magic first at Medmenham Abbey and later in the caves under Church Hill. The name the group gave to themselves was the Brotherhood of St Francis, or, more popularly, Dashwood's Apostles. They may have been up to no good, but if you believe they worshipped the devil then you believe it of half the then Government of England, for many of Sir Francis's Cabinet colleagues were fellow members of the Brotherhood. Much of their evil reputation rests on the Hellfire Caves that were dug into the hill below the church and mausoleum to provide chalk for the new road to High Wycombe. There is no contemporary evidence that the caves were used for evil practices, but the names given them today such as 'catacombs', 'robing room', 'inner temple', together with a recorded commentary designed to titillate the cash customers with the sort of details the organizers think they like to hear, invest them with mystery. The caves are extensive, running back into the hill for a quarter of a mile, and though they are now lit with electricity and furnished as restaurant, souvenir shop, and reproduction of a bodger's workshop complete with pole lathe, it doesn't take too much imagination to picture smoky, guttering lamps and cowled figures in the gloom, and hear the shrieks and whoops of their carousing.

Apart from the house and park, the real attractions at West Wycombe are the church on the hill and the Dashwood Mausoleum. The church is hidden from the road below, only the top storey of the tower and the great golden ball surmounting it can be seen rising above the classical columns of the Mausoleum, which itself stands out bold and clear. Not until you have climbed to the top of the hill does the church of St Lawrence come into view. The direct route from West Wycombe climbs steeply up the thickly wooded hillside, and as one labours up between the ancient, fantastic yews hung about with strands of ivy and with creepers as thick as a man's wrist it is easy to believe the tales of midnight trysts and secret rituals, but once through the wood and on to the heath the clean, invigorating wind sweeping the hilltop blows these fancies away. All is airiness and light; the Dashwood Mausoleum with its elegant columns and classical urns and frieze has never known a roof; it stands open to the sun and the sky, calm, peaceful; no more, now, than a graceful curiosity. One would not stand on the greensward within these walls and think of 'graves and worms, and epitaphs' or feel the sobering hand of death, as one might in even the humblest country churchyard.

As one does, indeed, in the quiet tree-girt churchyard that tops the hill above the Mausoleum, where the graves of great and small are clustered together in holy ground around the church. St Lawrence was an ancient church, originally parish church of the 'lost' village of Haveringdon. Only the ruined chancel and part of the tower remained when Sir Francis turned his attention to it; he had the nave rebuilt with a central altar, Corinthian columns, and a richly carved frieze with garlands; panelled the chancel arch behind the altar, paved the floor with marble, and commissioned a most beautiful and delicate painting of the Last Supper by Giovanni Borgnis for the lofty, stuccoed ceiling. All this remains today, and one has but to look upon it to know that assuredly this work was done innocently and with reverence, though the square nave with its unstained Georgian panes to the windows and plain, painted wooden pews set facing each other in a square before the nave altar are unconventional, to say the least.

It has been suggested that Sir Francis's intention in carrying out this work, as with rewriting the Prayer-book, was to make the Church and services more acceptable to modern man. The same pattern is there in our more evangelical churches today, with the Alternative Service Book, guitar accompaniments, padded seats and under-pew heating. The general opinion locally is that Sir Francis was a good man and a good landlord, providing work for his villagers in bad times with his road and his building works; that the Hellfire Caves are a mere tourist attraction, and that the Knights of St Francis was more a youthful indiscretion than a lifelong wickedness.

From West Wycombe village a footpath and a bridleway lead to Bradenham, another National Trust village, and the site of one of the four Chiltern Youth Hostels (the others are at Ivinghoe, Jordans and Lee Gate). The Georgian manor house, now used as offices, belonged to Disraeli's father, Israel d'Israeli, in the early 1800s, and it was the statesman's home until he bought Hughenden. Here he wrote the novels *Sybil* and *Coningsby*, and he is thought to have used the village and manor house as the setting for *Endymion*, where he wrote of 'the old Hall, huge gates of iron, high wrought and bearing an ancient date', and of a 'village green round which were clustered the cottages of the parish'. So Bradenham is today, with the church of St Botolph beside the gates to the manor house, the Old Red Lion, Old Forge, and cricket pitch on the village green. The road through the village leads to Bradenham Woods and thence towards Lacey Green and Speen, the heart of the Hampden country.

A busy day in High Wycombe

Aylesbury. The new Town Centre, Council offices and multi-storey
car park

Old houses by Aylesbury churchyard

The Market Square, Aylesbury

All Saints' Church, Wing, with its eleventh-century apse

The Plough Inn, below Whiteleaf Hill, the only pub on the Ridgeway
Long Distance Footpath

The Hampden Memorial at
Chalgrove Field

The Hampden Statue in the
Market Square at Aylesbury

"Just such cottages as the ordinary person might live in"—thatched cottages at Chalgrove

A quiet corner of Princes Risborough

A view across the Vale from Wainhill

Shirburn Street, Watlington

The Thames at Hambleden

Hambleden Mill

Hart Street, Henley

Looking towards Marlow Mills from the bridge

13

Aylesbury and the Vale

Aylesbury is another town that has been extensively developed in the last two decades. The ancient town was built on the summit of a hill with the tower of St Mary's Church making a landmark for miles across the flat lands of the Vale, but today the eleven-storey concrete finger of the new County Council offices towers above town and church alike, dwarfing all with its height and bulk.

Visitors to the town parking in one of the multi-storey car parks or disembarking at the new bus station might wander into the adjacent near-underground shops or the concrete wilderness of Friars Square, then drive out on the no-stopping one-way system, past the new Health Centre and the commercial premises of Hazell, Watson & Viney, and go away with a completely false impression. For around the church in St Mary's Square and along Parson's Fee and Church Street, the tiny, timbered houses of the old seventeenth-century town are still miraculously preserved. Here is 'Elseberie' as John Wilkes knew it when he lived at the Prebendal House with his new bride, as Cromwell's troops knew it during the Civil War when it was a Parliamentary stronghold; even, in part, as Henry VI knew it when he brought his Queen to the King's Head Inn for her honeymoon. Narrow courts and alleys lead from the square to George Street, Castle Street and Temple Square where houses of every period jostle together in a crowded, delightful conglomeration of styles; squat and timber-framed or crooked and tall, with bulging plaster walls, sway-backed roof tiles or elegant Georgian fronts, these houses turn American tourists pink with pleasure.

One of the Georgian houses in St Mary's Square has a Sun Insurance Fire Tablet on the wall above the front door. These tablets are rare today. They date from the time when most fire engines were owned by the insurance companies who sent them out to minimize the company's liability in case of fire. When a fire was reported the brigades came running, but unless your plaque said you were of their flock they would be likely just to stand by and enjoy the blaze.

The County Museum is housed in one of the lovely old sixteenth-century buildings in Castle Street, a house that was refaced with chequered brick in Georgian times. In its brief descriptive leaflet the museum describes itself as being 'for and about the people of Buckinghamshire', a claim which is taken seriously by the staff who go to endless trouble to answer questions and generally make their museum attractive. Anyone who has taken sandwiches to their popular lunchtime lectures will readily agree that this is so. The museum keeps an index of all known archaeological sites and finds in the county, and as the Biological and Geological Record Centre it also maintains records of plant and animal distribution and of rock exposure. Among the items on display are examples of all the old Buckinghamshire crafts and trades, lace-making, straw-plaiting, chairmaking, etc., and some stuffed and mounted white Aylesbury ducklings. The great size of these birds compared with wild ducks is always a surprise.

From Church Street it is but a step through Pebble Alley, where the last of the old Town pumps is preserved, to Kingsbury and Market Square. Market Square, with its War Memorial and Clock Tower and statues of Lord Chesham and John Hampden, is a square no longer, and the twice-weekly market is now held in the new complex in Friars Square. But Kingsbury, once the site of the residences of Norman and Plantagenet kings, retains its old triangular shape and its old pre-war look. Along a narrow alley nearby is the town's most spectacular piece of architecture, the black-and-white King's Head Inn. This heavily timbered and gabled fifteenth-century survival started life as guest house to the Franciscan monastery founded in Aylesbury in 1386. No trace remains of the monastery, but the name is commemorated in Friars Square and Friarage Road, part of the inner ring road that keeps traffic from the centre of the town.

The King's Arms has rested many famous heads upon its pillows in the course of 500 years; Henry VI spent part of his honeymoon there; Cromwell slept the night there in 1651 after receiving a delegation to congratulate him on the Parliamentary victory at Worcester, and later Sir Austen Layard, the explorer of Nineveh and Babylon, stayed there when he was M.P. for Aylesbury from 1852 to 1857. The inn was presented to the National Trust in 1926 by the Rothschild family, who had owned it for fifty years, and the Trust's policy has been to preserve it as a working inn.

There seems to be some doubt as to the exact date when Aylesbury became the county town. Traditionally Buckingham had the charter, and certainly the Assizes were held at Buckingham for centuries, but Aylesbury gradually usurped the functions of government, and when the new County Hall and the gaol were built there in 1720 it seemed that the title had passed by default. Buckingham fought back, however, with a bill in Parliament, and the title continued to be disputed until 1845 when the Assizes moved to Aylesbury, and with gaol, Assizes and County Hall Aylesbury's claim was finally established.

Florence Maybrick, the Victorian poisoner, served out a fifteen-year sentence in Aylesbury Gaol for poisoning her husband with arsenic. She had been sentenced to death in spite of her vehement protestations of innocence, but there was some dispute over the medical evidence and the sentence was commuted to 'life'. On her release she returned to her native America and wrote a book about her trial and sentence in which she once more reiterated her innocence, but she is still known as 'Florence Maybrick the Poisoner'. Earlier, in 1844, another poisoner had been hanged from the balcony of the County Hall for murdering his wife with prussic acid. This case attracted much publicity at the time for the murderer, John Tawell, was caught after his description had been signalled by the new electric telegraph. He, therefore, was the first criminal to be caught by such means, a triumph preceding the capture of Dr Crippen, whose description was sent out by wireless.

In 1970 the County Hall, a handsome Georgian building in Market Square which housed the Assizes and Quarter Sessions, was set on fire by an arsonist and the whole interior gutted. Fortunately the fire was extinguished before much damage was done to the structure and before the flames could spread to the nineteenth-century Corn Exchange next door. Within a year, the building had been totally repaired, the old interior being so faithfully reproduced that even the new woodwork was artificially darkened to simulate antiquity. Not that there is need to simulate antiquity in a town mentioned by name in the *Anglo-Saxon Chronicle*; under the date 571 occurs the entry: 'This year Cuthulf fought with the Britons at Bedford and took four towns, Lenbury, Aylesbury, Benson and Ensham'.

The cruciform foundations to St Mary's Church were laid at the time when Henry III was rebuilding Westminster Abbey, and the square thirteenth-century church tower has risen bravely above Aylesbury ever since. In the 1850s, though, when Sir George Gilbert Scott was called in to restore the church, he found the structure so neglected as to be almost beyond saving. Indeed, an architect called in before him had declared the church beyond repair, and so ruined that it would undoubtedly fall down before he could get back to Euston. An extensive rebuilding programme was the remedy, and most of the old Norman church disappeared in the process. Little more than a century later an Appeal Committee was again asking for funds to restore the fabric, which once more was in urgent need of repair. They were not, this time, asking for the £16,000 that the Victorian restoration had cost, but for £500,000. It had been decided that if work was to be done on this important building at the heart of the town it should be done for the benefit of the whole population, and not for the Anglican community alone. Under the Appeal Committee's auspices the interior of the church was redesigned as a centre for 'prayer, recreation, work, play, relaxation and worship', and for use not only on Sundays but on every day of the week.

The work took three years, and 7th May 1979 saw the reopening and rededication of the church, a ceremony that was followed by a month-long Festival of Arts, Music and Drama. A new choir gallery and stage were built below the beautiful sixteenth-century West window, and the late twelfth-century font, now the only piece of Norman work in the church, was replaced in its original position inside the West door. For worship, a portable altar is sited at the great crossing beneath the tower, and for private prayer the chapel of St Luke and St John, where all the memorial tablets were put at the time of the Victorian restoration, has been closed off entirely from the body of the church and given its own door to the churchyard, a door which is always open.

Life in the town is continually changing; the Greater London Plan of 1944 marked Aylesbury as a 'good unit, representative of administrative and industrial activities', and thought its population 'capable of easy expansion to a maximum of 60,000' in and about the town. Today the Aylesbury Vale District Council administers a population of 120,000 spread over 109 parishes, and the number is ever rising. In 1977 there were 45,000 residents within the confines of the town itself, residents enjoying the best of all worlds: a modernized antiquity, 'big town' shops and facilities, and all around the green, spreading countryside of the Vale.

The very words 'Vale of Aylesbury' call up visions of a favoured land, of fair farming country chequered with hedges, and of isolated farmhouses and neat villages relieved by tall church spires. The visions are not too far from reality, though the face of the countryside has changed in recent years with the change in farming patterns. Those rich hedges that once patched the fields with edges of lacy blossom have been grubbed out on many farms to form great fields more easily worked by today's mechanized methods. This takes away the homely patchwork of the years and gives the Vale a downland look. In one place at least this look is not new; Creslow Manor Farm near Whitchurch is known for its 'great pastures'. One vast 300-acre meadow here has been kept since medieval times to graze sheep and cattle for the King's table. John Westcar owned this pasture at the turn of the eighteenth century and had great success with his beasts; in 1799 he sold a prize ox for £100, an almost unbelievable price at that time. He was the first farmer to see the potential of the new canals for transporting livestock and sent his animals to Smithfield on the Grand Union, saving them a 40-mile walk.

Whitchurch runs into Oving in the west, the two together making up the largest of the Vale villages and according to Sir John Betjeman probably 'the best of the lot'. Ancient Oving with its pretty cottages and wide green verges is modest as a village maiden, and Whitchurch would be as quiet and unobtrusive but for the A413 to Buckingham which unfortunately forms the main village street, but in their time these villages have been busy and important places and they are redolent with history. Lying between them, though closer to Whitchurch than Oving, is the site of the great moated castle built in King Stephen's reign by Hugh de Bolebec, whose father came over with William the Conqueror. It was fashionable for such men to build themselves castles in the manors they were granted for their trouble. Often the castle was little more than a fortified hall-house, but Hugh de Bolebec was more ambitious than most and his castle was a grand affair. His descendants allowed it to go to ruin, however, and by the time of the Civil War it was unoccupied and the walls were crumbling. Cromwell ordered it to be demolished, and today only a few grassy mounds survive for its epitaph.

Making a third to these villages is tiny Creslow, smallest parish in the county which yet boasts the county's oldest house. Creslow Manor House was built during the 50-year reign of Edward III, when England's economy was founded on wool and sheep grew golden fleece. There would have been wealth enough then in Creslow's great pastures to build a manor house that might endure for half a millennium. Now much changed, restored and added to, the manor is privately occupied and serves as farmhouse to Creslow Farm.

Oving is the site of the 'Quinque via' mentioned in the old records of Buckinghamshire, the meeting of five ways, 'British trackways', Lipscombe called them. These five ways can still be seen on the map today. All the Vale would have been accessible from Oving, whose church was built 200 years before the Manor House at Creslow. One of the five ways from Oving leads to North Marston, a mile to the north. This village unwittingly contributed to the building of Balmoral through a local land-owner, Camden Neild. A barrister by profession, this man was the worst type of absentee landlord, never spending a penny on any of his farms, and he held several in the county, whilst always exacting the last coin in rent. He lived a frugal bachelor existence in London, and on his death left all his property to Queen Victoria. Estimates of Her Majesty's windfall vary from a quarter to half a million, but whatever the sum the bulk of it was spent on Balmoral, though a small part was spent on restoration to the chantry at North Marston church and a stained-glass window to Neild's memory.

North Marston has a great claim to fame in Sir John Shorne, rector there from 1290 to 1314. The saintly Sir John won renown by his claim to have wrestled with the Devil and confined him in a boot, or a horn, or perhaps it was a lamp? Anyway, the feat was depicted in stone and glass in churches throughout the south of England and commemorated in the rhyme:

> Sir John Shorne, Gentleman born,
> Conjured the Devil into a horn.

However, he seems to have escaped.

More to the point as far as North Marston was concerned was the rhyme telling of Sir John's fame as a healer.

To Master John Shorne
That blessed man borne
For the ague to him we apply.

He blessed the waters of a local well, a chalybeate spring, and effected a number of cures for scrofula, the King's Evil, so called because it was supposed that it could be cured by the touch of the King's hand. Anyone claiming to cure scrofula was on to a good thing, since it is a disease which, if left alone, will eventually heal of itself. It barely exists in this country today, the symptoms being treated early with antibiotics. That being said, it must be admitted that Sir John's chalybeate spring proved medically beneficial for centuries. It was still in use as the village well during the cholera epidemics of the 1830s, and North Marston had no deaths at that time although people in the surrounding villages suffered sadly. After Sir John's death his shrine was a place of pilgrimage. Foxe, in his *Book of Martyrs*, stated that 'some [Dissenters] were compelled to make pilgrimage to Sir John Shorne'. The shrine proved very profitable for the village, until Sir John's remains were eventually taken off to St George's Chapel, Windsor.

The thirteenth-century church of St John the Evangelist at Whitchurch has also seen its share of famous men pass through the Saxon doorway. Dr Lipscombe, the historian, Sir John Smythe, Chief Justice in the reign of Charles II; Rex Whistler, the artist, who lived at Bolebec House, and Cornelius Holland, who was granted Creswell Manor by Charles I but turned his coat in the Civil War and was one of those who drew up the charges against the King, though he did not sign the death warrant.

Westwards from these villages the lanes lead mile upon mile across the flat lands of the Vale. Take the right turnings and you might come to Waddesdon, to Quainton, to Pitchcott or to the Claydons: East Claydon, Middle Claydon and Steeple Claydon. The Claydons are Verney country, and its history, together with that of Bernwood and Boarstall and all this part of Buckinghamshire, is told in fascinating detail in the four volumes of the Verney Memoirs. Though no more than ten miles from Aylesbury as the crow flies, these villages on the edge of the Chilterns are some of the most remote in Buckinghamshire. They are on a direct route to nowhere, and no matter from where you set out to find them, you may be sure you will be driving to

and fro between the flat cornfields in a seemingly aimless
fashion for many miles before you arrive.

Quainton, or more accurately Quainton Road, was the
terminus for the Wotton Tramway, a light railway laid down by
the Duke of Buckingham. The Duke also constructed the
Aylesbury and Buckingham line which ran via Quainton from
Aylesbury to Verney Junction. His ambition was to extend the
tramway to Oxford and to connect the Aylesbury and Buckingham line with London and the North, an ambition in which he
was abetted by the Metropolitan Line Chairman, Sir Edward
Watkin. Had they succeeded, Quainton Road would have
become a very important junction, but their plans came to
nought, the Wotton Tramway never went further than Brill nor
the Aylesbury and Buckingham than Verney Junction. The
lines just pottered on until 1935, when they were both closed.
That should have been the end of Quainton Road, but in 1969
the London Railway Preservation Society was looking for a
home for the old steam locos it was trying to preserve and it
came upon the unused goods yard at Quainton, so a railway
museum was born.

The Quainton Railway Society now has more than thirty
steam engines as well as several diesels, the largest collection of
London & North Western coaches in the country, and over
18,000 square feet of loco sheds to house them. An ever-growing
membership is privileged to work on these ponderous, gleaming
trophies, 'have a play', as one of them described it, and there are
open days when members of the public are welcome to go and
watch. A special diesel is chartered on these open days to run
hourly on the otherwise disused line from Aylesbury to
Quainton Road.

Besides working on the restoration of the rolling stock and
generally helping to support the museum, members train to
work as signalmen, drivers, guards, etc. It beats the old 00
Gauge on the bedroom floor any day.

All this huff and puff has brought an unexpected popularity to
Quainton village, of which Sir Arthur Bryant wrote as having
'the still unbroken peace of centuries'. On the edge of the village
green is the oldest market-cross in Buckinghamshire, and the
church boasts more monuments than any other in the county,
the oldest being a brass in the chancel dated 1350. The really
lovely Winwood almshouses by the entrance to the churchyard,
all gables and dormers, date from 1687, there are seventeenth-

and eighteenth-century farmhouses and plenty of pretty cottages, and to complete the picture the tidy remains of a nineteenth-century windmill. One can but admit to a sneaking feeling that it will probably all still be there when the Quainton Road Museum and all its trophies have mouldered gently away.

In truth, we are lucky that Quainton is still here, that Oving and Whitchurch and the villages to the east of the A413, Aston Abbots, Cublington, Dunton, Stewkley and Wing, are still here. But for the courage and determination of those who live there those villages would be deeper drowned than any threatened by reservoirs, they would be flattened under six feet of airport runway concrete.

Perhaps this is the place to say a little about airports. The Vale has the misfortune to be a large, flat stretch of land strategically sited between London and the industrial Midlands, and covetous, philistine glances are constantly turned in its direction by those charged with finding room in this over-populated island for the miles of runway needed for today's jumbo jets. In vain do preservationists protest that by the time such a monstrosity is built technology will have taken us beyond the need for it; in vain do residents gird their loins to protect their houses and fight off the threat. Every five years or so a new proposal to use the Vale is mooted and the cudgels have to be taken up all over again.

The defence of the Vale between 1969 and 1971 by the Wing Airport Resistance Association is a classic of its kind. A committee under the chairmanship of Desmond Fennell, a local resident, produced such irrefutable and vehement arguments to the Roskill Commission that sat to decide the appeal as to convince one that, had the Commission decided against them and let the construction go ahead it might have led, not to a third London Airport, but to a second Civil War. The Association mustered support from all over England; locally they took statements from men and women whose forebears had farmed the same land or lived in the same village since Domesday; they pointed to the beautiful Norman doorway of Stewkley church, the ancient apse at Wing, the whole history and way of life represented by the Vale, and near-dared officialdom to lay so much as a finger upon it.

They were right, of course; and of course they won. It is hoped they won not because of any economic argument but because the Commission was moved, as any English person should be, by the mute evidence of the Vale itself. By the peaceful rolling acres and the story written in stone on every village green, of men born there that died in two world wars to protect their lovely heritage, as their forefathers had died at Agincourt. When the fight was all over and the battle supposedly won, the Friends of the Vale of Aylesbury under their President, Sir Arthur Bryant, collected and printed a most moving anthology of writings about the Vale.* It should be compulsory reading for any who plan airports in the future.

---

* *Country Like This:* F. Weathered & Son, 1972.

14

Whiteleaf, Thame and the Witchert Villages

Winter or summer, before most of us have breakfasted on Sunday mornings, the car park at the foot of Longdown Hill is already half-full of cars disgorging the sort of dogs favoured in the Chilterns, labradors, setters, retrievers, Dalmatians and basset hounds, all intent on taking their owners for a good run over Longdown or Whiteleaf Hill. Hours later the exhausted owners will descend to the valley and gather at the Plough Inn, on the road towards Askett and Whiteleaf village. The Plough is known today chiefly for its selection of thirty-eight different cheeses. Once, though, it was renowned for the tradition kept up by the landlord's wife of baking a cherry pie in the shape of a coffin every year on the 17th June to commemorate John Hampden's death, and the fact that his body rested at the inn on its way home to Hampden for burial.

The Patriot was mortally wounded at Chalgrove and died a few days later at Thame. There is no more memorable account of his death than that written in 1950 by the Chiltern poet and essayist, J. H. B. Peel:

The death of Hampden is an epic, like that of Nelson and Wolfe and H.M.S. *Rawalpindi*. On Saturday, the 17th of June, 1643, at a little after four o'clock in the afternoon, Prince Rupert of the Rhine rode from his Uncle's stronghold at Oxford—his trumpeters, it is said, bringing even the dons to their windows; his gay Cavaliers glittering and jingling in the bright sunshine. The King's men were out to harry the rebels.

They bivouacked that night in the woods above Stokenchurch, and at three o'clock next morning, as the sun was rising above Ibstone, they fell upon Chinnor, and burned it, and slew some of its men. Smoke and a rising sun spread the dreaded news—the Prince was out again! Hampden had long expected such an attack. On the previous day he had ridden into Watlington, to inspect the defences there, and he was at Watlington when the news of Rupert's sally reached him. He acted swiftly. To Lord Essex at Thame he despatched couriers post-haste, requiring a force to be sent to Chiselhampton Bridge, which (as he knew from long familiarity with the countryside) the Prince must re-cross in order to enter Oxford. Meanwhile, he himself set out at the head of a small body of troopers and dragoons to waylay the enemy until Lord Essex's men arrived. Hampden's friends protested that he need not undertake such an adventure: as Colonel of Foot (they said) he was not expected to play the Subaltern of Horse. The protests he ignored.

The Prince was encountered sooner than the Roundheads had calculated, and before Lord Essex's reinforcements had arrived. (In fact, these never set out, for Lord Essex foresaw whither the revolution was leading, and had no mind to speed its progress.) Rupert, for his part, turned about when he saw the Roundheads, whom he at once attacked. The battle was fought near the Oxford-shire hamlet of Chalgrove, in a place known as Chalgrove Field—where dead men's bones are still ploughed up—marked now by the second of the two monuments that Lord Nugent erected to Hampden's memory. Hampden charged, at the head of his men, but received a bullet wound, and was seen to turn away from the fighting: 'A thing,' as Lord Clarendon observed, 'he never used to do, and from which it was concluded he was hurt.' Very near at that hour was Pyrton, the home of his first love, but the enemy barred the way thither, and he made instead for Thame, having first to clear the wide brook below Haseley. He was seen to gather himself for the great effort. He clapped his spurs and set his horse to the brook. He cleared it, although he was dying. At Thame they took him to the house of a surgeon, one Ezekiel Browne, where for a time he lingered, but his wound began to fester, and after intense suffering he died, thinking to the last of his unhappy country.

His own regiment, the Buckinghamshire Greencoats, escorted the body home to Hampden, where he was buried at the church within his own gates. In the ensuing years there was some dispute as to the cause of his death, some saying his wound was caused by his own pistol having burst. As a consequence the body was exhumed in 1828 to settle the matter. Lord Nugent, then M.P. for Aylesbury, was prime mover in the matter, and he it was who unwrapped the body from its grave cloths. Plainly the dead hero had been treated with all reverence; three tightly wrapped layers had provided his winding sheet, and a con-temporary account of the exhumation describes the face still fleshed and so well preserved that the expression could clearly be seen. The hair on the dead man's head and his beard were still a 'full auburn brown'. There was no wound at the shoulder, but an amputated hand was found wrapped in a separate cloth, seeming to prove the claim that his death had been the result of a sad accident.

From behind the Plough Inn a path goes up steeply between the tall, straight trunks of the beech trees, over the leaf-fall of centuries, to attain the ridge again at Whiteleaf Hill where the largest of the Chiltern chalk hill figures, a great cross on a wide triangular base, is carved on the hill face overlooking the Vale of Aylesbury. On a clear day this cross can be seen for forty miles.

The true history of Whiteleaf Cross is not known. The *Victoria County History* suggests it is an ancient cross, and that together with Bledlow Cross on Wainhill, further along the scarp towards Chinnor, it is contemporary with the Long Men of Wilmington and Cerne Abbas. H. J. Massingham compared it with the Uffington White Horse, and adduced evidence of its antiquity from the round barrow excavated on Whiteleaf Hill. He suggested that the alignment of the cross with the earthworks on Pulpit Hill, with the barrows on Five Knolls Hill at Dunstable, and with Ravensborough Castle, is significant. Again, the writer Ian Rodger, who is quoted in Chapter IX in connection with the apse at All Saints', Wing, and who can see Whiteleaf Cross from his home at Brill, felt for many years that it was connected with Celtic ritual, and that if the proper sightings were taken at sunrise on 31st October, the Celtic New Year, it would be found that the first rays of the rising sun would fall on Whiteleaf Cross. Having waited for years for the right conditions, he was able to take his sitings in 1980, only to find that the expected alignment was not on Whiteleaf but on Beacon Hill, further along the ridge. Ian and Joan Hay in *Hilltop Villages of the Chilterns* suggested that Edward the Elder caused both the Chiltern crosses to be cut to mark his victory over the Danes at the beginning of the tenth century when the Danelaw was pushed back to the far side of Watling Street. This seems plausible, as the crosses mark the two sides of the Risborough Gap. Arthur Mee, on the other hand, says the cross at Whiteleaf is 'believed to have been cut in the seventeenth century'.

Certain it is that the first possible record of the cross is in a Charter of 903 which mentions a 'boundary mark'; all else is speculation. The first undisputed mention of Whiteleaf Cross is in an Act of Parliament of George IV's reign commanding that the cross be kept in good condition and regularly cleaned, and laying upon the owners of the Hampden estate the responsibility for doing so. Like Rycote Chapel, the cross is now officially an ancient monument, so presumably comes under the care of the Ministry of Works. Dr George Lipscombe, the Buckinghamshire historian, writing in 1837, reported that the cleaning of the cross 'is now borne by the neighbourhood and never without a merry-making'. This Dr George Lipscombe was a medical man, village doctor at Whitchurch, in the Vale of Aylesbury. He impoverished himself to produce his book, *The History and Antiquities of the County of Buckingham*, which was published in 1847, and died a pauper. Nevertheless, the book was a major work and he is still regarded as an authority and much quoted.

The view from the top of Whiteleaf Hill shows the peaceful Vale stretching wide and fair to the horizon. There are the towns of Aylesbury and Thame; there the ancient villages of Quainton, Long Crendon, Ludgershall and Brill; there in the west is Chalgrove Field where Hampden was ruined; there the 'violet-embroidered Vale' that Milton knew, the 'goodly Vale' of which Michael Drayton sang in 'Polyolbion' in 1612, and there the 'witchert' villages of Haddenham and Dinton, Cuddington and Chearsley, Upper and Lower Wichendon, Bishopstone and Ford.

Witchert is unique to this part of the Vale of Aylesbury. It is a thick, white, sticky clay which occurs in a four-foot layer just below the surface. Dug out and puddled, it becomes plastic and easily worked, and left to dry it forms a brick-hard substance which endures for centuries. Unlike wattle and daub or lath and plaster, the witchert requires no support, and although it was sometimes used as infill in timber-framed houses it more often stood alone. Like Devonshire cob, the walls were as much as two foot thick at the base, tapering to half that thickness at the top, and their superb insulating properties made houses that were cool in summer and warm in winter. They were built with deep overhanging thatch to take the weather clear of the walls from the top, and on three-foot-high flint plinths to keep them dry at the foot; essential precautions these, for once the witchert is allowed to get thoroughly wet it softens and simply collapses and washes away. When freshly dug the substance could be shaped and worked with ease, and the houses it built with their characteristic rounded, whitened walls and deep thatch were picture-book cottages. Some writers have described them as 'Spanish-looking', but they are wrong; these cottages are as English as mead and elm trees and the pink coats of hunting men, a fact never more evident than where misguided efforts have been made to smarten them up with iron gates and grilles and coloured lanterns. Another distinctive feature in these witchert villages is the prevalence of tall, curving white walls in place of fences, walls that once were crowned with thatch but now sport little 'roofs' of overhanging tiles or slates to protect them from the weather. To wander around these villages is to be set back in time by centuries. It is so easy to picture them as once they were, the cottages separated one from another by grass and field flowers, with narrow paths crossing to and fro, chickens and geese scratching and crooning about their daily business of finding themselves a bite to eat, and ducks dabbling in the ponds. Perhaps, too, an old lady seated before her door with a lace pillow on her lap and her man nearby with adze and spoke-shave, paring a chair-seat from cherrywood. Little Chearsley, with its thatched inn beside the village green; Nether Winchendon, the classic English village, where sixteenth- and seventeenth-century houses with infill of russet brick under thatched or tiled roofs make contrast to the witchert, and where the Gothic overlay on the Manor House hides a medieval stone mansion; and Cuddington, an unspoiled delight, with neat thatch, deep-eaved cottages, and a working pump on the village green. Nothing in the Vale can compare; it is a taste of Old England.

Haddenham, stretched along its lanes, was a gift for the developer, but around the church and Manor Farm all is unchanged, and along nearby Flint Street the terraces of neat, clear-paned Regency houses still stand, their doors opening directly on to the street. The remaining witchert houses lie along 'tails' of narrow, walled alleys which need to be explored on foot to savour their antiquity. Haddenham was one of the villages of the Vale where Aylesbury ducklings were raised for market, a trade more attractive in retrospect than in fact. The breeding sets were kept near the house in semi-cellars or little bothies alongside; they would be sent off to the pond during the day in the manner of children let out to play, and called home at night for feeding and bedding. The eggs they laid, (and a good duck would lay every day during the season) were 'set' under broody hens, and when the new ducklings hatched they were kept for eight to ten weeks in fattening pens in the cottage gardens. Just once during their short lives they were allowed down to the pond for a swim to freshen their feathers, and the sight of hundreds of ducklings waddling to the water in an excited, quacking stream was memorable. Best prices were made when green peas were on the table, and the cottage women, for it was women's work, aimed to have their birds fattened and ready then, killing them off progressively a few each day while the season lasted.

Long Crendon is another village stretched out, like Haddenham, along the lanes, but more kindly treated in the matter of development, perhaps because no less than seventy-six of its houses are listed buildings, three of them Grade 1. The beautifully preserved timber-framed Court House by the church, with its over-sailing upper storey, seems a fitting present to have been given by Henry V to his bride, Catherine de Valois, after Agincourt. That upper storey is just one long room inside, with a Queen-post roof of superbly carved timbers. It was built as a Staple Hall, but it has served many purposes over the centuries and is still used today, for an infant welfare clinic, among other things. This Court House was one of the first properties to be acquired by the National Trust.

It is impossible to single out all the lovely buildings in this old village; timber and thatch, wattle and daub, chequered brick, mellow stone, Long Crendon has them all. But one more building must be mentioned. Long Crendon Manor in Frogmore Lane was fifteenth century, and the King-post and tie-beams to the hall roof date from that time. Part stone, part timber-framed, crowned with a Jacobean chimney-stack, the manor is a mixture of styles and additions of the sixteenth, seventeenth and eighteenth centuries, and is, as they say, an eyeful!

Needle-making was the trade in Long Crendon in the eighteenth and nineteenth centuries, the village craftsmen producing a variety of high-quality sewing, sail-making and surgeons' needles. But mechanization put an end to the laborious and expensive work of the hand-grinder, and by the middle of the nineteenth century the trade had moved to the industrial Midlands. This must have been a bad time for the village people, for the lace-making which had been a lucrative source of extra income for centuries began to decline, driven out by cheap, machine-made Nottingham lace and foreign imports. It is surprising that the village survived so well, having lost both its sources of prosperity in the space of a few short years. So important was lace-making to the Buckinghamshire village women that cottages were built with a separate room or 'work-house' where the lace could be worked in spotlessly clean conditions. This tiny space was often no larger than a cupboard, but always with a very large window for the light. 'Pillow-point' or bobbin lace the work was called, from the straw-filled pillows used to mark out the patterns and the bobbins that were twisted and threaded around the pattern pins, pillows and bobbins that would be passed down in the family, usually from grandmother to granddaughter, skipping a generation, as the daughters would still be active lace-makers when their own children were of an age to start. Young girls would be set to the work very early, being quite proficient at the simpler patterns and earning money by the time they were seven or eight years old, and from then they would be captive to the trade until their sight began to fail them in old age. The craft served them well, earning them twice the wage of an agricultural worker, though the long hours of close work bent their backs and ruined their eyesight.

The ancient town of Thame, where Hampden died, is at the hub of these villages. The first mention of the town seems to be in the *Anglo-Saxon Chronicle*, which reports that the Archbishop of York, who was also Suffragan Bishop of Dorchester, died there in 971, but a settlement had probably existed on the site since before Saxon times. Thame received its first Charter in 1227 and developed as a market town, serving the farms and villages of the surrounding countryside. The townsfolk were renowned for their independence long before Hampden's time; there was trouble with the monasteries early on, then one of their number was prominent in the short-lived Agrarian Revolt of 1594. Many of John Hampden's classmates at Lord Williams' Grammar School were with him in his Ship Money protest, and the Bailiff of Thame Hundred refused to collect the tax. There was much support for Cromwell in the town, Church and State being so closely identified at that time that a man would support either the King and the established Church or Cromwell and nonconformity. Today 'freedom' tends to be identified with political freedom; in the seventeenth century it more often meant religious freedom. After the Civil War a census recorded a hundred 'Utter Dissenters' in Thame, and a meeting of Presbyterians and Anabaptists at the house of Edward Howes attracted twice that number. This congregation subsequently founded a chapel in Sun Yard, and a school where John Wilkes, the eighteenth-century champion of the freedom of the Press, was educated. Many remained loyal to the King, however, and during the troubled years of the Civil War Thame was England in microcosm.

The town was fought over continually during the war; the Royalists sought to use it as a base for assaults on Aylesbury and the Parliamentarians as headquarters for attacks on Oxford, and in between they harried each other about the countryside. Skirmish followed skirmish as each chased the other out; there was fighting along the High Street, and the townspeople never knew whether they would be billetting Cromwell's troops or those who held to the King. The fabric of the town seemed not to have suffered too greatly when tally was taken at the end of it all; some damage to the church, which was used to confine prisoners and stable the horses, and the desecration of Lord Williams's tomb, is all that was recorded.

Thame's quite exceptional long, broad High Street is less changed than most since those days. Sixteenth- and seventeenth-century half-timbering, over-sailing upper storeys, thatch, hipped gables, and diamond-shafted chimneys all survive; these and the strikingly picturesque Birdcage Inn, the narrow alleys of the Buttermarket to the left of the Town Hall, and the many gracious Georgian houses, all added to the town's present charm. Yet there are always changes and improvements, as at the nineteenth-century Maltings in the High Street, where the old grain store and the long, low malting chamber have been converted into apartments and mews flats, an imaginative and attractive way to provide new homes without losing the character of the area.

A mile or two to the west of the town, on the A329, is Rycote Chapel. It was built as a domestic chapel to Rycote Great House at the time of the Battle of Agincourt, though it is not recorded if Richard Quatremain, its founder, was one who 'outlived the day and came safe home'. A signpost 'To Rycote Chapel' takes the curious on a drive across Rycote Park to where the tiny Perpendicular building stands beside its great yew tree, a buttressed building of local limestone faced with ashlar, and with windows of clear glass. Inside, the building is a delight. With chancel and nave under a single wagon-vaulted roof, it is but 62 feet long and 18 wide, with a toy tower 8½ feet square. A spattering of gold stars decorates the roofs of the sixteenth-century two-storey family pew and of the Royal pew that was built for Queen Elizabeth, and the same decoration can be seen in the curves of the deep-blue vaulted ceiling between the close-set crimson-painted roof staves. The effect is startlingly pretty.

Old though the chapel is, it is a mere babe by comparison with the great yew tree that shades it. Twenty-six feet in circumference, the tree is said to have been planted in 1135 to commemorate the coronation of King Stephen.

The stepped gables of Rycote Great House nearby mark it as contemporary with Chenies Manor, and indeed its builder, Sir John Williams, prospered at much the same time and in much the same way as Sir John Russell who built Chenies. The house is not open to the public, and is privately occupied as apartments. Sir John Williams, later Lord Williams, obtained great wealth as Henry VIII's Administrator of Revenues from the Dissolution of the Monasteries. He owned many other manors as well as the Great House, including Thame Park, formerly Thame Abbey, which the King granted to him personally. Some of this wealth was returned to Thame on his death in the funds he left for the founding of Lord Williams Grammar School, and Almshouses.

15

Princes Risborough and the
Villages of the Icknield Way

'A small market town lying 8¾ miles south of Aylesbury, on the road from Aylesbury to High Wycombe', is what the *Victoria County History* had to say of Princes Risborough in the time of the Old Queen, and a small market town it is still. Though on a direct rail link to Marylebone, it lacks any trace of suburbia and is a true country town, more akin to Thame or Watlington than to High Wycombe or Aylesbury. There are still thatched cottages among the shops in Bell Street and many examples of Buckinghamshire brick and flint, while the antique shops off Market Square are becomingly housed in seventeenth-century timbered buildings. The Market Hall that stands in the square, brick above wooden posts, was built in 1824; the market is still held on the ground floor and the Parish Council meets in the room above. At the time this hall was built the old custom of cooking a bull and a boar each Christmas Day and distributing the portions 'smoking hot from the copper' at five o'clock in the morning ready for Christmas breakfast, was still alive in the town. Four bushels of malt and four bushels of wheat were made into beer and bread and given away at the same time.

The town was known as Earl's Risborough from 1243, when it was held by the Earls of Cornwall, but a century later it passed to the Black Prince and the name was changed. The Black Prince, who also held Berkhamsted, built a castle at Risborough of which little now remains but a few grassy mounds. The manor remained in Royal hands until 1628 when King Charles I, so fatally connected with the Chilterns, conveyed it to the City of London in part payment for his debts. Later it was sold to Peter Lely, Court Painter to Charles II. Princes Risborough's lovely Manor House dates from Lely's time, though at first sight it seems Georgian. This dainty house is owned by the National Trust, and has been described as the most live-inable of the Trust's properties. There is seventeenth-century panelling in the drawing-room and an attractive Jacobean staircase with a baluster carved whole from a single piece of wood, a fine memorial to an unknown village carpenter. The house is secluded from the town behind sturdy perimeter walls, and though it is open to the public only two rooms are shown. Several paintings from the National Gallery were sent here during the war for safe-keeping.

Princes Risborough's church of St Mary is undistinguished apart from its steeple, unlike the Perpendicular church of St Dunstan at Monks Risborough which dates from the fourteenth century. 'A noble Church', Arthur Mee called it, with chancel and porch 'built by men who would still be wondering at the news of Joan of Arc'. St Dunstan's was restored in Victorian times by Street, but still intact are all the lovely carvings of men and angels that were there to welcome the Black Prince. Monks Risborough is an older settlement by far than its princely neighbour, and first to bear the name 'Risborough', derived from 'Hrisebyrgan be Chilternes etese' or 'Brushwood by the Chiltern eaves'.

Just off Market Square, bare and modern by the roadside, is the Catholic church of St Theresa of Lisieux designed by Giuseppi Rinvolucri. It is as different in style and conception from St Dunstan's as could well be imagined, being built 'in the round' like the new Liverpool Cathedral, though in truth it follows the design of the very earliest English churches of the time of St Augustine. St Theresa's is a tribute to the faith of Father Dreves, parish priest in the 1930s, who decided that his people needed a better place of worship than the tin hut they had been using, and made a pilgrimage to the patron saint at Lisieux to pray for the money to build one. He needed £10,000, for which one might say £100,000 today, but he felt he might make a start if he could collect £3,000 to begin with, and it was for £3,000 that he prayed at Lisieux. No one who knows his story could say that prayer is not answered, for within a week of his return he was handed a cheque for just that sum by an anonymous benefactor and within two years his church was completed. By 1945 the whole sum had been found, though six years of war had intervened.

To either side of the road from Risborough to Kimble lie the unspoilt villages of Askett and Whiteleaf. Whiteleaf is little more than a single street of picturesque old cottages on a by-lane, but Askett, all thatch, green leaves and flowers, is everybody's idea of the typical English village—though so neat, trim and expensive-looking that it seems unlikely to house many typical English villagers! Great and Little Kimble lie together along the B4009; their most outstanding features are the two churches of St Nicholas and All Saints. St Nicholas's at Great Kimble is the church where John Hampden's famous Protest hangs, a church that was originally fourteenth century, but was heavily restored by the Victorians. All Saints' at Little Kimble, though, was too small and insignificant for them to trouble with, so it presents to us today the same simple face it has shown to generations of village folk since it was built in the thirteenth century. St Francis preaches to the birds in the East window, and around the whitened walls are a series of medieval wall-paintings, 'the Bible of the poor'. From All Saints' to the market town of Watlington the Roman Icknield Way, in the shape of the B4009, runs straight and level by some of the oldest villages in the Chilterns, leaving the wooded hills for the Oxfordshire plain.

The road seems bare and scrappy after the lushness of the hill country, and the luckier villages are those that lie undisturbed to the side of it. Saunderton, which the Romans knew, lies well off the route to the south, on the road that cuts through the Hampden country towards Great Missenden. At first sight you could be forgiven for thinking that Saunderton is little more than a suburb of Princes Risborough, but leave the ribbon development of modern houses and shops and take the byway to Saunderton Lee, and you will find old farms and farm cottages and sheep grazing the hills, all as it has been for centuries. Near here, within living memory, was held the oldest sheep, cheese and hop fair in southern England, indeed, some say it was the oldest fair in the land. There is a story, too, that when the Conqueror rode to Berkhamsted to receive the formal surrender he left his troops to find their own way to London, and they crossed the hills at the Risborough Gap. Their progress can be traced, it is said, by the devastated villages along the way. If this is true, and it would take a better historian than I to verify it, Saunderton could well have been one of the villages that suf-fered, for it certainly existed at that time. There was a Romano-Celtic village here, on the spring line. All these ridge villages were sited along the spring line, very necessary in the water-scarce Chilterns.

Most of the signposts from Saunderton seem to point to Bledlow Ridge, an evocative name for a rather ordinary place; but turn north instead of south and a mile or so along the lanes is Bledlow, ancient, impressive Bledlow, lying on a loop that leaves the B4009 at Pitch Green crossroads and returns to it half a mile further on, having skimmed around a touch of medieval England in its course.

Bledlow's name is said to commemorate a battle fought between Danes and Saxons, and to derive from Anglo-Saxon 'Bledlaew', the Bloody Hill, though Volume 2 of the English Place-names Society's book gives the derivation as 'Bledda's Hill or Barrow', from an Old English personal name. The village is quite beautiful, and worth a day's journey to see. On both sides of the way that leads to the tiny Norman church set on its green mound are thatched cottages, timber-framed, with tiny Tudor bricks in herring-bone infill. The Manor House, built in the early-eighteenth century, boasts a fine old weather-boarded barn, and the whole village is soft, peaceful, tree-girt, and a balm to the soul. The flint church of the Holy Trinity was built before 1200; it has a Norman doorway, a twelfth-century font with fluted bowl and foliated base and rim, of a type unique to the Chilterns, and elegant windows with quatrefoils. In the porch is a tribute to a stout little band of bell-ringers who in 1921 tolled a 'Peal of Doubles, 5040 changes Being 3600 of Grandsire and 1440 of Bob', all completed in three hours and three minutes.

The best way to approach Bledlow is as man has done for centuries, on foot from Chinnor or Wainhill through Bledlow Great Wood. Here the old Ridgeway is a deep-hollowed path between the trees, worn down through the soft chalk by the footfalls of the ages. On the way you might pass the tiny group of houses at Chinnor Hill, where old brick-and-flint stands cheek by jowl with fine examples of modern architecture, deep in the heart of the wood at the end of a winding lane. Places such as this are the best habitations on earth for those of quiet mind.

Chinnor, down below in the valley, is one of the places that has suffered from lying athwart the Icknield Way. H. J. Massingham in his *Chiltern Country* said that Chinnor had 'repudiated nature and beauty', and certainly there are few traces now of the old, quiet town that once it was. There was a village here as early as the fourth century B.C.; traces have been found of Iron Age settlements and of Roman and Saxon occupation. The inhabitants of Chinnor and nearby Kingston Blount had rights of cordage and pannage in Chinnor Woods at Domesday, while the rich, fertile common fields remained unenclosed until 1854. There were three different sets of open fields here in the Middle Ages, Upper and Lower Fields and

Littlemore, as well as Breachfield, lying towards Wainhill.

People have flocked to Chinnor since the war and there has been much new building to accommodate them so that the town is rather like a flower that has outgrown its strength, but it is not quite the 'bleak village consisting of numerous dismal council estates' that Pevsner describes it as. Some traces of antiquity remain. The rot first set in during the Civil War, when the town was sacked repeatedly. In 1624 the Earl of Essex had 500 troops stationed there in preparation for an attack on Oxford, and in 1643 came the pitched battle which Hampden set out to avenge, after which the Royalists set fire to the town. Later a Royal emissary was sent to collect taxes in Chinnor, taking even the 'clothes and linen' of those who refused to pay. A troubled village, with a troubled history.

High in the woods above Chinnor, Bledlow Cross is carved into the face of Wainhill. Once the Bledlow and Whiteleaf Crosses marked the break in the hills known as the Risborough Gap, but though Whiteleaf is cleaned and scoured the cross on Wainhill is overgrown and smothered by beech scrub and juniper. It can still be traced out though, if your eyes are sharp enough to spot it on the hillside above the Ridgeway. The chalk is still bare after years of neglect; indeed, a book first published as recently as 1946* has a picture of Bledlow Cross showing it plain on a grassy hillside, though even then the threatening junipers were there in the background.

Wainhill (correct pronunciation 'Wynnel'), Chinnor Hill and Crowell Hill brood in splendid, wooded majesty a mile distant from the villages on the plain, and Chinnor, Crowell, Kingston Blount and Aston Rowant, none of which has stood for less than a thousand years, look across the stony fields towards these green hills and ask a blessing. At Crowell the Icknield Way cuts through a tiny village where the area of the parish has remained unchanged since Saxon times, and where the last strip of common field in Oxfordshire was enclosed in 1886. Thomas Ellwood, the Quaker, was born here at Ellwood House, a sixteenth-century building with hipped roof and oriel windows, chequered brick façade and diamond chimneys, now the oldest house remaining in the village. The Rectory and the Catherine Wheel Inn are both nineteenth century, and the tiny church of the Nativity of the Blessed Virgin Mary was rebuilt in

* *Chiltern Footpaths*, Annan Dickson, Chaterson Ltd, 1946.

1878. Only the Norman doorways and the medieval tiles under the communion table show its age, and the age of Crowell village. This C. of E. establishment shares a vicar with Aston Rowant, and it shares its church with the Catholic congregation; Mass is said alternately with Anglican Communion, and both religious communities use the church hall.

Kingston Blount, next along the way, is another village bisected by the road; it has been added to in recent years but has suffered much less than Chinnor, though the mixture of styles evident as one drives through lend the village a slightly raffish, seaside air. There are thatched cottages, brick-and-flint, plain, red-brick Victorian houses with chequered fronts, and even some well-preserved tongued-and-grooved boarding. Kingston Blount was once famous in the furniture trade as specializing in rush-seated ecclesiastical chairs, and there is a busy, workaday air about the place.

There is a Nature Trail at Aston Rowant, a village that takes its name from the Rohant family who held the manor in the fourteenth century. It is the last of this string of villages before the wastes of the M40 motorway slice across the land, a village that lies amid fields to the north of the B4009 and one that you might never find except accidentally, as you walk the footpaths. Though the Norman church of St Peter and Paul has been heavily restored, there is still some fourteenth-century glass and some interesting, later, monuments, including a sadly romantic tablet to eighteen-year-old Susan Henrietta Mangin, 'simple as the flowers she loved'. This is a friendly and beautifully kept little church; every surface shines, including the old horse-plough before the altar, and the tall gas bottles of the calor heaters have been fitted with neat, ecclesiastical coats. Apart from a few cottages by the church, there is little else here save the trim buildings and white picket fences of the Aston Rowant Stud.

In the days when the small private railway ran from Watlington to Princes Risborough there was a station here at Aston Rowant, and another at Chinnor. The line was sold to the G.W.R. in 1884, and before its closure in 1957 it was used for filming *My Brother Jonathan* and *The Captive Heart*. The Chiltern area is much favoured by film-makers, and not only for its picturesque beauty. Alexander Korda had a mansion near the vast studios at Denham, now the home of Rank Xerox; weird flats and film-sets could once be seen behind barbed wire across the fields near Fulmer; and although the studios at Elstree are now no more the Beaconsfield Studios are still in business, and Hammer House of Horror have taken over Hampden House to make films there, so that one gets fascinating television glimpses of familiar, photogenic Chiltern locations like Old Amersham, Little Missenden and Hampdenleaf Wood.

The M40 motorway effectively cuts off Aston Rowant from Lewknor, the next village along the scarp, leaving the nineteenth-century Lambert Arms isolated in the middle. True, the motorway flies above the land on stilts so that access to the villages is not denied, but the approach roads and intersections of the junction separate the groups of villages to make all to one side appear to be Buckinghamshire and all to the other side Oxfordshire, whereas in fact the county boundary lies on the far side of Chinnor. Lewknor has begun to grow since the motorway was opened in 1975. It is still a charming and unspoilt village, with its thatched infant school beside the twelfth-century church, but one wonders how long it may remain so. In *Buildings of Oxfordshire* it is suggested that the great weather-boarded barn at Church Farm, where steep tiles cover massive timbers that were hewn and laid to the aisle roof in the fourteenth or fifteenth century, may have been an ancient Hall-house, a dwelling that consisted of an all-in-one solar where the lord and his retainers lived, ate and slept together in one great room. Signs of blackening on the central rafters, where smoke from the common fire would have found its way out, lend credence to this idea, which was first suggested by Mr Peter Salway.

And the history is not yet done, for a little further towards Watlington the castle that was built at Shirburn in 1377 still stands today. Shirburn, like Bodiam Castle in Sussex, was built of brick, most unusual at the time; four tower rooms rounded the corners of the quadrangle, and the domestic offices were built along the connecting walls. The castle has been much changed and modernized during the intervening years, and is still in use as a private residence today. It is one of the few great houses to remain utterly private over the years. No public access is ever permitted; all that one can see is miles of estate wall alongside the B4009, and the few estate cottages clustered at the castle gates. Old Shirburn Vicarage is in Pyrton village, a pretty little place on the road to nowhere, with a seventeenth-century Manor House and a diminutive thatched inn.

Anyone intent on a quiet country drive could do worse than follow the B4009 to Watlington from its start on the Aylesbury to Wendover Road. Given a little adventurous exploring down the side lanes, this stretch of under twenty miles can take in a dozen villages with their roots in medieval England, as well as the ancient towns of Watlington, Wendover and Princes Risborough. Not a bad score for a quiet afternoon.

16

Watlington and the
Oxfordshire Villages

If among the readers of this book there are those who long to live
in a country cottage snug under deep thatch, they could do worse
than make for Watlington and the surrounding villages of the
plain. Watlington is one of the most delightful small towns in
England, and though it has been brought within easy reach of
London and the suburbs by the M40 motorway, it still retains
the aspect and atmosphere of a nineteenth-century market
town. A traveller choosing to ride into town from the direction of
Lewknor on a snowy Sunday morning might trot along Shirburn Street to tether his pony outside the Hare and Hounds,
with only the road signs plastered over the ancient brick
arches of the seventeenth-century Town Hall to remind him
that Queen Victoria is dead and the motor car now king in the
land.

The Hall was built for the town by Thomas Stonor on land
belonging to the Manor of Watlington, which his father,
William Stonor, bought from Charles I. Thomas promised that
he and his heirs would keep the Hall in good order, and so they
did, until it was put in the care of the parish council in 1908. The
Hall was built in 1665, while the Great Plague was ravaging
London. Watlington suffered from the plague as other Chiltern
towns and villages suffered; as they suffered from the Black
Death in the fourteenth century and were to suffer again from
the cholera epidemics of the nineteenth, and the Stonors were
part of Watlington's history for all that time. First as farmers,
when they saw the fourteenth-century streets laid down to a
pattern which endures to this day, and the first thatched cottages built near the church; then as wealthy wool merchants,
when they saw the lovely timbered houses grow in Chapel Row
and Shirburn Street. Two hundred years later they saw the
Jacobean chimneys of The Lilacs rise in Brook Street, and later
still the Georgian terraces that brought elegance to the town,
and they were still about when all the nineteenth-century shop-
fronts were as dainty as the Old Tallow Chandler's which
survives in Couching Street. They knew the town when

Cromwell's troops were marching through, and the town knew them a century earlier, when they were sequestered for their Catholic faith with the fortune of centuries steadily leached away in fines.

It might be fair to say that Thomas Stonor's town hall did much to dictate the tenor of life in Watlington, for as the Hall promoted the market town's growth in the early years, so it has helped to inhibit the country town's growth in this century; no one in a hurry drives through Watlington twice. The twin obstructions of this Hall set fair in the centre of the town and the old, narrow streets, are enough to discourage all but those who come to Watlington for its own sake, so this is one of those blessed places that seem to exist only for the pleasure and convenience of those who live there.

From the town's centre roads wander in haphazard zigzags northwards to Pyrton, Cuxham, Brightwell and Chalgrove; west to Britwell Salome, Ewelme and Benson; east to Christmas Common and the Stonor country, and south through the woods to Nettlebed, Stoke Row and Checkendon and, eventually, to the Thames. Cuxham and Pyrton are the tiniest of villages. Planted, both, in Norman times, they seem to have taken to themselves no more than two or three houses in each of the centuries between. Though you might drive through Cuxham in a trice, the brief glimpse of flowers and neat thatch is enough to show why the Best Kept Village award rests here. Pyrton is more out of the way, and just a little more raffish. Pyrton church, where the records go back to 1115, is where John Hampden married his first wife, Elizabeth Symeon, one bright June day in 1619. Elizabeth's father, Edmund Symeon, had rebuilt Pyrton's medieval manor house, and no doubt saw to it that both events were suitably toasted under the thatch of the village inn. Similar events are still toasted under thatch at The Plough today.

There are ducks on the little brook that runs by the garden walls at Chalgrove, and fifteenth-century wall-paintings in its Early English church. The many thatched and timbered cottages in the centre of the village are pleasingly modest, just such houses as any ordinary person might live in. In some villages such cottages are so expensively restored as to take them beyond the pocket of the average home-owner, but at Chalgrove they appear as unassuming as the new houses and bungalows that surround them. This is a large village, almost as large as Watlington, with several shops, a new primary school, and much new building since the war.

On the edge of the village is Chalgrove Field, where the battle was fought between Hampden's men and the King's soldiers led by Prince Rupert of the Rhine. A large part of the battlefield is in use today as a civilian airfield, but at the lonely field's edge where the black earth is worked in long, straight furrows and ever and anon the bones of dead men are turned by the plough, a stark stone pillar has been erected to the memory of John Hampden, the Patriot. Above it skylarks sing their endless sweet song and lapwings wheel and call, flocking in dark clouds to the bare winter fields. This is the heart of that Civil War whose tale runs like a dark thread through the history of the Chilterns. Just as one cannot go to the smallest village in England without finding some memorial to the dead of two World Wars, so one cannot explore the Chiltern ridge without finding countless references to this other war, in street names, memorial tablets and folk memory. With the Parliamentary headquarters at Aylesbury and the King's troops stationed at Oxford, the Chilterns suffered badly. Apart from the battle at Chalgrove, there was a pitched battle at Holman's Bridge near Aylesbury engaging thousands, and another at Cropredy. Chinnor was raided repeatedly, as was Thame; heavy guns were brought to bear on Berkhamsted, and there were countless forays and skirmishes over the whole district. When they were not fighting, the troops of both sides were about the countryside, desecrating churches, trampling crops, stealing horses, and generally behaving as troops have ever behaved in time of war. Men of both armies were billeted about the countryside and they had to be fed, and one side or another was forever at the gates demanding taxes or levies. The citizens of Aylesbury were so incensed by the behaviour of the Royalist cavalry that they armed themselves with pikes and muskets and drove them from the town, but that was towards the end, when Cromwell's men were clearly in the ascendency. It was a long four years for the people of the Chilterns.

At Ewelme, two miles to the south of Chalgrove, the manor was held by Francis Martin, colonel in charge of the Parliamentary forces. He was stationed at Aylesbury, but seeing the damage done by Parliamentary troops elsewhere he commanded that Ewelme Church be locked and the key taken to the Manor House for safe keeping. This action saved from destruction one of the most beautiful churches in England. Built on the site of an earlier church by the great wealth of the Chaucer and de la Pole families, St Mary's, Ewelme rises above the village on a low hill, with the fifteenth-century school and almshouses of the de la Pole Foundation clustered below it. The story of the school and almshouses is told elsewhere in this book; suffice it to say here that to step from the church into this enclave is to step back four hundred years.

To any with a feeling for history the first sight of Ewelme church, brooding alone on its little hill top, is exciting. It could not more plainly say 'Here be treasures' if the words were blazoned across the chequered stone and flint in letters a foot high. It is built with a central nave, low, spreading north and south aisles, and a squat western tower. Inside, the great East windows and the glass of the clerestory roof make the church so light that its treasures of carvings and plaques, the Chaucer family tombs, and the elaborately carved ten-foot-high font cover with its tiers of arches rising to a spire, are most wonderfully to be seen. Chief among the treasures is the tomb of Dame Alice de la Pole, Duchess of Suffolk. If this tomb were in a town church it would have been necessary to protect it with disfiguring grilles against damage, but tucked away as it is in this little Oxfordshire village, hidden among lanes of bewildering complexity, it is open for all who find it to see and wonder. The tomb is fashioned of alabaster, most intricately carved, the canopy worked from a single slab. The Duchess lies in effigy above a tomb chest which holds her mortal remains, her hands folded in prayer, a coronet upon her head and the Order of the Garter, which she was granted in her youth in 1432, upon her left forearm. Between the stone arches which hold up this tomb and effigy can be seen a shrouded, emaciated figure lying on the cold stone floor, reminder that all this glory ends but in death. The Duchess lies alone, for her husband William de la Pole, Duke of Suffolk, was murdered at sea whilst on business for the King. He was ambushed, bundled into a small boat, beheaded over the gunwale and his body thrown unceremoniously to the fishes.

Dame Alice spent the next twenty-five years alone at Ewelme. The Duke had been her third and best-loved husband, and she had no wish to replace him. Ewelme was her own manor, inherited from her father Thomas Chaucer, son of that Geoffrey who wrote *The Canterbury Tales*. Through him Dame

Alice was related to Katherine Swynford, second wife of John of Gaunt, so that politics and intrigue were part of her life to the very end. Long after her death the Manor House at Ewelme was used as a country residence by Henry VIII, a circumstance which saved the church at the time of the Dissolution. Later, Edward VI gave the manor to his sister, Princess Elizabeth, and she spent happy years there in her girlhood, before the Throne cast its shadow upon her.

But Ewelme is not all church and manor; it has been well built up over the years, though it is still a beautiful village. As at Chalgrove, a stream runs under the walls of the houses along the main street, giving rise to a notice on the wall of one of the cottages: 'Take Note. All Persons found throwing any kind of refuse or allowing anything injurious to health to run from their premises into Ewelme Brook will be prosecuted.' The brook is a sweet, clear-running stream today, but one can imagine its condition when that notice was posted. The brook serves the great shallow ponds in the centre of the village where Ewelme watercress is still grown for market, as it was in Dame Alice's day. Bordering Ewelme in the east and spreading over a larger area than the village itself, are the married quarters to R.A.F. Benson. This aerodrome is the home of the Queen's Flight. Benson itself lies a mile further to the east, a pleasant village bordering the Thames, with more old inns for its size than any other village in the Chilterns.

Hidden among the lanes in the Watlington-Benson-Chalgrove triangle are the villages of Britwell Salome, Brightwell Baldwin, and Berrick Salome. These 'Salome' villages are said to take their name from the de Sulham family, who once held land at Britwell and at Henton. Berrick Salome lies on a pre-Roman route known as Hollandtide Bottom. According to local tradition the Empress Helena, mother of Constantine, rode along this route, and the churches at Berrick Salome, Ewelme and Abingdon were dedicated to her memory. The church at Berrick Salome still bears her name. St Helen's was originally Norman and still has its plain Norman doorway and a Norman font, but it was drastically restored in 1890 giving rise to a remark by Pevsner regarding the 'hideous application of all the trappings of fashionable late nineteenth-century domestic architecture to a church'. I quite like it.

Seeking out all these tiny settlements along the single-track lanes connecting them is a frustrating business. Often enough, in a car, one is through the village and on the way to the next before realizing one has arrived. This is certainly so at Bright-well Baldwin, and often so at Britwell Salome, a mile to the south of Watlington. But the drive through the secret, hedge-lined lanes is very pleasant; lanes between cornfields where field gateways or the rise of the land disclose meadows crowded with fat sheep, or with flap-eared pink and black pigs rooting between rows of but-and-ben pighouses. It is the same story to the south of the A423, the Henley to Nettlebed road, where the lanes run to Ipsden, Checkendon, Nuffield and Stoke Row. Here the country is slightly more hilly and wooded, more akin to the Chiltern Hills and less to the Oxfordshire plain, but still the villages seem to move about in the most unnerving manner, receding as one approaches, popping up on the left when the map clearly shows them on the right, dodging behind to disappear over the hill, and generally behaving as no respectable village should. Perhaps it is this ability to fade into the background which has kept them so small and secret over the centuries.

The church at Ipsden was built in the twelfth century. Together with St Mary's at North Stoke it belonged to the Abbey of Bec in Normandy, which accounts for much of the fine decorative work to the interior. Seventeenth-century Ipsden House, with its old wooden donkey wheel and dovecote of 600 nests, was once the home of Charles Reade who wrote *The Cloister and The Hearth*. He was born there in the year of Waterloo, half a century before the Victorians invented domestic comfort, at a time when even the well-to-do suffered the discomforts of cold and a poor winter diet. In his *Memoirs* he wrote: 'Ipsden was probably the coldest house in Europe, yet fires were all but unknown luxuries in its bedrooms, the halls and principal staircase were icy, and even in the livingrooms the beechen logs with their cheerful blaze emitted a minimum of heat. Ladies with bare necks and arms shivered in the dining-room and clustered round the hearthrug in the drawingroom.' Charles led a life of cheerful idleness until his thirty-sixth year, when he was called home to Ipsden to care for his aged father. Then the daily boredom of life in that cold, remote house where none but the tradesmen ever called drove him to entertain himself by writing, and by sheer hard work and determination he made himself one of the best Victorian novelists. 'I never wrote a book for the public until I was thirty-five,' he said, 'then at an age when most men's habits are fixed, I began my real life.'

Ipsden village is unremarkable at first sight, seeming to be no more than a single shop and a handful of modern bungalows, but further along the lane at Ipsden Farm is a beautifully preserved timbered granary raised on staddle-stones, and the same farm boasts the largest barn in England, 365 feet long, the eighteenth-century red-tiled roof held up by a forest of criss-crossed timbers.

The several lanes that lead from Ipsden to Checkendon form a bewildering maze. Local people would undoubtedly go around the edge of the wood by the bridle path, but the visiting motorist must drive amid the trees trying to follow the multiplicity of signposts that seem to point all ways at once. But the reward is there at Checkendon, an eye-catching row of pale, timbered cottages that might have sprung straight from the pages of an Elizabethan picture-book, with the Norman church across the green hardly changed in 800 years. A writer in 1935 reported this church as 'a typical Chiltern church, still relying for its illumination upon candles which, on winter evenings, shed a soft glow amid the prevailing darkness'.* Very pretty they must have been, twinkling on the brasses and casting shadows over the procession of apostles attending Christ in Majesty, painted by a thirteenth-century artist on the wall of the apse.

Old though the church is, Checkendon village is older. There is rumour of a wattle-and-daub church here when Offa was pushing south into the Chilterns, and the collective memory of the village goes back to the days when the Norsemen came in their longships and established the Danelaw; they left behind at Checkendon the tradition of decorating a pole on the village green with a sheaf of corn at harvest time, a survival of the old Norse habit of fixing ears of corn to their gable ends to feed Odin's pale horse of Death, so that it would eat the corn and pass by, leaving the dwellers under the roof in peace. Fewer people in Checkendon today are tied to the land and its traditions; they live quietly amid the cherry trees and do not trouble their prosaic heads with the old superstitions.

The narrow lanes that take the traveller from Checkendon to Stoke Row and Nettlebed or Ipsden Heath and Nuffield, wander and wind through little woods and copses awash with cherry blossom in spring and bright with bluebells. At Stoke Row the

* *Companion into Oxfordshire*, Ethel Carleton Williams, Methuen & Co., 1935.

cherry trees line the main street, and the heaths around Nettlebed abound in wild strawberry plants, their delicate sweet fruits hidden under the leaves from all but knowing eyes. For centuries Nettlebed was a town that made bricks. The deep red bricks that built Stonor Park were made there, and probably the bricks for Shirburn Castle, there or at nearby Crocker End. One of the Nettlebed brick kilns has been preserved as a monument to the town's one-time industry, though it looks a little out of place now surrounded by modern houses. This little town has not suffered too greatly from its position at the junction of four ways, to Wallingford, Reading, Henley and Watlington. The traffic cannot spoil its pleasant country atmosphere, nor detract from the beechwoods that surround it on three sides.

In Nettlebed Woods is Highmoor Trench, supposed to be part of Grimsditch, though in appearance it is very different from the long stretch of the Ditch to the west of Nuffield, where the Ridgeway Long Distance Footpath runs for over a mile beside it. Nuffield is always a surprise, an unassuming little place that one would not give a thought to but for its name, made famous throughout the world by that generous philanthropist William Morris, Lord Nuffield, who lies buried in the churchyard. This founder of the British motor industry is not to be confused, of course, with that other William Morris, poet, visionary, craftsman-designer, and member of the Pre-Raphaelite Brotherhood, who lived on the Upper Thames at Kelmscot.

The Fox at Bix, on the main road east of Nettlebed, pinpoints Bix village, which lies to the north of the road. Bix Bottom is the site of the Warburg Nature Reserve, largest of the reserves managed by the Berks, Bucks and Oxfordshire Naturalists' Trust. The lanes here wind on seemingly forever through the sombre, silent woods, and the lone traveller afoot or on a horse or bicycle, might think himself lost in an empty world. An impression that would be reinforced if he were to stumble upon the ruins of old St James's Church, abandoned in a field a mile to the north of Bix village, on the way to Maidensgrove. Tangled in nettle, blackthorn and ivy, the church is now little more than a few grave markers and some piles of stones, its death warrant sealed on the day the keystone fell from the chancel arch. The church was deserted in 1875 in favour of a new St James's built in Bix village.

The lane that leads from Bix village to Maidensgrove and on

to Russell's Water, Pishill or Stonor is the quietest under the sun. It is a lane that leaves the Oxfordshire plain and the flat lands that border the Thames and climbs to the hills again, a land where the only way to go is on foot or on horseback, climbing to Maidensgrove village then climbing again to Russell's Water, a perfect place where ducks dabble on the pond beside an ancient inn, and everything is as it should be. Pishill is little more than a church and a pillar-box, more of a name than a place. It lies on the way from Russell's Water to Stonor Park.

The Stonor family have been landholders in this part of Oxfordshire since before the Conquest. Their estate was increased eight-fold between Domesday and the end of the thirteenth century by the purchase of one free tenement after another, and by the beginning of the fourteenth century they owned at least a dozen, varying in size from ten to forty acres, scattered through Watlington, Pyrton, Pishill and Bix.

From Stonor to Skirmett or Turville in the Hambleden Valley is hardly more than two miles as the crow flies, yet one is centred on Watlington in Oxfordshire and the others on High Wycombe in Buckinghamshire, and it is more than the county boundary that divides them. Stonor was sheep, wool and farming country; Turville was bodgers and chairs and Buckinghamshire lace. Though so close, the two are hardly connected by a modern road, so that if a family was to move house from one village to the other the removal van would need to take a circuitous route that would take half the morning, probably through Christmas Common and almost back to Watlington.

Christmas Common is another reminder of the Civil War. It is said to get its name from the truce arranged there between Royalists and Parliamentarians for the Christmas of 1643. Bordering the village is the National Trust land at Watlington Hill, 108 acres of chalk down and copse overlooking the town of Watlington, a marvellous place for a good walk in early spring when lacy white blossom hangs on the blackthorn and yellow Brimstone butterflies flutter above the turf. Many walkers still remember the single-track railway that ran along the ridge to Watlington, bringing Watlington Hill within the orbit of London rambling clubs via Marylebone and Princes Risborough. Today those same ramblers would have to come by car along the M40, turning off at Stokenchurch or Lewknor after their run along that scenically satisfying and rarely busy motorway.

Watlington Hill is the last stretch of high heath before the Chiltern Hills fade into the level Thames-side plateau, where the river forms a great loop between Benson and Henley. From the top of this hill there are infinite views northwards across the patchwork of the Oxfordshire plain, and westwards across Ewelme Downs. From this hilltop, too, the twin peaks of Wittenham Clumps can be seen in the Sinodun Hills beyond the river. Wittenham Clumps guided men down off the ridge to the safe river crossing in the days when bears and wolves roamed the ancient yew forest around the flanks of Watlington Hill. This yew forest clothes the hillside between Watlington Park and Christmas Common, and is one of the oldest and largest forests of yew in southern England.

On the face of the hill overlooking Watlington is the last of the Chiltern chalk hill carvings, Watlington Mark. H. J. Massingham went into ecstasies over Watlington Mark, deciding on no evidence at all that it had been carved two-and-a-half thousand years ago as a pointer for the summer equinox. He was totally wrong, although he struck the truth by accident with a throw-away line about the mark being 'like the ghostly shadow of a church spire lying along the hill'. For the mark was made in the eighteenth century to the order of one Mr Horne, who could see Watlington Church from his window, outlined against the hill. He felt that the church should have a spire, so he had one carved in the turf on Watlington Hill and from his window church and spire seemed all of a piece.

And that is the true tale of Watlington White Mark, neither phallic nor Celtic, but the fruit of an old man's whim.

17

The Thames and the
riverside towns

Where the Thames rims the Chiltern country on its south-western boundary, a toe of the hills pokes down to the riverside towns of Henley and Marlow, Bourne End and Cookham, and to Pangbourne and Goring beyond the Henley loop. These are holiday towns, and it is the river that attracts the holiday-makers. They come to stroll along the towpath, picnic on the riverbank, fiddle about with a fishing net or perhaps take out a punt. Kenneth Grahame, who lived for a time at Pangbourne, knew about the fascination of rivers when he wrote his oft-quoted lines about 'messing about in boats', lines that have passed into the English language as a most apt description of an English national pastime.

True, these towns are not now so leisurely as once they were; on sunny bank holidays one coasts down lovely Remenham Hill into Henley nose to tail with a row of other cars and is hard-put to park when one gets there, yet quiet places are still to be found, places like Hambleden, 'Med'n'm' Ferry, and the towpath by Shiplake; warm, tranquil spots to stroll and dream or float gently along to the splash of oars, lapping up the peace of it all and savouring the haunting scent that Rupert Brooke described so well:

> The thrilling, sweet and rotten
> Unforgettable, unforgotten
> River smell . . .

Hambleden is the place for that evocative river smell. Here the Thames spreads itself into the weirs of Hambleden Mill and a series of narrow causeways cross the wastes of water to Hambleden Lock, passing precariously over the deep-running undertow and the foam of the falling water that once powered the mill. Moorhens hurry on long thin legs across little islands, hiding at the water's edge in clumps of tall Himalayan balsam, 'Policeman's helmets', as the flower is called. Along the far grassy bank willows bow gracefully to the water, sheltering private boathouses that give home to smart cruisers and varnished river launches with odd-looking, sloping 'slipper' sterns.

Hambleden Mill was grinding corn until 1958, but today it ekes out its retirement as a tourist attraction and marina centre. The whole peaceful setting of mill, cottages, backwaters and weirs is without parallel on this stretch of the river.

From Hambleden Lock the towpath on the south bank can be followed all the way to Henley, passing the Regatta course from Temple Island to the grounds of Phyllis Court, below the bridge. Along the way are yellow water-lilies, lilac milk-maids, bulrushes and water-forget-me-nots; sharp eyes will see the flash of kingfishers, as well as the more usual water-birds, wagtails, grebes, ducks, swans, coot and moorhen, and fly-offs from the heronry on the opposite bank at Fawley, while along the lovely stretch of greensward that fills up the half-mile between Remenham Club and the Leander boathouse, butterflies dance and dither across the turf.

Henley's history is told by bridge, church and inns. Many bridges spanned the river here before the present graceful arches were built by William Haywood in 1786. He is buried in the Baptistry of St Mary's Church, where he could hardly lie closer to his bridge, for the little group of church, almshouses and fifteenth-century chantry house stands right at the bridge approach, with only the width of the roadway between. Parts of St Mary's are older than the exterior suggests. The striking nave arcades are Early English, older by two hundred years than the lovely timbered chantry house with its great dark beams, hewn and set for their purpose in the days of the Rose of Raby. This chantry house has been used for many purposes in its time; chapel, priests' house, schoolroom, and annexe to the Red Lion Hotel which still hides it from view on its river frontage. It was bought back for the church in 1915 as a memorial to a former Rector, Canon J. F. Maul, and now serves as a very superior church hall.

The Red Lion itself can lay some claim to antiquity. It gave lodging to Charles I in 1632 on his way to Oxford, while the more plebeian Angel on the bridge was held by Cromwell's troops in the Civil War. Older than these two inns are the old White Hart and Catherine Wheel in Hart Street and The Bull in Bell Street, all dating back to the fifteenth-century. Henley's shopping centre lies but a stone's throw from the river, and abounds in old shops and picturesque little cottages. In New Street, by Breakspears Brewery, is the Kenton Theatre, offering both amateur and professional productions as well as a performers' theatre for young people. This theatre was built in 1805, and is said to be the fourth oldest purpose-built theatre in England.

All this said, the town's greatest attraction and its real claim to fame must be the Henley Royal Regatta. At Regatta time the whole town is *en fête*, the river bank by the Leander Club is gay with marquees and striped awnings, and old gentlemen in blazers and rowing caps strut about recalling the days of their youth. The first Henley Regatta was held in June 1839, when four crews raced for the Grand Challenge Cup and the whole affair was over in three hours. Today Henley Royal Regatta provides four whole days of racing, attracting crews from all over the world, and when the Royal Regatta is over there is still the Town Regatta to come in July or early August.

Marlow holds its Regatta the week before Henley. That, too, is an international affair, many of the crews entered for the Royal Regatta 'warm up' at Marlow first, though it is a considerable regatta in its own right with a programme that runs to over 150 races. As with Henley, the whole town celebrates, and at the heart of it all is Marlow Rowing Club, two members of which won a Gold Medal for England at the 1958 Olympics in the Double Sculls. Like Henley, Marlow is a prosperous, well-favoured town with a long history. It was already well established at Domesday, when it was listed as 'The land of Queen Maud in Desborough Hundred'. Many of the buildings in the shopping centre are Georgian behind their modern shopfronts: the house with five bays at the top of the High Street is Remnantz, where the Royal Military Academy was housed until it outgrew the building and moved to Sandhurst. This building, now used for offices, and Western House, a little further along, are said to have been designed by Sir Christopher Wren. Marlow Place, next to the Royal Cinema in Station Road, was built in the 1720s and was occupied at one time by George III; with its imposing entrance and classical pediment the house is described as a type 'unique in Buckinghamshire'.

Among the old houses surviving around Station Road and West Street is Shelley Cottage. The poet lived here for a year in 1816, drawn to the town by his friend, Thomas Love Peacock. Here his wife, Mary Shelley, is said to have written *Franken-stein*. Mary was Shelley's second wife; his first wife, Harriet, having drowned herself in the Thames.

Beside the river, opposite Lock Island, the towpath winds on to Spade Oak Ferry and Little Marlow. Here beside the towpath is the lovely white weather-boarding of Marlow Mills, a group of modern town houses built in 1968 on the site of the old mill which had stood below the weir since the Norman Conquest, until the last mill building was destroyed by fire in the 1960s. Above the weir is Marlow's famous suspension bridge, one of several to be built in various places during the nineteenth century to the same design by W. Tierney Clarke. He also designed the beautiful bridge that spanned the Danube between Buda and Pest, but that bridge was blown up by the Germans in 1944 to delay the Russian advance and today Marlow Bridge is the only example of Tierney Clarke's work still standing. During the 1950s when faults were found in the structure it was thought that this bridge, too, would have to go, but by dint of imposing a weight limit until the structure could be strengthened and subsequently building a bypass, the Council was able to save Marlow Bridge and give it a new lease of life.

At the approach to the bridge on the town side is the church of All Saints, a nineteenth-century Perpendicular church built on twelfth-century foundations. The church and the lovely old red-brick houses that line the approach to the bridge make a beautiful setting, and the park alongside borders Marlow's long quay, a very popular overnight mooring for holiday boats.

There is a particularly lovely, peaceful stretch of river between Marlow and Henley. The towpath is open on the north bank as far as Temple Lock, but between there and Hurley the private club and trailer park of Harleyford Manor closes off the bank except to club members. The Olde Bell at Hurley was unofficial Headquarters for General Eisenhower during the war. There are many mementoes there of the war-time days, and it is a popular tourist attraction still for American visitors. There is no access to the north bank until Medmenham Ferry is reached, when a lane opposite the fourteenth-century Dog and Badger on the Marlow to Henley road leads directly to the river. No ferry plies here now, but the shallow strand makes a handy launching site for small boats and the broad, grassy banks are popular for family picnics. There are board-walks to trail a fishing net from, and back-waters to explore where great crested grebes float with their babies nestled upon their backs. We owe the use of the river bank here to the first Viscount Devonport, who fought a successful action in the courts in the closing years of the nineteenth century to establish for all time that

Medmenham Ferry was a public place and should remain so. The shallow strand by the bridge here is one of the few places along this stretch of the river where small boats can be launched free. Unfortunately it is almost impossible to park a car; there's always a snag.

Up-river from Henley is Shiplake Lock, another favourite holiday mooring. Here the River Loddon, tree-shaded, green and mysterious, forms a back-water, while above the weirs a Thames Conservancy camping site provides idyllic holidays for those lucky enough to get a pitch there. Alfred Lord Tennyson was married in Shiplake, a quiet, old-fashioned town with a railway level-crossing where the branch line from Reading runs through to Henley. Further upriver, past Reading and Pangbourne, lies Goring and here the prehistoric Ridgeway crosses the river to stride on over the high Berkshire Downs. The town is still quiet and unspoilt, despite much modern development. There is an attractive mill weir beside the bridge, and countless little inlets along the tidy banks provide space for moorings and boat-houses to the gracious houses along the riverside. The élite of the nautical world seems to retire to Goring, where eyes that have narrowed against the storm of the seas can feast themselves on the gentle river flowing between steeply wooded banks. In one of the riverside boat-houses a steam-launch is kept. It can occasionally be seen queening its way through Goring Lock, paintwork glistening, brass shining, little white clouds puffing from its bell-topped smoke-stack; the most elegant sight on the river. There is no lovelier stretch of water than this in our area until one comes to Cliveden Reach, away down-river from Marlow, a bird-haunted, lonely stretch where the river ripples gently to and fro between wooded banks where the trees hang heavy and still over the water, forming caverns and shelters of leafy tangled branches. Only the little, cheerful calls of the water-birds disturb the silence, until a river-boat comes chugging by. Out of season is the time to see the river; on autumn weekends or mid-week in early summer it can be enjoyed at its quiet best.

Cookham is another favourite spot for overnight mooring, mostly along the south bank above the bridge where a broad green staithe stretches for half a mile beside the river. A short-cut from the river-bank leads through Cookham Churchyard to the High Street shops and restaurants. The church of Holy Trinity was originally Norman, but only the Norman north-west wall and one Norman window still remain. The lovely chapel of St Catherine with its lancet windows is early thirteenth century, and the whole enclave of church, rectory and churchyard shows the beauty of a well-kept church at its best. Across the road from the church is the Stanley Spencer Gallery, honouring Cookham's most famous son. Stanley Spencer was born in Cookham in 1891 and was so wrapped up in the town that he was nick-named 'Cookham' by his fellow students at the Slade. Once, in later life, when he was asked if he had ever painted in Paris he replied: 'No, why should I? What's wrong with painting in Cookham?' Many of his paintings have Cookham backgrounds, such as *Resurrection in Cookham Churchyard* and *Christ Preaching at Cookham Regatta*, and many of the figures have recognizable local faces. Alongside the paintings in his gallery is preserved the disreputable old pram he used to push through the streets bearing his easel and painting materials, together with the notice he put up when painting his landscapes: 'Mr Stanley Spencer is busy. Please do not disturb him at his work.' He hardly had time, on receiving his knighthood a few months before he died, to knock out the 'Mr' and alter it to 'Sir'.

There is still a strong artistic tradition in Cookham today; many practising artists, potters and sculptors live in or near the town, and a biennial Festival of Arts and Music is held in the church, rectory and grounds, a beautiful setting for such an event.

18

A place in the country

Commerce has played as great a part as poetry in shaping the modern Chilterns, for when Mrs Nathan Mayer de Rothschild decided that her boys needed fresh air and exercise and bought a few acres of hunting country in the Vale of Aylesbury to lure them away from their City desks, she decided more than she knew. So enthusiastically did those 'boys' embrace the life of English country gentlemen that they made great changes in the Chilterns and in the lives of many who dwelt there.

Within a few years three of her sons had bought estates in Hertfordshire or Buckinghamshire and built themselves grand mansions where they entertained crowned heads and statesmen and men of letters from all over Europe. In the succeeding generation two grandsons and a nephew did the same. It was Mayer Rothschild, the youngest son, who built the first Rothschild mansion, Mentmore Towers. Mentmore was built in 1851 to the design of Sir Joseph Paxton, who also designed and built the Crystal Palace in the same year; it was the scene of the auction of the century in 1977 when its fairy-tale contents, the result of several lifetimes' collections by a very rich family, were sold off by the Roseberys, who had the property by marriage from Mayer's only daughter, Hannah. The sale realized an unbelievable six and a half million pounds; and far from leaving the mansion a ruin or a shell, it was still 'stuffed with gilded opulence', to quote a contemporary newspaper report, when it was bought for a mere £240,000 by the 'World Government' followers of the mystic Maharishi Mahesh Yogi. Under their care Mentmore is being restored and renovated to 'recreate the spirit of dignity, elegance and charm' that once it had. Like other owners of stately homes, the World Government opens Mentmore to the public on Wednesdays and Saturdays throughout the summer, though visitors faced with, say, the Levitation Room, might find things not quite so stately-homes-like as expected.

Anthony, the second son, bought a 'ready-made' house at Aston Clinton in the 1850s. The house is gone now, but the remains of the 'Rothschild' village, with two Gothic-style schoolhouses built as a sixteenth birthday gift for Anthony's daughter Constance, and the Anthony Hall, built after his death by Anthony's wife and given to the village as a memorial to him, can still be seen there. In Sir Anthony's lifetime the village also received at his hands a lending library an evening school, and a domestic training institute.

Wherever the Rothschilds settled they wrought changes. Mayer Rothschild rebuilt Mentmore village whilst building stables and kennels there for his staghounds, and the hostel he built at Ledburn, a mile away, to house his stable lads is now the Hare and Hounds Inn. Tring was a poor place on the canal until Lionel, the eldest son, built his great chunks of black and white neo-Tudor in the High Street. Lionel bought Tring Park in 1872, enlarging and almost rebuilding the house there. When death duties forced the family to sell in 1938, most of the estate houses and farms were sold off to the existing tenants; the mansion was bought by the British Museum for use by the Natural History Museum, and the woodlands were bought by the Council for use by the public in perpetuity. This outcome would have pleased the Rothschilds. They are remembered to this day in Tring as just and generous landlords, as evinced by the terse comment of a local contemporary writer: 'It can be understood,' he wrote, 'that the best minds in Tring have not sympathized with any persecution of the Jews.'

Baron Lionel had also bought an estate at Halton in 1853, but it was his son, Alfred, who so far forgot his family responsibilities as to remain a bachelor all his life, who built the mansion there. It was built in the style of a French château, a forerunner to Waddesdon, all white and gold and with a huge chandelier matching the magnificence of the beautifully proportioned central hall. Ever a patriot, Alfred cut down his trees for pit-props when war came in 1914, and gave Halton to the War Office for the duration. He died early in 1918, and when the estate and contents were sold off after the war the estate was bought by the Royal Air Force, who are still in possession today.

Bachelor Alfred's younger brother, Leopold, bought Ascott House near Wing in 1874, a beautiful old timber-framed building built in 1606. Though he enlarged it beyond all recognition, Ascott is the only one of these Rothschild houses to look at all like a home, and it is the only one still lived in by members of the family. Leopold's son, Anthony de Rothschild, gave Ascott with all its contents to the National Trust in 1949, a generous act indeed as among the 'contents' is a priceless collection of Old

Masters and what is thought to be one of the finest collections anywhere of Chinese porcelain. The grounds at Ascott are justly famous; thirty acres of specimen trees and shrubs, golden yews, Japanese maples and dark copper beeches, and on one of the terraces the Roman numerals of an evergreen sundial planted in box, encircled by the legend 'Light and shade by turns, but love always'.

Last of the Rothschild houses to be built and by far the grandest, Waddesdon Manor arose on its hilltop west of Aylesbury in the 1870s, under the hand of the French architect Gabriel Hippolyte Destailleur. It was built for Baron Ferdinand de Rothschild, one of the French branch of the family. Although the land was purchased in 1874 and the work commissioned immediately, it was fifteen years before Waddesdon was completed, a frou-frou of towers, bays, columns, dormers, staircases and pediments all carried out in mellow Bath stone. Seen in sunshine it seems to float like a fairy castle over its green, rolling parkland. A parkland replete with fountains, terraces, Italian sculptures, an aviary, a pergola, a herd of smoke-brown Sika deer, and a daffodil valley. Baron Ferdinand was born in Paris and lived in the Continent until he was a young man; he wanted a French château built at Waddesdon and spared no expense to realize his desire. He seems to have got his money's worth.

Waddesdon was left on Baron Ferdinand's death to his unmarried sister, Alice. Although she loved the house and cared for it during her lifetime, Alice felt Waddesdon was too grand to live in and preferred her own house a mile away at Eythrope. When she died the estate passed to their great-nephew James, who left it in his turn to the National Trust. The Trust's first task after opening the manor to the public was to make a catalogue of contents. That was twenty-two years ago, but so vast is Waddesdon's collection of treasures, of French furniture, carpets, paintings, tapestries, china, documents, and every kind of *objet d'art*, that although ten volumes of the catalogue have been completed to date, another seven are still to come. It is impossible for the visitor to take in all this magnificence at one go; one is apt to come away so gorged that brain and eye are bemused by it all, and several visits are necessary before a clear picture emerges. A good argument for joining the National Trust, as members get in free!

In the closing years of the nineteenth-century, Rothschild

hospitality was renowned. The Prince of Wales was a frequent visitor to one mansion or another, and the Queen herself demanded to see Waddesdon, being driven around the grounds in a bathchair drawn by a small pony. Lionel's stag parties at Tring, where one or two Cabinet Ministers would always be among the guests, and Royalty too, more often than not, were famous, while across the park at Halton the cultured Alfred, 'the finest amateur judge in England of eighteenth-century French art', was reputed also to be the most generous and considerate host in all Europe, numbering among his guests such famous entertainers as Rubinstein, Liszt and Dame Nellie Melba. Not surprisingly, the Chilterns became a very popular area in which to have 'a little place in the country', as Society moved into the ambit of these lavish weekends and dinner parties.

On the other side of the scarp at Hughenden lived dear Dizzy and his Mary Anne, in a 'gentleman's residence' of warm red brick built in 1738. Disraeli bought the house in 1848 for a purchase price of £35,000 and lived there with his wife, the former Mrs Wyndham Lewis, in perfect amity and happiness for thirty-three years. Indeed, the house has the feel of a happy home, its rooms neither too big nor too grand to be comfortable in. There is the urge to work in that library where the books run from floor to ceiling on all the walls, or to settle down quietly for an afternoon's sewing in that drawing-room overlooking the garden; while the Blue bedroom actually seems to welcome one to slumber, unlike the museum pieces one sees in some of the stately homes.

When Mary Anne died in 1872 Disraeli was inconsolable. He found on sorting her papers that she had lovingly preserved every single piece of paper he had written on during their time at Hughenden. Disraeli had been thirty-five years old when they married, and already a Member of Parliament. Of their wedding Mary Anne wrote in her diary: 'Married on 28th August 1839 at St George's Church, Hanover Square. Lord Lyndhurst and Mr Scrope, my cousin, were present at the ceremony. Dear Dizzy became my husband.' During their time together they reconstructed the house and replanted the park, carrying out the work a little here and a little there as time and income permitted, as any ordinary householder might do. Disraeli lived on at Hughenden for nine years without her, continuing to work in the park and to write his books in the bare little study on the first floor, but he pined for his Mary Anne, and until his death all the Hughenden notepaper bore a broad black mourning band in her memory. In 1877 Disraeli entertained the Queen at Hughenden, a year after Her Majesty had created him Earl of Beaconsfield. They lunched in the Gothic dining-room, and afterwards the Queen planted a tree in the park. When he was dying, three years later, the Queen sent a message asking if he would like to see her. He declined, and his reported reply displays the wit and irreverence that made him such good company throughout his life: 'No,' they say he answered, 'she'd only ask me to take a message to Albert.'

Hughenden is now a National Trust property, and lost in a maze of winding lanes to the north-west of Aylesbury is another National Trust property, Claydon House, seat of the Verney family since 1620. In the latter half of the eighteenth century the second Earl built a great mansion there with matching east and west wings and a vast central rotunda, hoping to rival the glories of the Duke of Buckingham's house at Stowe. Lord Verney bankrupted himself to provide nothing but the best and finest for Claydon, with the result that in 1783 most of the contents had to be sold off to meet his creditors. But he got poor value in his structure: the foundations were so shoddy that the central rotunda and the east wing with its magnificent ballroom started to crumble soon after his death, and had to be demolished. Only the Palladian west wing now remains, but that is sufficient to show how spectacular Claydon must have been in its heyday. Beautiful rococo carvings by Luke Lightfoot smother the walls and ceilings with a delicate profusion of scrolls, wreaths, swags, friezes and medallions, intricately and perfectly fashioned. The cornices are superb, the great doors of heavy Spanish mahogany hang beneath beautifully fashioned pediments, and the visitor's progress from room to room is attended by gasps and exclamations as magnificent ceiling is followed by magnificent ceiling followed by gorgeous staircase . . . No man could have a finer memorial.

The second Baronet, Sir Harry Verney, who inherited in 1827, married Florence Nightingale's sister, Parthenope, and in the first-floor museum a number of Miss Nightingale's photographs, letters and effects are displayed among the relics of the Verney family. The family has a proud history; Sir Edmund Verney was King's Standard Bearer in the Civil War, and when captured at the Battle of Edgehill he refused to surrender the

Waddesdon Manor, built for Baron Ferdinand de Rothschild

Stonor Park. The private chapel is on the right

Hughenden Manor, from the garden

Buckinghamshire brick and flint. The Lodge, Hughenden Manor

Fishing at Harefield

Locking through Cow Roast

Church House, Grove Lock, a redundant church converted sympathetically into a private dwelling

A pair of Chartist cottages today. Many of the two-, three- and four-acre plots are still intact, some used by their owners now for grazing cows and sheep for their freezers

Jordans. The Meeting House and William Penn's grave

The Church School at Ewelme. Through the gateway are the Almshouses

Pigotts. The original house and barns of Eric Gill's home

The Old Plow Inn at Speen

The Pink and Lily at Speen

Amersham Hospital. The Old Workhouse, designed by Sir George Gilbert Scott

Thame High Street closed for the fair

Chiltern steam

colours, declaring: 'My life is my own, my Standard the King's'. His life was forfeit, but even in death his hand would not relinquish the Standard, so the Parliamentarians hacked it off to bear the flag away, and the story goes that when it was recaptured his dead fingers were still clasping the stave. There are still Verneys in residence at Claydon today.

Two other families of ancient lineage long settled in the Chilterns are the Stonors at Stonor Park and the Blounts at Mapledurham, both in Oxfordshire. There can be few homes in England as beautifully set as Mapledurham's Tudor Manor House in its enclave of water-mill, church and almshouses. It stands beside the family's original timbered house of Mapledurham Gurney built in 1489, guarding the water-meadows to the Thames beside a tree-shadowed weir. The present manor was started in 1588 by Sir Michael Blount and was completed by his son, Richard, who was killed at Oxford during the Civil War. Two magnolia grandiflora, oldest of their kind in England, attend the castellated porch to the front entrance, making a wonderful display in late summer against the mellow Tudor brickwork. Inside, the house is cool and elegant; generations of Blounts look down from the pale walls, and the quiet good taste of Mapledurham's solid old English furniture and restrained furnishings is very pleasing.

In the small boudoir which adjoins the salon is a portrait of the poet Alexander Pope, by Kneller. They didn't tell us at school as we studied *The Dunciad* or *An Essay on Man* that Pope was a mannikin who never attained as much as five feet in height, nor does the portrait show it; but it was so, though his works, the proud look in his eye, and the delicate tracery of his features prove that in heart and in mind he was as other men. He was ardently attracted to the peaches and cream beauty of Martha Blount, and if he was not permitted passion at least he could be attentive and entertaining. History paints a charming picture of his capering in the park as a youth hand-in-hand with Martha and her sister Teresa, dancing between them. Though Martha's looks were to be ravaged by smallpox, Pope continued faithful until her death in 1763, fifty years after their first meeting. First editions of all his works were given to the Blount family, and many books from his library are to be found at Mapledurham today.

Well down-river from Mapledurham, Cliveden stands high above the Thames overlooking the river near Maidenhead. The 'vast, balustraded pile', as the National Trust Guide has it, was commissioned in 1850 by the Duke of Sutherland from Sir Charles Barry, who also designed the House of Commons. He retained the great terrace, 400 feet long by 25 feet wide, which was all that remained of William Winde's house built in 1666 for the notorious Duke of Buckingham, and allowed the present house to rise symmetrically above it. Stone-built in the style of an Italian *palazzo*, with nine tall, pedimented first-floor windows above nine matching ground-floor bays and an extra flanking bay on each side to give balance, Pevsner describes it as one of Sir Charles's best mansions.

If the interior is disappointing (only part is on view, as the mansion is let by the National Trust to America's Stanford University), the grounds are ample compensation. The house is situated on a bend so that the view is along the river rather than across it to the opposite bank, and vistas draw the eye continually down to the placid water far below where it broadens into Cliveden Reach, with the steep, richly wooded banks rising above. One of Cliveden's attractions, in fact, is that it can be visited on a trip along the river by hire-boat from Maidenhead. The river trip, a walk in the many acres of woodland, tea, a wander round the rose-garden and back to the river again, passes an idle afternoon in summer most admirably. In recent years the Festival of Cliveden open-air theatre has been staged in the water-garden during late June and early July. Superior refreshments with home-made food, strawberries, and wine are on offer for an hour before the performance starts and during the intervals, and musicians play interlude music and overtures from the islands.

Evidently the National Trust is alive to the possibilities of entertainment on the grand scale at Cliveden, for one of their issues of *News from the N.W. Home Counties* advertises a Cliveden concert with Cristina Ortiz, Piano, tickets to 'include a glass of champagne'. They are but following a Cliveden tradition, for when George II's son, Frederick, Prince of Wales, was in residence before the Duke of Buckingham's mansion burned down, he enlivened the time with family entertainments of masques and plays, many of which he had written himself. It was at one of these entertainments that Thomas Arne's 'Rule, Britannia' was heard for the first time. Prince Frederick was one of the few members of his family to be popular in his time. Unfortunately he never came to the throne, meeting a ludicrous death at Cliveden through being struck by a cricket ball. A contemporary rhyme recorded the event:

Here lies Poor Fred, who was alive and is dead.
Had it been his father I had much rather;
Had it been his sister nobody would have missed her,
Had it been his brother, still better than another,
Had it been the whole generation, so much better for the nation,
But since it is Fred who was alive and is dead,
There's no more to be said.

During the 1930s when Lord and Lady Astor owned Cliveden, the house again resounded to applause as the 'Cliveden Set' were entertained by such outstanding fellow-guests as Charlie Chaplin. But the war put an end to their larks, and Lord Astor gave Cliveden to the National Trust in 1942.

Stonor Park is another house that, like Claydon, lies in a maze of narrow lanes, this time between the Thames and the M40, above the Henley loop. The first Stonor built his house here in the twelfth century, and in all the years between Stonors have lived at Stonor Park, so that the present owner, Lord Camoys, can write in his booklet about the house: 'My family has always lived here. A Stonor built the first house, and the estate passed from father to son in direct succession, except three times when brother inherited from brother, for eight hundred years.'

By the fourteenth century Richard Stonor owned a 'fair house' on the site, consisting of buttery, hall and solar, with a family chapel built alongside, as well as sixteen manors elsewhere. His little timber dwelling is still there, incorporated in the great house that stands at Stonor Park today. The mansion lies in a slight hollow, overlooking lawns to the front and a small formal garden to the rear, amid acres of rolling park and woodland grazed by a herd of fallow deer. The first impression of the house is of sheer size; tall white casements set in pale Tudor brickwork under a steep-tiled, dormered roof, brickwork which in part is but a façade upon the older flint and timber building beneath. The twelfth-century flint and stone chapel with brick tower has been used for worship through all the intervening years, at times perilously so, for like the Blounts at Mapledurham, the Stonors were Catholic recusants. They refused to take the Oath of Supremacy when Henry VIII broke away from Rome, so that from the time of Sir Thomas More's execution until James I came to the throne the family were forced to retire from all public affairs and conduct themselves very quietly at home, paying their annual fines for refusing the Protestant Oath, at one time to the tune, in today's currency, of £50,000. When James's Act of Indulgence came to their rescue the family was so reduced financially because of repeated fines and penalties that all their property was gone save the house at Stonor, and not until the Emancipation Act of 1829 were they truly safe from persecution. On the top floor at Stonor is the room where Edmund Campion, the Jesuit preacher, set up his printing press in Elizabethan times and hid from the authorities before his later capture and martyrdom.

It is our good fortune today that private owners of lovely estates such as these open their doors to us all in an effort to preserve their inheritance and make it self-supporting. They each have their pet methods of keeping the cash bells ringing. At Chenies Manor on the Hertfordshire/Buckinghamshire borders, Colonel and Mrs McLeod Matthews organize Medieval Banquets and Historical Cookery Courses centred on their Elizabethan Manor House and Physic Garden, and most of the houses open to the public run souvenir shops and serve afternoon teas. Personally, I am grateful to them. Now that the gates are unchained and the walls are down we can all have the pleasure of enjoying these lovely old buildings that are our national heritage, together with the furnishings, pictures and *objets d'art* they house, without the responsibility and expense of keeping it all tidy and in good repair.

19

The Grand Union

If the Duke of Bridgewater, that 'Father of Inland Navigation', were to return to earth and climb the 172 steps of his monument at Ashridge, he could gaze across country to where one of the most ambitious of his offspring, the Grand Union Canal, potters through Berkhamsted on its way to the North.

The canal gives a new view of the prosperous Chilterns; an old-fashioned, industrial, workaday view that has a flavour all its own. On some stretches ominous black iron warehouses and gaunt factory buildings tower so close to the edge that they see their faces in the dun-coloured surface, on others waterbirds nest beneath overhanging trees along the banks, swifts skim low over the water and iridescent mayflies dance above the towpath. Miniature hump-backed bridges carry country lanes across where the cut runs through meadow land; side streams lead off to weirs, marinas and boat-basins; isolated houses, lock-keepers' cottages and the occasional inn remind us that not everybody lives on a boat, and small colonies of narrow boats prove that some lucky people still do. It is a place apart, a once-busy highway that for a century carried the cargoes of an industrial nation, now quiet, isolated, by the world forgot. A place for dreamers, idlers, fishermen, and the slow-moving, chugging boats with sun-dazed holiday-makers sprawled about their decks and along their cabin tops.

The Grand Union loops around the eastern edge of the Chilterns, touching Rickmansworth, Berkhamsted, Tring and Ivinghoe before passing out of the district at Leighton Linslade. It was one of the last major canals to be added to the Inland Waterways system, starting life as the Grand Junction Canal built to join London with Oxford and the canal systems of the North. By the time the Grand Union Canal Company took over, the canals in Britain were already doomed as working water-ways, and today the Grand Union is a lonely back-water serving the leisure industry. Pleasure boats there are in plenty during the summer months, a very few residential boats where people live all the year, and some thirty miles of towpath to attract walkers, fishermen and bird-watchers.

How the change from a working canal came about is, some

say, more a matter of politics than progress. The narrow boat, drawing its load to the rhythm of one old single-cylinder semi-diesel and worked by families living aboard, must have been the most economical bulk-cargo mover the wit of man could devise. More so when it was horse-drawn. But its day is gone, and today there are hardly any working boats on this section of the canal, just one or two coalers and a working pair that ply from Brentford to Boxmoor carrying lime-juice. For the families that worked those boats along the canals life was far from easy. Never a nine to five job, it was hard physical work for everyone. Women with babes in arms would be called up to help work the boats, and quite small children sent on ahead to open the lock gates. The standard width of canal lock-chambers was normally 7 feet, and although the locks on the Grand Union were built to a 14-foot standard, working narrow boats were never more than 7 feet wide. Life in the cabins was cramped and crowded; cupboard doors let down to form beds and tables, and in summer the heat from the round-bellied cooking stoves was unbearable. But there was colour everywhere in the brightly painted 'Roses and Castles', there were birds, river creatures and wild flowers along the banks, and friendliness at canal-side inns. Life on 'the Cut' had its compensations.

Now that the canal companies and the working boats are gone it is left to the British Waterways Board to keep the canals clear and the locks repaired, and to a new breed of canal people to find a new use for the waterways; people who love the back-waters for their peace and quiet magic, people of imagination and enterprise, like Fred Good of the Goodwill Marina at Cassiobridge. Fred had always loved the water, and when he left the Navy at the end of the war he bought a cabin cruiser and moored it on the Thames, the first Norman Twenty to be registered on the river. In those early years it was fun, but by 1970 there were too many boats on the Thames for comfort; he became tired of waiting up to three hours on sunny summer weekends to get through a lock, and turned his eyes to the quieter waters of the canal. Finding a mooring at Black Jack's Mill between Harefield and Rickmansworth, he was so plagued by people begging the loan of his boat for holidays that he began to think about hiring out boats professionally. At this time he was a business executive in his late forties with a son who wanted to work for himself. He considered the figures: 1.9 boats per mile using the canal against 9.1 boats per mile using the

Thames. He thought about his life in business and felt that if he didn't make a fresh start he had nothing to look forward to but old age. He decided to look for a boatyard, and with his son, Steve, he set out to walk the towpath northwards from Brentford, investigating every suitable patch of land. Lead after lead came to nothing, but they persisted and six months later, as a cold, wet February day was fading into night, they found what they were looking for, a stretch of hard-standing by a derelict factory site at Cassiobridge, where the A412 from Rickmansworth to Watford passes over the cut. For once nothing went wrong. Rickmansworth Council, who owned the land, was persuaded to lease them the canal frontage, and their order was placed for a hire fleet of three new narrow boats, as many as they could afford.

They had no electricity, no sanitation, no water laid on; their office was a narrow boat moored by the towpath, their workshop a plank across two calor-gas bottles, but that first year they were booked throughout the season to 90 per cent of capacity. After a while the electricity cable was laid, and the local Health Officer came along with a divining rod and found a stop-cock by the gate, so they had fresh water. When the hire-boats came in on a Saturday morning there were just two hours to check the contents, clean the boats, empty the Elsans, change the linen and generally get ready for the next hirer. The entire family turned to and helped, and if a boat broke down at some inaccessible place along the cut, they had to work out the nearest approach by road and then walk sometimes miles along the towpath carrying tools or gas bottles or batteries to attempt a rescue. It wasn't easy, but it was a start.

Seven years later Fred and Steve no longer hire out boats; their three little Goodwills have come to the end of their working lives. Instead, they build and sell boats, and hire out moorings on their new marina. They spent five years negotiating with seven different authorities to get all the necessary permissions to dig out a marina at Cassiobridge, and so great has been the increase in leisure traffic on the Grand Union during those five years that the hundred boat berths they made are all taken. So Fred can look across his desk at his secretary typing the letters in her bikini and think with some satisfaction: 'If only the boys at the Office could see me now!'

Goodwill's moorings are all for leisure boats; residential moorings on the canal are very hard to come by. There are a few

at Harefield, by Widewater Lock, on one of the flooded gravel
pits that are strung out like pearls all the way from Denham to
Rickmansworth. The canal enters the Chilterns at Denham,
and from there to Widewater the channel is separated on both
sides from these man-made lakes by stretches of bank and reeds
that give home to countless waterbirds. Their small sounds echo
across the quiet water, familiar to the boat-dwellers as sunrise
and sunset: the wing-beat of ducks as they riffle down and
skiddle across the water, and the haunting, eerie call of the wild
geese as the skeins come winging in, a call that raises prickly
hairs on the back of the neck and sets the heart yearning for
strange, faraway places. All this the canal people are heir to,
with the sight of the wind lifting the surface, and the slap of
water against the boat sides; and if they take a dinghy across to
the Horse and Barge for a sundowner there is no one to breath-
alyse them on their uncertain way home.

The lock beyond Widewater is Black Jack's Mill, where there
are some of the most coveted moorings along the canal. The
banks are bordered by gardens, willows droop over the water
and there are even a few thatched cottages to add to the view.
Later, the canal runs through a lonely wasteland, the haunt of
fishermen and bird-watchers. Along the water's edge are ox-eye
daisies and codlins-and-cream, the towpath is bounded by
hedges of blackberry, honeysuckle and wild rose, and in early
autumn the boggy hinterland is a mass of glowing orange
balsam. (And, alas, giant hogweed. Where did that plant come
from?) At Rickmansworth the Council have used the classic
salesman's ploy of turning an objection into an objective by
utilizing what might have been an unsightly wasteland for
their Aquadrome. The gravel pits here, within a stone's throw of
the centre of Rickmansworth, have been naturalized, the banks
mown and trees allowed to soften the contours. Club houses and
changing-rooms have been built and the area developed for
water-skiing, swimming and sailing.

Beyond the Aquadrome, at Batchworth, there is a double lock
and a confusion of weirs and waters as the River Chess comes in
from the left and the Colne from the right, while the River Gade
accompanies the canal on to Cassiobury Park and Grove Mill.
There is a long string of residential moorings beside the water-
meadows between Batchworth and the next lock, Common
Moor, but after that the canal is very much a back-water, built
up on both sides with modern housing estates and factories. It

bursts into the country again at Cassiobridge to pass through Cassiobury Park, where it forms a great attraction. On any sunny weekend boat crews can be assured of an admiring and envious audience as they tackle Cassiobury Lock. An all too helpful audience, very often, causing the nervous boatman to drop his precious lock key into the cut, and other disasters.

Cassiobury Lock is reputed to have a history of disasters. It is said to be haunted by the ghost of a gigantic negro, so big and powerful that he could jump the 14-foot lock chamber. In the early years of the canal this negro harried the boat crews at his master's bidding, cutting their mooring ropes, dropping the paddles of the locks, stealing their lock keys, and generally causing havoc. In those days the boats were worked by all-male crews who earned enough to keep their families decently ashore; only as the waterways became generally less prosperous and wages fell to poverty level did the boat captains resort to housing their families, wives and children, aboard. Eventually the troublesome negro was killed by an enraged boatman who hit him over the head with one of the very lock keys it was his delight to make off with. The story goes that many years later a great hollow oak in the Park was struck by lightning, and inside it was found a cache of some three hundred lock keys, rusted together into a useless mass. The lock key, which acts like a windlass handle to raise and lower the paddles, is an essential tool to the boatman, for without it he cannot work his boat through the locks.

Some beautiful bridges cross on the way to Hunton Bridge, but from there to Berkhamsted the canal runs between the railway and the A41, keeping company with watercress beds, allotments and the backs of factories. At Castle Wharf, Berkhamsted, Mike and Lindsey Foster run their Bridgewater Boats hire fleet, smart and handsome traditional narrow boats, each with its distinctive 'Bridgewater Boats' plaque. Anyone hiring one of these boats and turning its bows to the north will cruise through the prettiest stretch in the Chilterns on the way to Grove Lock, the last before the canal passes into Bedfordshire. They will go through Cow Roast, where another new marina complements the old whitewashed cottages to either side of the lock, and on towards Tring, where trees form a leafy tunnel and the overhanging branches are reflected green in the still water. Bright dragonflies hover above the surface, and wagtails busy themselves about the towpath where a few anglers sit placidly by their lines.

At Bulbourne Junction the Wendover Arm goes off on the left, a narrow canal with 7-foot locks that is navigable for only a short distance, and further on at Marsworth Junction the Aylesbury Arm also leaves the main channel. This arm is navigable all the way to its terminus at the Aylesbury boat basin. The narrow water runs all the way through flat land and cornfields, where lapwings feed in flocks that rise like clouds when disturbed, voicing their unmistakable cry. Other birds there are in plenty; larks sing overhead, herons flap lazily off towards the reservoirs, and in the sedge tiny bright-eyed reed-buntings tack their diminutive nests to the reeds.

There are a few residential moorings at Aylesbury, and a long string of temporary moorings by the Grand Junction Arms at Bulbourne, a favourite spot for holiday regulars like Eric and Tricia Parrott of the narrow boat *Maud Gracechurch*. They are among the fortunate few with residential moorings, being based on the Regent's Canal at Maida Hill. Tricia says that their boat, which looks so awkward and difficult to manoeuvre when moored by the towpath, practically steers itself. She maintains that the canals are so beautifully engineered that they take the boats along with the minimum effort, each curve, lock-entry and bridge-abutment being designed to position these long boats correctly in the stream and give least resistance to their progress. This must have made a great difference when the boats were horse-drawn, and the distance they might travel in a day depended on the strength and staying power of the boat-man's horse.

Beyond Bulbourne the nine Marsworth and three Seabrook locks take the canal down from the Tring summit on to the level plain. Though the canal uses the Tring Gap to cross the Chiltern Hills it still makes quite a height, and every time a boat passes over the summit 200,000 gallons of water flow back down the canal. The restoration of this lost water to the summit level was a great headache for the early canal engineers, and though the Wilstone, Marsworth and Startopsend reservoirs were created to top up the channel, it was still necessary to install a pumping station at Northchurch to draw up fresh water through a bore-hole in the chalk to maintain the supply. During the long, dry summer of 1977 the position became so serious that the locks were closed for all but four hours every day, and queues of boats could be seen waiting their turn to lock through.

Even when the canals are full progress is slow. The channels were built to flow at no more than 1 m.p.h., and the official speed limit for boats is 4 m.p.h. This is a very necessary restriction, particularly on the narrow canals, as a greater speed would not only damage the banks, but would create a wash and sweep the water away from under the boats, leaving their propellers turning in air. The slow rate of progress, combined with the time taken working the locks, means that a walker on the towpath will come up with the same set of boats time and again in the course of a stroll, and in some places will even outstrip them. This is particularly true where the boat crews are busy with the thirteen locks on the stretch from Bulbourne to Ivinghoe; while they are sweating at the paddles or dashing on from lock to lock to make ready, a walker can idle along the towpath enjoying the views across the reservoirs and catching an occasional glimpse between the trees of the great square tower of Ivinghoe Church.

At Grove Lock, the last lock in the Chilterns, the canal runs almost under the walls of the tiny church of St Michael and All Angels. Writing of this church in 1831, Lipscombe said: 'That part of the interior which is used for Divine Service is separated from a porch (which during many years was a mere lumber room) by a partition of rough boards. The Font and Communion Table stand in the outer division, and are only very rarely moved into the church; but the whole is much improved of late years, and now has six regular and neat pews, instead of a range of forms and benches.' So far is Grove from a village or settlement of any size, that matters can hardly have improved for it from that date, and in 1971 the church was made redundant and sold for conversion to a private dwelling.

The present owners, one of whom is an archaeologist, bought the building part-converted two or three years later, and have finished the conversion and added an extension on the back. As they have a Grade II Listed Building on their hands they cannot take too many liberties with the structure, nor do they wish to, and it is surprising that they have managed to make such a comfortable and interesting home whilst changing so little. Sunlight filters through the lovely old glass of the East window into their sitting-room in the nave, the pulpit stands under the stairs that lead to the galleried bedrooms, and the kitchen occupies the former vestry, which once was separated from the main body of the church by a curtain. When their extension was built the original Norman door was found behind a Victorian chimney-breast, and herring-bone pattern Norman foundations outside in the churchyard. Part of the original floor to the Norman chancel was found under what is now the garden when the electricity cable was laid, and when a hole was dug inside for the main support beam to the bedroom gallery a skeleton in a stone coffin was found beneath the floor. There was no name-plate to the coffin and the church records make no mention of the interment, though only an important person would have been accorded the honour of burial inside the church. It was decided to fill in the hole and leave coffin and contents at peace in their ancient resting place.

St Michael's was the smallest church in Buckinghamshire. Though its records go back to 1222 and the Norman foundations prove it older by far, all its history is now told by the plaque at the gate:

> St Michael and All Angels.
> Made redundant, 1971.
> Bell dated 1676 taken to Westonbirt, Glos.
> and Norman Font to Llantrisant, Anglesey.

20

Some Chiltern settlements

England has always had room for minor prophets; no man with an idea, a germ of a notion, a vision that might change the lives of men, will lack souls to follow him, and though as a result he may spend his life hand-in-hand with trouble, yet at the end some positive good may remain. Such a man was Feargus O'Connor, nineteenth-century Protestant-Irish Radical, journalist, orator, twice Member of Parliament, a man to dream dreams and paint from them such pictures as would stand the world on end. O'Connor's dream was of a property-owning democracy, but he dreamed it a hundred years too soon.

When Feargus O'Connor came to England from Ireland he attached himself to the Chartist Movement, a group whose aims were universal male suffrage, vote by secret ballot, payment for Members of Parliament, and the abolition of the property quali-fication. Very obvious and ordinary aims, we would think today, but the Chartists were hounded for their effrontery. The leaders of the movement were on the whole reasonable and moderate men; they mistrusted O'Connor and his oratory, a mistrust that was not unfounded, for the Chartist Movement has no history beyond 1860, and Feargus O'Connor and his Land Movement did much to bring it down.

It was at the Chartist Conference of 1845 that O'Connor revealed his Great Dream; by joining together in the collection of thousands of small subscriptions working men could purchase plots of land and settle there such lucky ones among them as should be chosen by ballot. Sums as small as one penny a week could raise £5,000 in fifty shilling shares, and buy 120 acres of land, providing sixty settlers each with two acres, a cottage and a cow. These properties could then be mortgaged for a sum sufficient to buy land for seventy-two more, whose property could in turn be mortgaged to settle more, and more . . . and more . . . All it needed was faith, and enough subscribers. To his audience of working-men it was a vision of Heaven, and though the Chartist leaders declared the idea basically unsound and would have none of it, O'Connor carried the rank and file and at that very meeting the Chartist Land Company was formed.

Hopefuls rushed to join from all over the country; at one time there were 60,000 members and the Land Company had funds of £90,000, collected from tiny weekly subscriptions. The task of accounting, undertaken by volunteers, proved enormous and impossible; legal requirements were ignored as taking too long and the acquired plots were wrongly registered in O'Connor's name; what is more he clearly treated them as his property. The inevitable happened, difficulties piled up until they were insurmountable, the bubble burst, thousands were dis-appointed in their hopes, and in 1851 the Land Company's operations ceased. But progress had been made, and when Feargus O'Connor died in 1855, discredited and insane, he left behind for a monument 256 trim cottages in five separate settlements, built to his design and often with his own hands for tenants transported from poor-law institutions and the slums of industrial cities to live as English yeomen on good English land. The five settlements were at Lowbands, within view of the Malvern Hills, Minster Lovell in Oxfordshire, Snigs End near Tewksbury, Great Dodford in Worcester, and Heronsgate, near Rickmansworth, in the Chilterns.

Heronsgate was the first of the Land Company's purchases. One hundred and three acres of freehold land to the south of Long Lane, Rickmansworth, in the county of Hertfordshire, bought in 1846 and named 'O'Connorville'. Here were built thirty-five cottages on plots of two, three or four acres, to be allocated by ballot of all fully paid-up members. The cottages were mostly of two storeys, soundly built of brick faced with stucco, in semi-detached pairs, and to the rear of every house was a yard with cowshed, stable, pig-pen and wash-house. To families used to living higgledy-piggledy in one room, they must have been paradise.

There was a schoolhouse on the estate, but no church for O'Connor disapproved of religion; no shop, and no ale-house. All the Chartist estates were 'dry', and O'Connor never tired of declaring that the subscriptions to his land company were 'snatched from the beer-house or gin-palace'. An inn soon opened, though, just beyond the confines of the estate, in the Land of Liberty. The inn stands in Long Lane today, and the sign before its door still bears that odd name: 'The Land of Liberty'. On 1st May 1847, the thirty-five lucky settlers moved into their houses to find their allotments tilled, manured and ready-planted with root-crops, wood for kindling stacked by the door, and a sack of barley meal provided for bread. And every male householder was entitled to a county vote. A grand meeting was held to show off 'Labour's Own Land bought with Labour's Own Money', and though a local man protested that the Land Company was no more than a lottery and that it would take forty-seven years to house even the present subscribers, a branch was started at Chorleywood that day and several new members enrolled.

Sadly, many of the new yeomen failed to prosper. Crop failures took their toll, livestock failed to thrive. The death of a pig or cow is a misfortune if it is one of a herd, a disaster if it is the sole provision of milk or meat for the coming winter. The two-acre plots in particular were not really large enough to support a family, and in the depressed 1840s there was no work available locally to help out. Despite loans from the Land Company for the purchase of seed and manure, despite the remission of rent in cases of hardship, despite the fact that O'Connor readily dipped into his own pocket when appealed to, one by one the settlers gave up in despair. Leases began to be offered for sale on the open market, and when the Land Company was finally wound up and the estate sold off, only three of the original settlers had been able to save enough to pay off their borrowings and take up their freeholds. It is significant that two of these three had come from rural backgrounds.

The name 'O'Connorville' appears on no map today, and when nostalgia or curiosity drives the descendants of those first lucky winners on the Chartist football pools to Heronsgate to seek out the settlement and see how it was, they find that in some curious fashion it is both greatly changed and changeless. The layout of the estate is still the same, most of the Chartist cottages are still there, yet the area now presents an aspect of comfortable prosperity undreamed of by O'Connor's 'Blistered Hands, Unshorn Chins and Fustian Jackets', as he loved to call his followers. Today's residents gaze out over park-like vistas, over swimming-pools, tennis courts, paddocks and croquet lawns bounded by neat hedges and smart post-and-rail fences. Pheasants shriek where hens once scratched, cow-sheds serve as garages or stables, and pig-sties as garden sheds. Few of the cottages are unaltered. Most have been enlarged to twice the size and more. Sometimes the change is so drastic that the old building is detectable only by a narrow casement, a plain gable-end, or a distinctive patch of plaster decoration; sometimes the extensions have been so cleverly added that the original cottage remains intact, stressing the new building's humble origin. In one case only the cellar and part of the kitchen remain, the present house having been built above and around them, and often these changes have been wrought by a succession of owners each adding something new, as the differences in the brickwork will testify. The narrow estate roads are unchanged, still only 9 feet wide and still bearing the names of the towns from which the Chartist settlers came: Halifax Road, Stockport Road, Nottingham Road and Bradford Road. Only Cherry Tree Lane is new, its pretty, rural name belying the fact that it is far less of a 'lane' than the four 'roads', and far more adequate than they for the motor cars that are a necessity today. We see the ghosts of the old Chartists sadly shaking their heads and saying with G. K. Chesterton that 'a new people takes the land, and still it is not we', for most of these houses are owned by people at the top of their profession and these are the heirs to that educated, enfranchised, property-owning democracy of the Chartist vision.

The twentieth century has caught up on Heronsgate. Already the ghost of the lady that walks in Ladywalk Wood is disturbed by the sight and sound of traffic on the North Orbital—M1 Extension, not five hundred yards away across the fields. Once her haunting-ground was secluded and quiet, surrounded by meadows and country gardens. The residents fought hard to keep it so, but they lost. The motorway was built, and inter-continental juggernauts snarl across the rolling Hertfordshire countryside threatening their front door, while their back door is in danger from the proposed M25, which will not only take a chunk of Feargus O'Connor's land for its construction but will isolate Heronsgate in a wedge between two motorways.

Not ten miles from Heronsgate, across the border in Bucking-hamshire, is a settlement which owes its life to a man whose vision was profounder and more enduring than that of poor Feargus O'Connor; it is the Quaker Meeting House, Guesthouse and village at Jordans, lying on a quiet lane between Chalfont St Giles and Beaconsfield. Older by two hundred years than Heronsgate, its origins go back to a handful of George Fox's Quakers meeting for worship in the kitchen at William Russell's Old Jordans Farm in 1659. They met secretly and unobtrusively, drifting like shadows by night, in continual danger of arrest and imprisonment. Many of them saw the inside of gaol, though their only crime was a desire to worship according to their conscience. Their obstinate refusal to accept the ministry of the established church led to many practical problems. They could not marry in church, were summoned and sometimes imprisoned for non-payment of tithes, and they were refused burial in consecrated ground. So to provide decent burial for their members, in 1671 the Jordans Meeting bought a quarter of an acre of William Russell's land to use for a burial ground. This most modest start has grown over the years until today the Quaker settlement at Jordans comprises a modern village with shop, school and village hall, a Guesthouse and Conference Centre, the Mayflower Barn, the Meeting House, and that first little graveyard, now greatly enlarged.

A small plot of land beside the burial ground was bought in 1688 after King James's Declaration of Indulgence (principally intended to help his Catholics) freed the people of England to worship as they saw fit, and within three months a simple Meeting House had been built by members of the Jordans Meeting, with their own hands. This Meeting House survives almost unchanged today, looking surprisingly fresh and new from the outside, for all its age. Inside, the plain cream-washed walls, brick floor and simple wooden benches lend peace and simplicity to this place where Quakers have met for worship every Sunday for three hundred years. The mellow light filtering through the original glass of the diamond-paned windows settles on a facsimile of the Act of Indulgence. Signed by the King, it hangs framed on the wall next to a copper-plate list of names of those buried in unmarked graves in the old burial ground. When first built, the Meeting House had a living-room and kitchen at one end with two bedrooms over, and though these rooms are intact, they are not now used for their original purpose. Today the living-room serves as an entrance and ante-room, one of the bedrooms is a reading-room, and the other, which was built with removable wooden screens giving access to the proceedings in the Meeting House downstairs, now has these screens permanently removed to form a gallery to seat an overflow of twenty-eight people. Very necessary at Meetings for burial. Framed on the walls of this gallery are letters written by the old Quakers; to George Fox whilst in prison from his follower William Penn, from Penn's second wife, Hannah, written from Philadelphia, describing her unhappiness in 'this dreadful land', and from the faithful Thomas Ellwood.

This isolated Meeting House attracts an average gathering of seventy souls to Meeting each week, including visiting Quakers from all over the world. For apart from its interest as one of the first Quaker Meeting Houses (the oldest was built at Hertford in 1670), it is a place of pilgrimage to the many famous Quakers that lie at rest in the burial ground. William Penn, who founded Pennsylvania, is there with his first wife, Gulielma, his second wife, Hannah, and ten of their sixteen children; Thomas Ellwood, one of the most faithful of the early Quakers, is there with his wife, Mary; Isaac and Mary Pennington, Gulielma's mother and stepfather, who were fined of almost all their possessions for their faith, are there; and Joseph Rule, called the 'White Quaker' from his habit of making his clothes from undyed cloth, is there too. It is said that at his burial flakes of snow fell upon his coffin, a last touching memorial to the White Quaker.

Many of today's visitors to Jordans are Americans who come not only for the Quaker connection but for a quite accidental connection with the Pilgrim Fathers through the Mayflower Barn. This barn was bought by the Jordans Meeting in 1911, when it was found that the years which had mellowed the burial ground and softened the mounds above the graves of the faithful had dealt harshly with Old Jordans Farm. The house where their first meetings were held so long ago had been allowed by its owners to go to ruin. The Meeting decided to buy the farm, funds were raised, and farmhouse, granary, stables and barn, together with seven acres of land, were acquired for use as a Quaker Guesthouse. The great farm barn had been known for years as the Mayflower Barn because it was said to have been built with timbers from a ship called *Mayflower*, broken up at Harwich in 1624. By one of those odd coincidences that make life the joy it is, a Cambridge historian, Dr Rendel Harris, who had been researching for years into the fate of the *Mayflower* in which the Pilgrim Fathers had sailed for the New World in 1620, was at a memorial service at the Meeting House in the 1920s when he heard mention of the Mayflower Barn. Scenting a connection, he traced the purchase of the timber for the barn, and was able to prove that this timber was indeed from the ship he was seeking. Scorn has been poured on Dr Harris's conclusions, and admittedly it seems astonishingly far-fetched that the remains of the ship that carried the founders of New England to America should have been hauled to Buckinghamshire to build a barn, and that the founder of another American state should return to the same corner of Buckinghamshire to be buried within its shadow, but Dr Harris was a trained, respected historian, and is worthy as such to be believed. The evidence is set out in his book published by the Manchester University Press in 1922. The Mayflower Barn is one of the best preserved seventeenth-century barns in Buckinghamshire. It is large enough to hold a hundred people seated, and the many uses to which it is put as part of Jordans Guesthouse and Conference Centre include music recitals, lectures, wedding receptions, art exhibitions, and activities in connection with a host of conferences held here by organizations as diverse as the American Genealogy Society, the Samaritans, and the Society of German Beekeepers.

The purchase of the barn and Old Jordans had barely been accomplished when in 1915 it was learned that land belonging to Stony Dean Farm, on the other side of Jordans Lane from the Meeting House, was to be sold, and that a speculative builder was interested. The thought of the precious peace of Jordans Meeting House, the resting-place of so many faithful Quakers, being destroyed was not to be entertained; a sum sufficient to buy the land was raised by subscription, and it was decided that when the war was over a Quaker village should be built there. The Purchasing Committee resolved to 'aim for community of ownership of the land and a co-partnership system in regard to the houses'. Like Heronsgate, most of the houses were to be built for working men, in this case not yeomen but craftsmen, and not all of them Quakers. Right from the start it was intended to be a mixed village, though the terms in which the initial announcements were made and the publications in which they appeared ensured a certain similarity of outlook among the first residents.

As soon as the war was over a start was made on laying out the estate, and in 1919 the first bricks were laid. It had always been intended that village industries should be established 'to provide well-made things from the best materials', and the Committee felt that the first task of the village industries should be to build the houses. Capital was provided and wooden workshops sprang up in one corner of the village green. All the building trades were represented among the intended residents, together with blacksmiths, gardeners and furniture-makers. A company was registered in the name of Village Industries Ltd of which all the men were shareholders, the minimum share being £1. By 1920 there were sixty-five people living in Jordans Village, the roll including bricklayers, cabinet-makers, gardeners, joiners, a plumber, a storekeeper and a clerk. All would have helped to build the houses they lived in, as all were in time to help build the village hall, lay the roads and smooth the village green. Village Industries Ltd also contracted for alterations and extensions to the Guesthouse at Old Jordans Farm, and it ran the village store. By 1922, however, the company was in financial difficulties, and in spite of the Jordans Management Committee announcing stoutly that financial success was 'subsidiary to our main object of building up a society of men and women who make no distinction between different forms of labour', in 1923 Village Industries Ltd had to be wound up. The workshops on the village green were demolished, the shop taken over by the Committee as a village co-operative, and the building operations taken over commercially by some of the workmen who banded together to operate as builders on their own account. The dream of a self-supporting community of craftsmen was over.

As with Heronsgate, however, the dream was not in vain. Fred Rowntree, the Quaker architect, had well designed his terraces of neat red brick-and-tile workmen's houses and set them around a generous village green, and by 1923 the craftsmen of Village Industries had built four of these terraces, together with twenty-one other single or semi-detached houses on leasehold plots. They had levelled the ground and built the roads, opened a claypit and produced distinctive, hand-made bricks, felled trees for lumber and made in the wood-yard floorboards, rafters, doors and window-frames, and the blacksmiths had beaten out individually designed sets of latches and door-handles for each house. And when all was done and the houses built, they had made gardens. Not only that, they had helped to make a caring community from a disparate group of strangers from many walks of life, and that community and those houses still flourish today. So what do you see—the ultimate failure of a commercial endeavour, or the living community that is one more triumph in the progress of man?

The enlarged farmhouse at Old Jordans is now a Quaker Guesthouse, and those who travel half-way across the world to see the Meeting House and Mayflower Barn or to visit relations and friends in Jordans village readily find accommodation there. A few days spent in this quiet haven in the Buckinghamshire beechwoods will cheer a careworn face and lift the saddest spirit. Even to sit at tea in the Guesthouse dining-room which was once the old farmhouse kitchen and still has inglenook and bread oven, uneven floor and old, polished tables of single oak planks, is restful. This serenity is open to any passer-by; tea is provided at modest cost, refreshment to the soul comes free.

At the other end of the Chilterns beyond Watlington, tucked into a fold of the Oxfordshire plain, is God's House at Ewelme, a settlement far older than either Heronsgate or Jordans. 'God's House' was the name given by its founders, Alice, Duchess of Suffolk, and her husband William de la Pole, the Duke, to the medieval almshouses and Grammar School they founded when the church was built to give homes to thirteen poor men and to provide schooling for the children of the village.

From the West door of the church tower a low-covered passageway and a set of steps lead to a cloister where thirteen dormered, red-brick almshouses are set about a square. By today's standards they were diminutive: one tiny living-room with sleeping space under the thatch, looking out on to a paved courtyard with well and winding-gear. But at a time when only the grandest houses were built of brick, the almshouses must have been thought palatial. The Foundation provided for the almsmen and two clerics to be housed free, and to receive a small yearly income in return for their duty which was to pray daily in the church for the souls of their patrons.

A step from the almshouses, and completing the settlement, is the lofty, angular Grammar School where the children of Ewelme have learned their letters since 1437. This is the oldest building in England to have been in continuous use as a school, and it is notable that it has remained a free school; so many of the medieval foundations meant to give free schooling to poor scholars became fee-paying in the eighteenth and nineteenth centuries. Originally an open hall with high, timbered roof, the interior of this beautiful old building has been refitted inside for use as the Ewelme C. of E. Primary School, without interfering with the structure or altering its appearance from the outside. The tall, square chimneys that are carried right to the ground on the west wall, the simple outline and beautiful proportions of the building, are as they ever were. The rich, red brick glows in the sunlight, and the entrance doors of English oak have weathered to silver over the years, their carvings so worn as to be discernible more by touch than by sight. None of the books gives a name to the architect of this medieval settlement, though the Guide to St Mary's Church, Ewelme, says 'the style suggests that the workmen came from the Duke's chief manor at Wingfield in Suffolk'. The chequered stonework of the church suggests the same.

This is no poor Foundation, and when in 1971 it was decided that the almshouses must be modernized, there were funds in hand to do the job properly. The whole interior was replanned, and now behind the thirteen doors about the square there are only eight apartments, each of four rooms instead of two, and each with bathroom and toilet in place of the old outside bathhouse and lavatories which stood in what is now the schoolhouse garden. But the Duke of Suffolk's Trust provided for thirteen almshouses supporting thirteen almsmen, so five modern apartments have been built in Ewelme village to bring the number back to thirteen. At the start of the refurbishing there were only five residents left in the old almshouses, two almsmen and three widows. One of the old men was too ill to get to church, and about that time, too, St Mary's was for two years without a rector or regular church services. Although a rector has now been appointed, he has four other churches in his charge as well as St Mary's. Sadly, as a result of these changes, the obligation upon the almsmen to pray daily in the church for the souls of their patrons has lapsed. Dame Alice and her poor murdered husband have no bedesmen now, but the medieval gem they founded, so soundly and reverently built at the start and so lovingly cherished for half a millennium, is in itself a prayer, and perhaps it will suffice.

21

Literary Associations

Writing of the Chilterns as late as 1950, J. H. B. Peel described a hamlet where the nearest shop was an hour's walk away, as was the nearest bus-stop. Travellers along the lane to this hamlet in the winter months, he said, did not exceed three or four a week. In those days there was a waiting list two years long for any make of new car, and many Chiltern villages were as isolated as this hamlet. Living in such remote places was cheap; a substantial detached house could be rented for as little as £50 a year, and cottages could be had for a pittance, enabling writers and artists to live within reach of the publishers and galleries of the capital and the libraries and museums of Oxford. So many of them, in fact, chose the Chilterns for a base that the difficulty is not who to put in, but who to leave out.

In the 1930s Eric Gill lived at North Dean, in Hampden country, gathering about him his 'Guild of Medieval Craftsmen'. Sculptor, printer, writer, designer, Eric Gill made an art of life itself. As Annan Dickson, who wrote the previous *Portrait of the Chilterns*, said: 'To him all Art was one Art, and his philosophy of the art of living made his writings a penetrating analysis of the ills of civilization. On this hilltop in a clearing, ringed about by quiet woodlands, he was the presiding genius of a living, working community, where every visit gave one fresh visions of higher hopes for the future.' Eric Gill is dead now, as is the writer of those words, and lies at peace in Speen Churchyard. Perhaps his best memorials are his carvings of the Stations of the Cross in Westminster Cathedral, and the beautiful typefaces he carved which have entirely changed modern printing, Gill sans, Bunyan and Perpetua. His autobiography makes good reading.

Annan Dickson himself was well known in the Forties and Fifties as a writer on country life and on the Chilterns in particular, but he was overshadowed by another Chiltern man, H. J. Massingham, who lived at Long Crendon and wrote for the *Field* and the *Spectator*, and edited the Nonesuch edition of Gilbert White's *The Natural History of Selbourne*. City born and bred, H. J. Massingham was a man with an abiding love of the countryside and a great delight in country ways. He was also a

man on whom Fate played a particularly cruel trick; one evening whilst cutting ivy from an ash tree he fell and cut his leg on a
piece of rusty iron. The accident cost him the leg, a sad fate for
any active man, particularly for a walker and a country-lover.
Nevertheless, some of his best work was done in the fifteen years
that remained to him. Perhaps his faith was a consolation, for
like Eric Gill and G. K. Chesterton, who wrote 'The Ballad of the
White Horse' while living at Beaconsfield, Massingham was a
Catholic convert.

There are still people in Beaconsfield who remember the
flamboyant figure of G. K. Chesterton stumping through the
town towards his favourite spot by the bar in the White Hart,
there to dispute and argue over an anything but quiet drink
with any who cared to take him on. When he saw Beaconsfield
just after the First War Chesterton described it as 'a sort of
village'; no one could so describe the town today. He was living
in London at the time, collaborating with his brother and
Hilaire Belloc in their weekly magazine *The New Witness*, a
name that was changed later when Chesterton took over the
sole management to *G. K.'s Weekly*.

Chesterton was as prolific and bounteous a man as his vast
figure suggested; he had the energy of ten, and a stream of
articles, poems, stories and books flowed from his pen, much of it
devotional in character. At Overroads, their first Beaconsfield
home, and later at Top Meadow, he and his wife kept open house
to their hundreds of friends including his erstwhile partner
Hilaire Belloc, a man with the soundest ambition any man
might have:

> If ever I become a rich man
> Or if ever I live to be old,
> I will build a house with deep thatch
> To shelter me from the cold.
>   There will the Sussex songs be sung
>   And the Sussex tales told.
> I will build my house in a high wood
> Within a walk of the sea,
> And the men that were boys when I was a boy
> Will sit and drink with me.

Belloc was born a Frenchman and a Catholic. He converted
himself to an Englishman and both the Chesterton brothers to
Catholicism, and lived to attain his house in Sussex.

Another frequent visitor at Top Meadow was Father O'Connor, priest in charge at Beaconsfield's Catholic church. He was the acknowledged model for Chesterton's famous detective, Father Brown. When G. K. C. died in 1936 he was buried in Father O'Connell's churchyard, and lies there beneath a monument designed and executed by his friend Eric Gill. His own words from 'Child of the Snow' might supply a memorial:

> At night we win to the ancient inn
> Where the Child in the frost is furled,
> We follow the feet where all souls meet
> At the inn at the end of the world.

During his Beaconsfield years, the 1920s and 1930s, Chesterton saw the start of the changes that were to come upon the Chiltern countryside, and indeed upon much of the land of England; the change from a principally agricultural to a principally urban community. He saw the first Chiltern farms sold for development and the first new estates grow upon the land, and was among those who fought to keep the necessary development within bounds. His was one of the first voices, too, in his poem 'The Secret People', raised against the new race of bureaucrats that he saw taking over this country, and, indeed, the world:

> They have given us into the hands of new, unhappy lords,
> Lords without anger or honour, who dare not carry their swords.
> They fight by shuffling papers; they have bright dead alien eyes;
> They look at our labour and laughter as a tired man looks at flies.
> And the load of their loveless pity is worse than the ancient wrongs.
> Their doors are shut in the evenings; and they know no songs.

'Smile at us, pay us, pass us,' he said, 'but do not quite forget, That we are the people of England, and we have not spoken yet.'

The people of the Chilterns spoke to effect over Wing Airport, and, earlier, to prevent a major road disturbing the peace of the Quaker Meeting House and burial ground at Jordans. We are not always so Secret a People. After Chesterton's death his secretary, Miss Dorothy Collins, ran Top Meadow as a home for unmarried mothers. During the War she also took paying guests, one of them being the novelist Angela Thirkell, who used Beaconsfield in general and Top Meadow in particular in her war-time novel *Cheerfulness Breaks In*.

John Masefield came to the soft Chiltern countryside before the First World War, renting a farmhouse in Great Hampden in 1909, a man in his thirties struggling to support a family with his pen. He had published nothing of note since his *Salt Water Ballads*, seven years before, and thought his muse had deserted him, but his time in the Chilterns gave him peace and a quiet mind and in 1911 he published in book form his best-selling poem *The Everlasting Mercy*:

> So up the road I wander slow
> Past where the snowdrops used to grow
> With celandines in early springs,
> When rainbows were triumphant things
> And dew so bright and flowers so glad,
> Eternal joy to lass and lad.
> And past the lovely brook I paced,
> The brook whose source I never traced,
> The brook, the one of two which rise
> In my green dreams, in Paradise*

The work was a resounding success and John Masefield never looked back, publishing another long poem *Reynard the Fox* in 1913, followed by several novels and more books of poetry. He moved from Great Hampden in time, but for the rest of his life was never far from Hampden country, living first in Oxfordshire and later near Abingdon. In 1930 he was made Poet Laureate by King George V. It is easy to see the fascination of this sailor-poet for the Sailor King, born to a throne and nurtured in regal isolation. One pictures him, least free of any man in the kingdom, reading Masefield's 'Wanderer's Song':

> A wind's in the heart of me, a fire's in my heels,
> I am tired of brick and stone and rumbling wagon-wheels;
> I hunger for the sea's edge, the limits of the land,
> Where the wild old Atlantic is shouting on the sand . . .

and sighing wistfully, and appointing the writer to be his own poet, his singer of songs.

Later, the poet and essayist J. H. B. Peel, a great friend and admirer of John Masefield, came to live in Hampden country at

---

* An account of the writing of this poem can be found in *People and Places* by J. H. B. Peel, Robert Hale, 1980.

Hotley Bottom where he wrote much about the Chilterns, including his own poem *Mere England*, a hauntingly descriptive book in rhyme and blank verse of this beautiful countryside he knew so well. He went on to make a name for himself as a writer on country matters, probably the best of his generation, with a dozen or so books on the subject and a fortnightly column in the *Daily Telegraph*.

We could speak of other Poets Laureate in connection with the Chilterns. John Masefield's predecessor, Robert Bridges, was not actually a Chiltern man, though his house at Boar's Hill at the Berkshire end of the Ridgeway overlooked the Chiltern countryside. Nor, in truth, can we claim Tennyson, who was certainly writing *In Memoriam*, the poem that first brought him fame and secured his future as Poet Laureate to Queen Victoria, whilst courting Emily Sellwood at Shiplake in the 1840s. He must have rued the safety and companionship of those Shiplake days in the year after his marriage when, having rented a grand house in Surrey which proved to be haunted, he found himself at midnight fleeing down the Surrey lanes pushing his already pregnant wife before him in a bath-chair:

> While I live, Owls!
> When I die, GHOULS!

Not unconnected with the Chilterns, too, is our present Poet Laureate, Sir John Betjeman, with his well-known enthusiasm for Metroland, though his home is at the other end of the Ridgeway, at Wantage. Sir John crossed swords with H. J. Massingham in the *Chilterns Magazine* of 1949 on the touchy subject of the Victorian glass in Chetwode Church. The *Chilterns Magazine* was a short-lived post-war quarterly which ran to only about seven issues, but attracted many good writers during its short life. After its demise the seven issues were published in book form; some Chiltern libraries still have copies.

Near to Chetwode, at Gawcott, the Victorian architect Sir George Gilbert Scott was born; his father was Perpetual Curate there. This gentleman is said to have had a hand in the design or restoration of no less than 474 churches and about 200 other buildings, including the Albert Memorial. He it was who designed the red-brick workhouse in Whielden Street, Amersham, that forms the core of the present Amersham Hospital.

In Victorian times Charles Reade wrote *The Cloister and the*

Hearth at Ipsden; Grote, of *Grote's Greece*, lived at East Burnham Park, and built himself a house there called History Hut; Maria Edgeworth of *Murder in the Red Barn* fame lived in a Georgian house at Gossoms End, and Mrs Humphry Ward at Stocks House, Aldbury, entertaining her nephews Julian and Aldous Huxley there in their school holidays. The present century saw Jerome K. Jerome at Ewelme, where his grave can be seen in the churchyard; George Orwell (then Eric Blair) growing up as a boy at Shiplake, W. B. Yeats renting the Red House, now a bookshop, in Thame; Gilbert Cannan, a member of the Bloomsbury Group and friend of Lytton Strachey, making his cottage at Hawridge a week-end retreat for his literary friends; and J. M. Barrie a frequent visitor at Egerton House, the home of the Llewellyn Davies family at Berkhamsted. Nearer our own time, Laurence Meynell, poet and critic, lived in Waller's old house at Coleshill, and T. S. Eliot spent the years of the Second World War in a modest house at Marlow. Kenneth Grahame wrote *The Wind in the Willows* at Pangbourne, and Hugh Lofting wrote *Dr Doolittle* at Maidenhead, both in the form of letters to their children; George Orwell's *Animal Farm* was conceived at Gerrards Cross; Robert Frost, the American poet, wrote for a while at Beaconsfield, and as is well known, Graham Greene sat down to write his first novel at Berkhamsted.

The next person to attempt a Portrait of the Chilterns will want to mention such present-day writers as David Mabey of *Food for Free* fame, Gordon Beningfield who wrote and painted *Beningfield's Countryside*, and Ruth and Alastair Fitter, with a life's work on nature guides behind them, all of whom are living and working in the Chilterns at this time. There might be mention too of Edmund Crispin, the writer of detective stories, at Chesham, of Roald Dahl, Val Biro and H. C. Todd, all writing in or around Old Amersham, and of the poet Jean Kenward, whose work is read regularly on the radio and published in the better magazines. Undoubtedly there *will* be mention of Dame Rebecca West, living near Ibstone, and Sir Arthur Bryant, well known in the Vale of Aylesbury. But before we leave this section we mustn't forget the Chilterns' most famous literary man, John Milton.

Milton was a London man at heart, and an internationalist. He spent only a little time at Chalfont St Giles in retreat from the Great Plague, and it must have irked him to be even for so short a time away from the centre of things. But his rural retreat was dictated by youthful associations; his grandfather had lived near Oxford, and Milton spent many years of his boyhood there. When he came down from Cambridge he lived for six years in his father's house at Horton, near Thame, where he wrote 'L'Allegro' and 'Il Penseroso', and his masque, *Comus*, and where he met and married a Chiltern girl, Mary Powell.

After their marriage they moved to London, relying on his friend Thomas Ellwood, the Quaker, to keep him in touch with the free-thinkers of the Chilterns. For though he is best remembered today as the blind poet who wrote *Paradise Lost*, in truth Milton was a political activist and a very advanced thinker. His *Areopagitica* was the first treatise to be published in defence of the freedom of the Press, written in the days when an unguarded word could land you in prison. 'When complaints are freely heard,' he wrote, 'deeply considered, and speedily reformed, then is the utmost bound of civil liberty attained that wise men look for.' He was one of the first, too, to speak out in favour of divorce, declaring incompatibility to be as great a hindrance to a happy marriage as physical infidelity; only in the last decade, with 'marital breakdown' now the sole admitted cause for divorce, have we caught up with his thinking. Were Milton alive today, his work would be found in the columns of the *New Statesman*, and the poet himself on the benches of the House of Commons, expressing opinions well to the left of centre.

'Give me the liberty to know, to utter and to argue freely according to conscience, above all liberties.'

22

'Queen Elizabeth slept here'

The thread which, however remotely, connects us with our forebears is one which brings to us a warm personal pride in their activities. Writing a book such as this, therefore, is easy, since in any company all are ready with anecdote or legend. The subjects range wide, the old tales gain with telling, and the unthinkable acts of yesteryear are recounted with fascinated, awed relish.

'You know there was a man burned at Chesham?' might be the hesitant start, and then the tales come tumbling out. Of the Dinton Hermit, the Mad Hatter, the Maharajah's Well, the Miller of Mansfield, the 'Absolute End' . . . and

Village statesmen talk with looks profound,
And news much older than their ale goes round.

Take that Mad Hatter, the 'Haberdasher of Hats'. His wits were addled in the Parliamentary Army, when his skull was cleft by a sword at Holman's Bridge. He ran amok, was sentenced to death by Cromwell, pardoned, and dismissed the service, to open a hat shop at Chesham. He got ever odder as the years passed, dressing in sackcloth, drinking nothing but water and eating turnips and grass, claiming that any man could live on three-farthings a day. (Some say three-farthings a week, but that does seem unreasonable.) The town eventually tired of his eccentricities and he was beaten for a madman and put in the stocks. Taking the hint, he removed to Uxbridge where he survived for many years as a pamphleteer, styling himself 'The English Hermit—Wonder of the Age'. Lewis Carroll immortalized him in *Alice*, and though the town drove him out, Chesham now claims him for her own.

Not far away at Chesham Bois lived a lady named Hester Sandys, mother of four sons and nine daughters, not a record for her time, but the chronicler Thomas Fuller thought her worth a mention. He wrote 'Her children so exceedingly multiplied that this lady saw 700 extracted from her body. Reader, I speak within compass, and have left myself a reserve, having bought the truth hereof from a wager I lost.' Dangerous things, these wagers; one such lost Fingest's church bells to Hambleden.

John Bigg, the Dinton Hermit, was another victim of the Civil War. Once secretary to Simon Mayne of Dinton Hall, who was among those who signed the King's Death warrant, Bigg was widely believed to have been the masked executioner who carried out the sentence, a belief that was doubtless without foundation for the deed was done with such accuracy and despatch that the executioner was unlikely to have been an amateur. Whether or no, the events of the time turned his head and Bigg took to living in a cave, eating what he could gather from the fields and hedgerows and what his friends would give him. He carried three bottles at his belt, for milk, water and small beer, and patched his clothes and boots as they wore with odd strips of leather. Continuing thus for thirty-six years, he became a grotesque figure in his patched and mended clothes and with boots grown gross from layers of leather. One of these vast boots is preserved in the Ashmolean Museum, and is said to be built up of over 1,000 pieces of leather.

Victim of a different war, Louis XVIII of France kept court for the seven years of his exile at Hartwell House, near Aylesbury. Other exiles joined him, and the house was filled until not one more person could be squeezed in. Many of the principal rooms were partitioned, cupboards pressed into service as bedrooms, nobles slept in the servants' quarters and servants slept under the stairs and on the kitchen floor. The Duc de Berri and his entourage took over the lodge, while the Duchesse d'Angoulême had to be content with a woodman's cottage. The King was something of a scholar—not for nothing was he dubbed The Sage of Hartwell—and he bore his years of exile philosophically. Not so his Queen, who found life at Aylesbury hopelessly dull after the grandeur and excitement of the Russian Court of her girlhood. She was reduced to easing her rage and frustration by knocking the heads off the carved figures that decorated the balusters of the grand staircase, before dying of boredom in 1810. A twentieth-century restorer has created an effect here by replacing the missing heads with representations of such contemporary notables as Churchill and G. K. Chesterton.

When the King was recalled to France after Napoleon's downfall he commemorated his stay in the Chilterns by planting an English Garden at Versailles, Le Jardin Anglais, a faithful reproduction of the Queen's garden at Hartwell. A contemporary writer reported that of all the hundreds of French

nationals that had flocked to Hartwell during the King's stay
there, not one remained after he returned to France. It was a
different story at Turville where General Dumouriez had taken
residence. He refused to return to France when Louis was
restored, and lived on at Turville until his death in 1823. But
then, he was in receipt of a British Government pension,
(doubtless index-linked) awarded for his services to the War
Office in the fight against Napoleon.

Shakespeare, they say, once spent the night at Grendon
Underwood and there conceived the plot for *A Midsummer
Night's Dream*. He was found asleep in the church porch by a
pair of constables who turned him out as a vagrant, but he got
his own back by writing them up as Dogberry and Verges in
Much Ado. Even then he wasn't finished with the Chilterns, for
he had yet to write about Cymbeline, King of the Britons, whose
castle stood on the hill above Kimble. Not much of the Chilterns
is to be detected in that crazy, mixed up tragi-comedy, but it does
hold the loveliest funeral dirge in all English literature:

> Fear no more the heat o' the sun
>   Nor the furious winter's rages;
> Thou thy worldly task hath done,
>   Home art gone, and ta'en thy wages.
> Golden lads and girls all must
> As chimney sweepers, come to dust . . .

Master Shakespeare must have found the Chilterns a handy
staging-post between London's Globe and his native Warwick-
shire.

In disputes with authority a show of ignorance is often better
protection than a suit of armour, and of more value than right on
one's side. Edmund Burke, who was perpetually hard-up and
continually being dunned by his creditors, could spot a bailiff at
fifty paces. One day when he was labouring in his own fields, a
task he always enjoyed, he was hailed by a pair who were clearly
armed with a summons and after his blood. 'Where's Mr Burke?'
they demanded summarily, whereupon Burke pulled his fore-
lock and replied that Master was away from home and not
expected back for a month. Thirty years later the owners of
those same fields fell out with the Rector of Beaconsfield, who
was claiming more at tithing than local custom allowed for. The
Rector took them to law, and lost, and they put him in his place
by setting a stone on the Parish boundary at Holtspur announc-

ing: '3rd May, 1827. Boundary stone of the Manor and Parish of Beaconsfield. The custom of Tithing in this Parish is (and has been immemorially) by the Tenth Cock and Eleventh Shock.'

Much of the friction between Priest and Parishioner, and much of the Church's power, vanished when tithing fell into disuse. It was finally abolished by Act of Parliament in 1936, but it left its mark in such phrases as 'Parson's Pig', for the runt of the litter, and in street names such as 'Parson's Fee', as well as in the magnificent tithe barns which still stand about the countryside. The man at the head of this particular rumpus, the Reverend John Gould, was arrested for debt after first his children and then his wife all died cruelly of the cholera, and finished up in Newgate from whence he issued forth every Sunday to take the services in Beaconsfield Parish Church.

Another case of mistaken identity is recorded in the name of the Miller of Mansfield Hotel at Goring. This Miller was a happy-go-lucky midlander who accidentally entertained the King to a feed of his own deer. Finding himself lost in the forest whilst hunting at Sherwood, Henry II was offered a bed for the night by the kindly Miller, who had no idea of his guest's identity. Anxious to please the guest, his wife served up for supper what she called 'Lightfoot pasty', of which the King ate heartily before remarking innocently that it tasted like venison, but of course it couldn't be since all deer belonged to the King. Without further ado the Miller told him plainly that indeed it was venison, that what the King didn't know he wouldn't grieve over, and that he had several more carcases up in the roof. Imagine his chagrin next day when the rest of the hunting party rode in looking for the King, and fell on their knees before his overnight guest. He saw the gallows noose dangle before him, but, grateful for his night's lodging, the King magnanimously appointed him Overseer of the Forest on condition that he put a stop to all this poaching.

This tongue-in-cheek attitude is reflected in the tale of the Maharajah's Well at Stoke Row. A member of the Reade family of Ipsden House took service in India during the latter half of the nineteenth-century, and one day, when being entertained by the Maharajah of Benares he took to reminiscing about home and told how, as a boy, he had seen one of the village boys receive a sound beating from his mother for going to play before carrying out his daily task of fetching water from the next village, for Stoke at that time had no fresh water supply of its own. The

Maharajah's eyes widened in horror and he exclaimed: 'Do you mean to tell me there are villages in England where fresh water cannot be had for the asking?' So touched was he at the thought that he made immediate arrangements from his own doubtless limited means to have a well sunk at Stoke Row, which still stands to this day, decorated with a miniature Indian elephant and a dainty dome well-head on tiny pilasters. At that time there was a water shortage in the Chilterns, water was dearer than beer, and they had to cut 368 feet down through the chalk before they reached the water-table.

A verse about 'Tring, Wing and Ivinghoe' crops up in all the books on the Chilterns, usually in a piece of doggerel connected with the Hampdens, and almost always accompanied by the remark that the verse excited the imagination of Sir Walter Scott who misheard Ivinghoe as Ivanhoe and used it for the title of his book.

> Tring, Wing and Ivinghoe
> Hampden of Hampden did forgoe
> For striking of ye Prynce a blow,
> And glad he might escape it so.

The Hampden referred to is not Ship-money Hampden, but a much earlier member of the family, and the 'Prynce' is the Black Prince, with whom he came to blows over a wager. (These wagers!) The verse might seem more authentic if there was any record of any member of the Hampden family ever having owned lands at Tring, Wing or Ivinghoe.

Another version of the rhyme is given in a book first published in 1902.*

> Tring, Wing and Ivinghoe,
> Three churches in a row,
> Take your shoes and stockings off
> And jump over them.

This sounds like a children's counting game, and is attributed to 'Old Betty', a lady of Tring who died at the end of the nineteenth-century, in her 110th year. 'Farmer and labourer alike knew Old Betty,' the book says. 'She was fond of her snuff, and when asked how she did invariably announced that she was well

* *Highways and Byeways in Hertfordshire*, H. W. Tompkins, Macmillan, 1928.

enough but that her [snuff] box was empty. There was a touch of Meg Merrilees in her, too; for she would rail on occasion against those who endeavoured to enclose common land, plough public footpaths, prosecute the poacher, or infringe the gleaner's immemorial rights. She went "a-faggin" every harvest, and was over 100 years old when she last went gleaning in the fields.' She would have been at home in the Chilterns today, enrolled in the Chiltern Society and doing her best to tame the twentieth-century for the sake of

> . . . the country places,
> Where the old, plain men have rosy faces,
> And the young, fair maidens
> Quiet eyes.

The district has its occasional ghost: Henry VIII, of course, stumbling through the corridors at Chenies Manor, and the Prelate, Henry de Burghersh, who was Bishop of Lincoln in 1330 and made the mistake of enclosing a stretch of common land into his Park at Fingest. He is said to have appeared after his death to one of his retinue, dressed in Lincoln green and with the bow and arrows and horn of a huntsman, saying that God was displeased with him for stealing from the poor and had put him in charge of the park, refusing him his eternal rest till retribution should be made. He had indeed committed a great crime, for the common lands were the only place where a landless man could pasture his beasts and grow food for his family. When this land was taken, the poor starved.

St Osyth, who appeared to the faithful in Aylesbury Churchyard after her martyrdom at the hands of the Danes, was expiating no crime, but simply expressing dissatisfaction at her appointed resting-place in the crypt. She desired to lie at Chich Priory, near Colchester, where she had once been prioress, and upon her bones being removed there she appeared in the Chilterns no more.

A few Chiltern houses can claim that 'Queen Elizabeth Slept Here': Chenies Manor, Bradenham Manor, and Hampden House (where, incidentally, a stretch of Grim's Ditch was filled in and levelled to facilitate the Royal Progress). Henry VIII was at Moor Park, Ashridge and Ewelme; Berkhamsted Castle saw one Royal dynasty after another over a period of five hundred years, and Burnham Beeches was one of King John's favourite hunting grounds. 'The Absolute End' is the whimsical name given to the village store at Cadmore End, and 'The man burned at Chesham'? That was poor Thomas Harding, who shared the fate of Latimer, Ridley and Cranmer. Perhaps he heard in his agony Bishop Latimer's voice at his ear: 'Be of good comfort, Master Harding, and play the man. We shall by God's grace light such a candle in England this day as, I trust, shall never be put out.'

23

Natural History

In spite of the excellent system of roads, railways and motor-ways that brings the remotest of its inhabitants within daily commuting distance of London, in spite of the doubling in size since the war of High Wycombe, Aylesbury and Chesham and the near-suburbanization of Rickmansworth and Amersham, most of the Chiltern area manages to remain splendidly rural. No Chiltern dweller worthy of the name will miss the sight and scent of massed bluebells in spring nor the crunch and crinkle of beechmast underfoot when the trees are bare, and in high summer it is some compensation for a working day spent in the airless city to be able to walk to and from the station through lanes white with waving cow-parsley or across heaths alive with bird-song.

Several factors combine to bring about this happy state of affairs, not least the maintenance of the Metropolitan Green Belt. For many years between the wars the London Society urged that a Green Belt be set around London to put a stop to the untidy development of the suburbs. In the 1930s the London County Council resolved to do something about this and the Green Belt Act became law. Two million pounds was set aside by the L.C.C. for the purchase of suitable stretches of land, in addition to sums spent by various local authorities. Other areas were simply declared 'Green Belt' and therefore automatically protected against further development. In the Abercrombie Report on the future of London published immediately after the war the principle was reiterated, and lands at Amersham, Gerrards Cross and Chorleywood and Moor Park Golf Course were specifically mentioned. Although there is still constant demand from developers for building land, the 1938 Act Still protects the whole area of the Chiltern Hills from encroachment by Cobbett's 'Great Wen'.

Another force in the preservation of the area is the deter-mination of its residents that their lovely heritage shall not be destroyed. This has been evidenced on many occasions by public objections to development, and never more strongly nor more effectively than between 1969 and 1971 when a third London Airport was proposed for Buckinghamshire. Had this airport been built, the villages of Wing, Cublington and Stewkley with their Norman churches and medieval cottages of timber and thatch would have been levelled to the ground, and the beautiful Vale of Aylesbury ruined beyond redemption.

The Wing Airport Resistance Association organized the entire population of the district against the proposal, publicizing its enormity in the most ingenious ways so that for months one could hardly pick up a magazine or read a newspaper without finding Wing and the airport mentioned, and as one drove along the A413 towards Buckingham one found notices by the wayside and among the flowerbeds with such announcements as 'Airport perimeter would start here' or 'Main runway would finish at this point'. What weight all this lent to the Roskill Commission's eventual recommendation that the airport be sited elsewhere one cannot say, but it was a fine effort, and showed the mood of the people clearly. Alas, even as this book is being written the people of Stewkley, Cublington and Wing again find themselves threatened with an airport on their doorsteps, and the old round of meetings, fund raising, letters to the Press, etc., has had to be started all over again.

Organizations such as the Chiltern Society, the Berks Bucks and Oxfordshire Naturalists' Trust, and innumerable tenants' associations and residents' societies are ever wary, and though there is much new building and a continually growing population, the delightful rural character of the area remains. There are still thousands of acres of rolling farmland, common flowers of wood, heath and hedgerow in abundance everywhere, and for those with eyes to see more unusual species are there for the finding. There are more varieties of wild orchids growing in the woods and on the chalk grasslands than in any other area in Britain: the rare monkey orchid and even rarer ghost orchid both grow in the Chilterns; pyramid, spotted, fly, bird's nest and bee orchids are all known, as are white and violet helleborines. Coral-root grows near Bradenham and in Amersham's Rectory Wood; chalk gentian grows at Ivinghoe, and on Pitstone Hill in April and early May there is still the pasque-flower. The list of birds, too, is impressive: nuthatch, long-tailed tit, tree creeper, green and lesser-spotted woodpeckers, dunnock, willow-warbler, green and pied wagtails, blackcap, chiff-chaff, brambling, skylark, reed-bunting, kestrel, sparrow-hawk, woodcock, and the languid, elegant heron are all to be seen, and there are still a few hobbies and buzzards, and several pairs of stone-curlew. Kingfishers flash along the river banks, and since the war the little ringed plover has come to breed beside gravel pits along the Thames and at the Marsworth, Wilstone and Startopsend reservoirs between Tring and Ivinghoe.

Many species of butterfly, too, gladden the eye. No less than five of Britain's seven native Blues have been reported in the Chilterns, also Speckled Wood, Orange-tip, Brimstone, Purple Hairstreak, Peacock and Dark Green Fritillary as well as the Marbled White, seen only rarely elsewhere in Britain but found in great numbers on the Buckinghamshire grasslands. Britain's second largest butterfly, the Purple Emperor, with its four-inch wingspan, suns itself on the tree-tops, and at Bernwood Nature Reserve in the Vale of Aylesbury the rare Black Hairstreak feeds its caterpillars on breaks of old, tangled blackthorn that are specially preserved for it.

Bernwood is managed by the Berks Bucks and Oxfordshire Naturalists' Trust (B.B.O.N.T.), which manages no less than twenty-three nature reserves in Buckinghamshire and eighteen in Oxfordshire, though not all of them come within the area of the Chilterns. Notable among them are the 247-acre Warburg Reserve at Bix with its woodland orchids and helleborines; the junipers at Chinnor; Kimble boxwoods (one of the three notable stretches of boxwood in Britain); the 22-acre Vicarage Pit Wetlands Reserve at Stanton Harcourt, established during the 1976 European Wetlands Year; the Waterfowl Reserve at Weston Turville; and the reed swamps of Parsonage Moor at Cothill in Oxfordshire, with early marsh orchids, comfrey, and devil's-bit scabious feeding caterpillars of Marsh Fritillary butterflies.

Some of the B.B.O.N.T. reserves are open to all, some restrict access to B.B.O.N.T. members only, and some are 'protected' sites on private land where access is not generally permitted, such as the sites in Buckinghamshire with the only British red helleborines known outside the Cotswolds, two of the three known sites of the military orchid, and both the known British stations of the ghost orchid.

Not all are large reserves, they vary from the 247-acre reserve at Bix, the only B.B.O.N.T. site to boast a full-time warden, to the tiny Bullingdon Bog site between Headington and Cowley in Oxford, an acre of calcareous fen growing grass of parnassus, bog pimpernel and marsh helleborine, thought to be the only such area of fen within a city's limits in the whole country.

B.B.O.N.T. also keeps an eye on sixty-nine scheduled road-side verges throughout the territory, and a length of disused railway track in Oxfordshire. Without the watchfulness of such organizations, where the work is entirely voluntary apart from the one paid warden at Bix, much of this natural habitat would not survive.

The National Trust is another organization to which credit must be given for the preservation of the natural beauty of the Chilterns. The Trust owns some 12,000 acres of woodland, heath and parkland in the area, most of it open to the public at all times, and has covenants over several acres more. The largest of these land-holdings is the Ashridge Estate, nearly four thousand acres of farms, beechwoods and chalk downland enclosed in the triangle where Hertfordshire, Buckinghamshire and Bedfordshire meet, and because it is National Trust land secured by Act of Parliament in perpetuity against change or destruction. Here on the hills are great stretches of sheep-cropped turf where cowslips grow so thick in summer one can hardly set foot between. Yet looking closer one finds greater riches still: burnet, felwort, rest-harrow, pretty yellow and purple vetches that feed the caterpillars of the Chalkhill Blue; harebell and clustered bellflower, and here and there, pushing shyly up between the grass-blades, tiny wild orchids.

Similar stretches of chalk grasslands are owned by the National Trust at Watlington in Oxfordshire and Coombe Hill near Wendover. Sadly, all these high chalk areas suffer from people, and since the designation of the Ridgeway Long Distance Footpath in 1973 thousands of eager feet have tramped away the turf along parts of the ridges, leaving the chalk bare. Good landlord that it is, the National Trust is aware of the dangers of such erosion and its wardens are doing their best to repair the damage by re-seeding, wiring off the worst areas and in at least one place diverting the long distance footpath so that the turf may regenerate. Certain parts have been 'patched' with plastic netting in an attempt to stop the erosion, and experiments are being made with different varieties of ground cover to see which gives best and quickest growth and which will best withstand the traffic.

The beechwoods which once marched in a great swathe across the middle of England are still a feature of the Chilterns. The map shows the famous Burnham Beeches, home of the oldest beech trees in Europe, as the largest uninterrupted stretch remaining; perhaps the purchase of these woods by the Corporation of the City of London in 1878 for the recreation of its citizens has something to do with its preservation. Certainly as a playground for City dwellers it is unparalleled. Unfortunately too many people are not good for woodlands either, and these woods suffer from fires and other vandalism. For all its size Burnham lacks the seclusion and quiet beauty of Wendover woods, the variety of remote Bix Bottom or the brooding silence of the Watlington woods, where in Watlington Park the ancient yews have trunks six feet across. There is a depth and density about the woods below Watlington Hill which excites the senses of a lone walker, warning him that here anything is possible and man but a poor thing, ephemeral as bird-song and as easily destroyed as any ant or beetle. Walter de la Mare could have had these woods in mind when he wrote:

> Very old are the woods, and the buds which break
> Out of the briar's boughs when March winds wake
> So old in their beauty are. And no man knows
> Through what wild centuries roves back the rose.

The air seems chill even on the hottest day, and only when the trees are bare in winter does the sun penetrate, shafting palely down between the branches. The more open beechwoods along the ridge are carpeted in spring with a dense haze of bluebells stretching unbroken as far as the eye can see, their heady scent drenching the senses, and when the bluebells fade their place is taken in lesser degree by wood anemone, wood sorrel, woodruff, herb Robert, wintergreen and Solomon's seal, while the dead trunks of fallen trees harbour plates of yellow sulphur tuft, tiny candle-snuff spikes and devil's butter, with earth-stars and horn-off-plenty flourishing in the autumn leaf-mould. All this gives the lie to the old tale of beechwood floors being 'clean' or 'bare', from lack of light. Quite enough sun and rain penetrates the leaf canopy, evidently, to nourish all these and more besides.

Wendover woods are less dense than Watlington, the trees seeming younger and fresher. Here bridle paths dissect the glade, and roadways and tracks cut up the woodland into compassable portions, giving access to small clearings where isolated, flint-built cottages shelter a few lucky souls. Though the same woodland flowers grow they are not found in such profusion, and the great glory of these woods is the beech tree.

When spring comes to Wendover the trees hang motionless against the blue sky, branch and twig forming a tracery where tiny new leaves lie damp and crumpled like babies' hands, and all the while the sweet, lilting song of wood-warblers fills the air.

One would not think better could be found, but on Pitstone Hill a little copse flourishes where, in a sparse spread of mixed woodland, brambles and wild roses flower profusely among the trees and the path edges are massed with wild flowers. In spring the prevailing wind swoops up from the vale setting the new leaves dancing and flattening the violets and primroses against the ground. Such harsh treatment should discourage them, but they must love the exhilaration of it for the violets flourish here from late February almost into June, with primroses keeping them company nearly all the way. So small is this glade that as one walks one hears skylarks trilling above the heaths ahead, and sees beside the Speckled Wood butterfly its heath-loving friends the yellow Brimstone, the Skippers and, occasionally, one of the Blues, strayed from the open hillside below. Even the vast spread of Pitstone Cement Works looks good from up here, with the sun glinting on its chimneys and lacy plumes of white smoke floating on the sky.

The country towards Fingest and Turville is less wooded; mostly farmland and heath and soft, rounded, copse-crowned hills where chalk shows white through the sparse green cover. Here the beeches survive only in the hanging woods of the dry valleys, spreading dark green fingers across the acres of pale heath and cornfields. In Oxfordshire, at Bix Bottom, the beeches are relieved by dark yews and plantations of Corsican pines, and by oak, ash and elm; but much of the green on the map between Nettlebed and the Thames signifies only scrub and saplings of birch, ash and hazel, though the same haze of bluebell carpets the ground in spring. Coppicing of beech and hazel was very common in the Chilterns when bodgers grew their long, straight poles to turn into chair-legs for the furniture trade. Such coppices make wonderful wild-flower habitats, but today the furniture trade looks elsewhere for its chair-legs and there would be none of this kindly habitat left in the Chilterns had not B.B.O.N.T. created or preserved a few coppices, such as Long Grove Wood at Seer Green, for the wild orchids and helleborines that grow there.

It would be surprising if this richness of natural woodland and heath did not attract many wild creatures. All the more common species of deer make their homes in the Chilterns, including a few red deer and tiny Chinese water deer. The little muntjak, an escapee from Woburn Park where it was introduced towards the end of the nineteenth century, is now seen all over the Chilterns, and roe deer are common above the Thames in the Henley loop, and in south Buckinghamshire. Fallow deer are widespread throughout the district, but particularly on the Oxford escarpment, and Sika deer, introduced into many private parks during the nineteenth century, are also found wild in Oxfordshire. Even in the built-up areas deer are common visitors; there have been reports of small deer in gardens at Chorleywood, and in the same area early one summer morning a magnificent stag was seen silhouetted at the end of a woodland ride, resembling exactly the great red deer of Exmoor.

Another parkland escapee is the Glis glis, the fat or edible dormouse. Walter Rothschild brought the Glis glis to Tring Park in the early 1900s, and it is now quite common in the small area around Tring and Beaconsfield, though it has not yet spread beyond the Chilterns. The creature is between six and seven inches long, grey in colour, with a tail like a squirrel. Not so pretty as the English dormouse, it has large, protuberant eyes and small ears on a head that seems too big for its body. It is not unknown for the Glis glis to winter in lofts and attics or garden sheds, though more usually it seeks out snug holes in the trees for hibernation. Badgers, foxes and grey squirrels are common everywhere; otters, of course, are unknown, though some coypu have spread across from East Anglia, and there have been reports of mink living near the rivers.

Another creature worth a mention, and perhaps one of the most important when one is considering the preservation of wild-flower habitats, is the common-or-garden rabbit, nibbling away at the grassland and keeping the turf fresh and short. Much of the lush, rolling Chiltern grassland is arable, laid to root and cereal crops, and much more is 'managed' grassland in private hands, feeding sheep and cattle. It is the fashion today for farmers to plough up natural grassland and re-seed with a few selected grasses which give best nourishment to grazing animals, treating the new growth with herbicides and commercial fertilizers. Grassland treated in this fashion is often botanically disappointing as the treatment kills off all the wild flowers, and the speedwell, corn-salad, marjoram, yarrow, eyebright, hawkbits, sorrel, dandelions and daisies that would otherwise have enriched the pasture are nowhere to be found. All the more important, then, that the wild grasslands of the great natural heaths—Dunstable Downs, Ivinghoe Beacon, Ewelme Downs and the surrounding hills, with their wonderful variety of downland flora, are preserved.

Unfortunately even natural grassland cannot be left to itself, as any lawn-owner knows. But for rabbits and occasional sheep that graze the turf and keep it short and sweet, the grass would soon grow coarse and rank and within a very few years the rich downland flora would be smothered. A few years more and scrub saplings and bramble would take over, taller flowers such as Michaelmas daisy, foxglove and rosebay-willowherb would come in, and the whole area would eventually revert to woodland again. The beginnings of this reversion were seen when myxomatosis almost wiped out the rabbit population in the Fifties and Sixties, and the preservation societies have been hard at work in recent years grubbing out the scrub growth that first took hold then.

24

Chiltern People

Hill and valley, town and farm, the face of the countryside is painted by those who live there. Only the immemorial rocks, the bones of the face, are changeless, the rest bear the stamp of man, for he it is who clears and cultivates the fields, lays the roads and fashions village and town, first for his survival and then for his comfort and enjoyment, and as we go about the land it tells us of the people who live there. In the prosperous Chilterns it tells us of a people who farm and build by the most modern methods, spend well at busy shops, drive distinctive motor-cars, and are spread fairly thinly by today's standards about towns and villages where they live in neat, well cared-for houses. In short, the ages of clearing and striving are past, and more than most in England today the people of the Chilterns are heirs to an age of comfort and enjoyment.

The families that have served the countryside for generations are still there, though the beechwoods that formerly sustained them are 'dead' woods today. Apart from some desultory felling and clearing, only the weekend walker or rider disturbs the glades which once were part of the countryman's life-support system. There were lime burners, charcoal burners, bodgers, men coppicing and felling, draymen working teams of great Shire horses to drag out the felled timber on sleds; and at a humbler level there were pigs rooting for beechmast while their owners trapped rabbits and game, bundled firewood, and collected blackberries, crab-apples, rosehips and sloes. Now Sir Bernard Miles's wily Hertfordshire yeoman and his doughty Buckinghamshire or Oxfordshire counterpart buys his packaged foods from the supermarkets like the rest of us; he may take home to his family a few farm eggs or vegetables, but for the rest he is just part of the Euro food chain, and more likely to work in clinical animal houses or where hedges have been grubbed out to form arable fields so vast that the furrows rise to the hilltop and disappear over the horizon, than in the woods and the small, friendly meadow and byre of former years.

Even those who live in the remote villages have alternatives today to agricultural work, and the men who now work the land do so from choice rather than necessity. He who rides a tractor to plough a straight furrow could as well take a lorry along the motorway, and those who tend the beasts to scientifically ordered timetables have a dedication and knowledge that would put many a shop or factory worker to shame. Such men come from all backgrounds to work on the land for the love of the outdoor life, like the young lad from Leeds seen out with his gun one morning in the Hampden country. He had one of those sullen faces that light up as their owner warms to his subject, and he told how, living out his boyhood in the city streets, he had determined that his life would be spent outdoors, though for one without family traditions or contacts the start had not been easy. In the end he'd answered an advertisement in *Horse and Hound* for a kennelman, and found himself at sixteen, too far away to live at home, looking after himself in a leaky caravan. He'd stuck it for two years before moving to his present job on a farm where he could live in, but he'd be moving again soon, he said, because it was all arable and he missed the animals. When he went back home at holiday times he found the boys he was at school with were earning twice his wage, but he didn't care. They were still kids, he said, and half-dead already.

So close to London and with so much post-war housing development along the routes of the railways and the new motor roads, a large proportion of the working population can but be commuters, though it is noticeable that every time British Rail puts up its fares a fresh forest of 'For Sale' notices arises in the villages around Great Missenden and Tring. But by no means all the non-agricultural workers are London commuters. The trading estates at High Wycombe, Chesham and Aylesbury take many of them, as do the nearby towns of Watford, Hemel Hempstead, Luton and Oxford, while the district is favoured for offices by such concerns as British Aluminium at Chalfont Park and the U.K. Atomic Energy Research Authority at Amersham. Nor are such associations as the Lions and the Round Table, who traditionally draw their members from people active locally in commerce and industry, short of support, as is evidenced by the good work they do for charities at home and abroad.

The same energy and enthusiasm that takes so many of these Chiltern people to the top at work is devoted to their leisure time activities. Few live far from tennis-court, swimming pool, cricket club or golf course, although the latter is often a little nine-holer laid out on common land, as at Ley Hill,

Northchurch, and Chorleywood. Drama and music societies abound; some, like the Misbourne Orchestra, the Tring Operatic Society, the Rickmansworth Players and the Actors' Repertory at Pendley, presenting most professional performances in theatres that have been incorporated into purpose-built public halls in the tradition of the old Intimate Theatres. The Elgiva Hall at Chesham is one such, and Watersmeet at Rickmansworth is another, although the Pendley Arts Centre near Tring, with its plain woodwork and bare brick, reminiscent of the Mermaid Theatre, serves the purpose with greater aplomb.

A notable change in leisure habits has been brought about since the war by new Leisure Centres with really superb facilities, like the High Wycombe Sports Centre on Marlow Hill, visible from the M40. This centre has a 50-metre indoor swimming pool, an indoor bowls hall, weight-training room, six squash courts, sauna and solarium, and a 35-metre sports hall that can accommodate 8 badminton courts, 2 volleyball courts, 2 indoor tennis courts, basketball, indoor hockey, five-a-side football, etc. Outside there is an all-weather pitch, athletics track, and climbing-wall. Chalfont St Peter has a more modest but still excellent centre on similar lines, which owes its existence to the enthusiasm and persistence of a small handful of local residents, while at Amersham-on-the-Hill the swimming pool and library complex is complemented by a new meeting hall and community craft workshops converted from old barns.

In 1947 a different kind of leisure centre was established at Gerrards Cross when a subscription list was opened to buy the house and grounds belonging to the old vicarage in East Common as a War Memorial. From small beginnings with a voluntary committee organizing a few club meetings on the first two floors and painting and sculpting in the attics, the project has grown until now the Gerrards Cross Memorial Centre has a full-time paid warden and is open day and evening for a multitude of activities from bridge to yoga, bicycle repairs to English for foreign students. By far the greatest demand here, as elsewhere, is for facilities for amateur painters. Eight classes a week cater for this demand at the Memorial Centre, reflecting an interest that is pronounced throughout the district. The Society of Buckinghamshire Artists and the Chiltern Painters are perhaps best known of the arts societies, but there are amateur potters, sculptors, pewter-workers, weavers and silversmiths producing very competent work which they exhibit at local Arts Centres, libraries and village halls all over the Chilterns, while private galleries, such as the Century Gallery at Henley, sell on a professional basis.

One gallery that has been a great success is the Three Households Gallery at Chalfont St Giles. Every year an Art Show is held on the green at Jordans, arising from the time when the cottages around the green housed pottery and craft workshops. After a particularly successful show in 1968 a group of artists and potters discussed among themselves the possibility of starting a gallery on a co-operative basis as a permanent showroom for their work, and by coincidence that very day one of them saw just the premises for such a venture. Built in 1630 and full of character, with exposed oak beams and leaded panes in its tiny shop windows, the place cried out to be used as an Art Gallery. Of the fourteen amateur artists on the founding committee, one was an accountant and one an insurance expert, and between them they managed to get financial backing to turn the dream into reality.

The Gallery was manned for the first few years on a voluntary part-time basis, and although it was several years before the venture was financially successful artistically it was a great success, fulfilling from the first what has always been its primary function, to sell art. At the very beginning the founders determined one thing, that whatever was put on show, be it prints, paintings, silver-smithing, pottery, sculpture or what you will, the Gallery would sell only the works of living, practising artists, and it would deal directly with the artist and with the artist alone. Some of these artists, like Edward Stamp and Janet Ledger, are now famous, and many who have displayed their first craft work at Three Households now sell professionally at shops and galleries all over the country.

Surprisingly, in this far from working-class area, the Workers' Educational Association flourishes, offering daytime and evening sessions in a variety of subjects, the former being a boon to retired people. Chorleywood, that classic example of a meritocracy, boasts a thriving branch of the W.E.A., sprung from a Current Affairs Class that used to meet during the war. One member of that little group was Bob Turney, who had been a City of London policeman. Bob should be hallowed in the memory of all wage slaves as one who beat the system: he drew his pension for longer than he worked. He lived at The Retreat at Chorleywood Bottom (formerly Younger's Farm), where he was reputed to have more books than Chorleywood Library. The Retreat had been in his family for generations, and still is. In his grandfather's time parties from North London used to journey out for Sunday School teas there, followed by races on the Common. Bob and his wife ran the place as a small-holding; his house was one of the few left in Chorleywood still to have rights of Commonage. The old gentleman was always ready with information about where the dewpond was and by which path the corpses were carried to the cemetery at Rickmansworth, before Christchurch was built. He was eventually made President of the W.E.A. branch he helped to form, and it was a standing joke among the members as to whether he was landed gentry or their only working man. A life-long Socialist and rationalist, it was sad to see him carried off at the end like any other mortal; he should have had a procession along Lower Road behind black horses and waving plumes with the Mayor in attendance, as he might have in France, 'Civil, and with the Band'.

When summer comes the Chiltern area is full of visitors, many of them from overseas. To entertain them there are summer carnivals and fêtes, school fairs, dog shows, garden festivals, barbecues, and horticultural shows with all the usual classes on the schedules: 'Six Roses, any variety', 'Sweet Peas, 6 sprays from seed', 'Delphiniums, one specimen spike', 'Dish of Raspberries', 'Cherry Cake', 'Jar of Marmalade', 'Bottle of Homemade Wine'. These shows mirror the life of the countryside, and competition is always keen. Many of the events have a rural flavour, like the Young Farmer Rallies, Goat Society's Show, Pony Club events, Foxhunter Trials, and the famous Kimble Point-to-Point, while some are more sophisticated, like the Aylesbury Motor Club's Askett Autocross which attracted over a thousand spectators in 1980, and the talk on Transcendental Meditation by the Maharishi at Mentmore Towers which drew only a fraction of that number. But for sheer spectacle it would be difficult to beat the Steam Traction Rallies.

There is a great following for steam in the Chilterns. Members of the Chiltern Traction Engine Club own some seventy engines between them, and more than one front garden boasts a gleaming Burrell or a Fowler tucked up under a tarpaulin. The Club's annual Steam Rally is a two-day event at upwards of thirty engines and road rollers gather from all over the Chilterns. With a road speed of about eight miles an hour and weighing up to thirteen tons, some would have started the day before and travelled all night to be sure of getting to the field in good time. 'Races' and demonstrations of working engines are staged to entertain the three thousand or more fans that stream through the gate during these weekends. The cost to the club members of such a rally is in excess of £5,000, so a good 'gate' is essential if the club is to break even. For the spectators, the sight, sound and smell of these great engines with paintwork and brass gleaming, whistles blowing, chimneys sending out puffs of acrid smoke, and boiler-suited, coal-grimed engineers hoisted aloft on the driving platforms like gods, whirling their brass-handled steering wheels with authority and aplomb, is thrilling and not a little awe-inspiring. Small boys gaze with envy and beg for rides and little girls squeal with delicious terror when the steam-whistles shriek their nerve-shattering warnings. All this, with the side-shows and stalls selling home-made cakes and candies, lavender bags, toffee-apples, honey and sarsaparilla, and a steam-organ churning out 'Daisy, Daisy', makes for a memorable afternoon's entertainment.

Along the Thames very different scenes attend the Regattas at Henley and Marlow in June. Alas, much of the old elegance of Regatta Week is gone, with roundabouts and hot-dog stands supplanting the champagne parties of yore. But there are still strawberries and cream if you know where to look and still private parties along the river bank where men in blazers and flannels escort fashionable ladies across the greensward, while nothing can detract from the dignity of the slim, silent boats flashing across the sunlit water.

Although it reigns supreme for rowers, the Thames is not now the only venue for Chiltern water-sports. It has been to some extent supplanted in recent years by the many sailing clubs that rent private water on reservoirs and on the many flooded, worked-out gravel pits in Hertfordshire and the Thames Valley. Chiltern gravel is much in demand, and although Residents' Societies and Local Councils almost always oppose gravel digging, ways are found to open new pits wherever extensive gravel beds are found. The construction of the North Orbital Extension in 1976 from Maple Cross to Hunton Bridge on the outskirts of Rickmansworth exposed a layer of gravel in the Chess Valley which is being worked, and where doubtless there will be a Chess Valley Sailing Club in years to come. Most of these clubs are for one or two classes only, and cater mainly for family sailors. Mirrors and Fireflies are popular. With their trim little club houses, usually built and kept up by the members, these sailing clubs are the social successors to the tennis clubs that flourished in the 1920s and 1930s.

County Show time comes in September, when the harvest is in and the year's work on the land almost over. The Bucks County Show is held each year at Hartwell Park, two miles south-west of Aylesbury, on the first Thursday in September, and here the farming community gathers as it has for centuries either to celebrate a good year or console itself for a bad one. The same scenes are enacted at such shows all over England; white-coated milkmaids leading their glossy prize-winners, shepherds with dogs and half-a-dozen docile, laundered sheep, fat ponies sporting rosettes, Young Farmer displays and competitions, and innumerable stalls selling everything from guns to candy-floss.

It is many years since Thame Show, held later in September, was allowed to occupy the broad High Street; the animals and events of the show proper have long been banished to a field outside the town, while the High Street and Market Square are given over to a vast, three-day fun fair with every sort of booth and sideshow. Great fun for visitors and good for trade, but devastating for residents who see the towers of helter-skelters rising to their rooftops and bear the canned music of the round-abouts and swings. Amersham residents suffer similarly in October at the time of the Amersham Mop, but their fair livens up the town for one day only before packing up and moving on, leaving only a drift of plastic and old boxes for the memory.

All this liveliness reveals a people that are active, committed, articulate. Their churches are full on Sundays, their elections energetically campaigned, their connections, both professional and private, are world-wide. When they stand around their family tables on Christmas Day to drink to Absent Friends they will be remembering loved ones on oilfields from Venezuela to Iraq; with V.S.O. in the Third World; on commercial engage-ments in Europe, America and the Antipodes; in medical, teach-ing and diplomatic posts in every part of the globe. And if, as you toil up their interminable hills, you pause to ask one of them: 'Does the road wind uphill *all* the way?' the chances are your informant will be well read and witty enough to answer in Christina Rossetti's words: 'Yes, to the very end!'

Sources

Arthur Mee's Buckinghamshire : Hodder & Stoughton.

The Book of Thame, Gerald Clarke: Barracuda Books.

The Buildings of England series, Niklaus Pevsner : Penguin.

The Chartist Land Company, Alice Mary Hadfield : David & Charles.

Chalfont St Peter, A Lost Village, Audrey Wheelband : Richard Sadler.

The Chilterns, Kevin Fitzgerald : B. T. Batsford.

The Chilterns, J. H. B. Peel : Paul Elek

Chiltern Country, H. J. Massingham : B. T. Batsford.

Chiltern Footpaths, Annan Dickson : Chaterson Ltd.

Chiltern Villages, V. B. Burden : Spurbooks.

Christchurch Chorleywood, the Story of a Church and Parish : George Bastin.

Companion into Buckinghamshire : Maxwell Fraser Spurbooks.

Companion into Oxfordshire, Ethel Carleton Williams: Methuen.

Country Like This, A Book of the Vale of Aylesbury : issued for the Friends of the Vale of Aylesbury by F. Weatherhead & Son.

The English Country Chair, Ivan Sparks : Spurbooks.

Hertfordshire, W. Branch Johnson : B. T. Batsford.

Hertfordshire Landscape, Lionel Munby : Hodder & Stoughton.

Highways and Byeways in Buckinghamshire, Clement Shorter : Macmillan.

History and Antiquities of the County of Buckinghamshire, Dr George Lipscombe, J. & W. Robins (1847).

A History of Moor Park, Hilary Armitage.

Jordans, the Making of a Community, Arthur L. Hayward : Friends' Home Service Committee.

Latimer, Keith Branigan : C.V.A.H.S.

Little Gaddesden, the Story of an English Parish, Vicars Bell : Faber & Faber.

The Living Land, a Natural History of the Chilterns, Michael Smith : Spurbooks.

Lost Villages of England, M. Beresford : Lutterworth Press.

Metro Memories, A Pictorial History of Metroland, Dennis Edwards and Ron Pigram, Midas Books.

Penn County of Buckinghamshire : C.P.R.E., 1932.

Portrait of Buckinghamshire, John Camp : Robert Hale.

Portrait of Hertfordshire, Brian Bailey : Robert Hale.

Quaker by Convincement, Geoffrey Hubbard : Pelican.

Rickmansworth, a Glimpse of the Past, ed. C. R. Burch : M. & R. Printing Services, Rickmansworth.

The Rothschilds, a Family Portrait, Frederick Morton : Secker & Warburg.

A Short History of Berkhamsted, Percy Bitchnell : White Crescent Press.

The Stonors, P. J. Jefferies : Nelson.

Understanding English Place Names, William Addison : Futura.

The Victorian County Histories of Buckinghamshire, Hertfordshire, and *Oxfordshire.*

View of the Chilterns, Brian Bailey : Robert Hale.

Unfortunately many of the above are no longer in print.

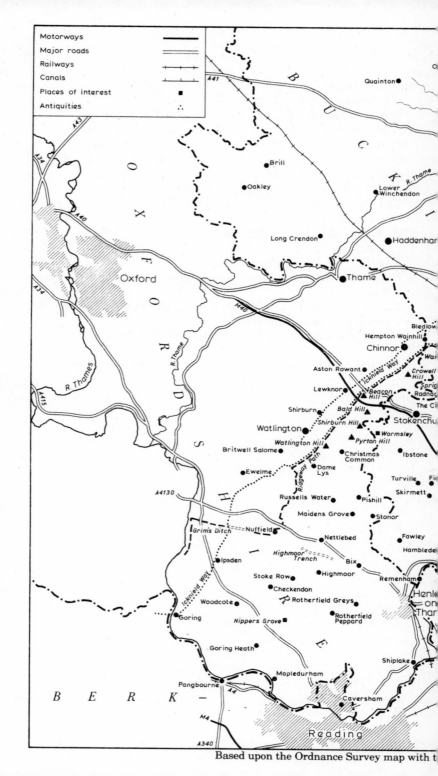

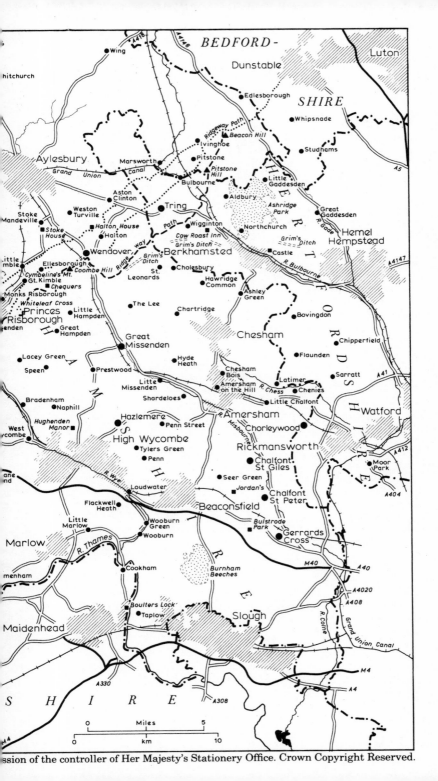

Index